# Rendition to Torture

Genocide, Political Violence, Human Rights Series

Edited by Alexander Laban Hinton, Stephen Eric Bronner, and Nela Navarro

Alan W. Clarke, *Rendition to Torture*

Lawrence Davidson, *Cultural Genocide*

Alexander Laban Hinton, ed., *Transitional Justice: Global Mechanisms and Local Realities after Genocide and Mass Violence*

Irina Silber, *Everyday Revolutionaries: Gender, Violence, and Disillusionment in Postwar El Salvador*

Samuel Totten and Rafiki Ubaldo, eds., *We Cannot Forget: Interviews with Survivors of the 1994 Genocide in Rwanda*

Ronnie Yimsut, *Facing the Khmer Rouge: A Cambodian Journey*

# Rendition to Torture

ALAN W. CLARKE

RUTGERS UNIVERSITY PRESS

NEW BRUNSWICK, NEW JERSEY, AND LONDON

LIBRARY OF CONGRESS CATALOGING-IN-PUBLICATION DATA

Clarke, Alan W. (Alan William)
  Rendition to torture / Alan W. Clarke.
      p. cm.
  Includes bibliographical references and index.
  ISBN 978–0-8135–5276–7 (hardcover) — ISBN 978-0-8135-5312-2 (e-book)
  I. Extraordinary rendition—United States.   2. Torture—Government policy—
United States.   3. Detention of persons—Government policy—United States.
4. Deportation—Government policy—United States.   5. False imprisonment—
United States.   6. National security—United States.   7. Extraordinary rendition.
8. Torture.   I. Title.
  KF9635.C53 2012
  342.7308'2—dc23                                           2011028852

A British Cataloging-in-Publication record for this book is available from the
British Library.

Visit our Web site: http://rutgerspress.rutgers.edu

Manufactured in the United States of America

For my partner and wife, Laurelyn Whitt,
and my parents, Buddy and Jo Clarke,
whose love and encouragement made this book possible

# CONTENTS

*Preface*                                    ix
*Acknowledgments*                        xiii

1    Introduction                                           1

2    Cultivating a Torture Culture                      16

3    From Eichmann and Carlos "the Jackal"
     to Reagan and Clinton                              60

4    Significant U.S. Renditions to Torture          91

5    State Secrets Privilege Trumps Justice:
     *Mohamed v. Jeppesen Dataplan*               117

6    The Illegality of the Iraq War and How
     Rendition Sparked It                              135

7    European and Canadian Complicity
     in Rendition and Torture                        159

*Notes*                     181
*Index*                     223

# PREFACE

$D$emocracies claim never to torture. Former president George W. Bush asserted that the "United States does not torture" because it is "against our values." Torture violates the most fundamental international norms, abhorred equally with slavery and genocide and punishable as an international crime. Most democracies, including Canada, Great Britain, and the United States, also make torture a crime under domestic law. No exceptions are supposed to be permitted; neither war nor the "ticking bomb" nor any other events override the prohibition, which has been declared utterly outlawed. Moreover, end-runs are likewise proscribed; a nation cannot export its interrogations, problem prisoners, or unwanted aliens to a scofflaw nation's torture chambers. According to Judge Irving Kauffman in writing the oft-cited *Filartiga* case, "the torturer has become like the pirate and the slave trader before him *hostis humani generis*, an enemy of all mankind."

What are we to make of extraordinary rendition? Of rendition to torture? After the tragic events of September 11, 2001, the United States turned to so-called harsh interrogation techniques that ordinary people would deem outright torture. Even that level of cruelty did not suffice, and some in the administration argued for even harsher interrogation tools. The United States picked up alleged terrorists from all over the world and sent them to countries that subjected them to the most brutal and medieval torture. Bones and lives were shattered as U.S. agents, using private corporate jets, carried the innocent and guilty alike to Morocco, Syria, and Egypt. The prohibition against torture fell away without appreciable resistance. As David Luban puts it, "American abhorrence to torture now appears to have extraordinarily shallow roots."

Other democracies complicity became crucial. A number of Western democracies, notably Canada, Great Britain, and others of Western Europe, eagerly assisted. Their aversion to torture also proved superficial, albeit perhaps to a lesser degree than the United States.

With hindsight, we can assess the multiple failures of rendition to torture. We hear the stories of innocent people caught up in the war against terror and mercilessly tortured. We can now evaluate the instances where torture led to false information that in turn led to expensive and sometimes disastrous errors. We continue to learn about the enemies made and the terrorists encouraged as our proxy gulags become a recruiting tool for al-Qaeda, al-Shabab, and the Taliban. But if torture and rendition to torture failed, and this book amply demonstrates that they did, why did their use seem so seductive? What made policymakers assume that such law evasion could work on any level?

This book attempts to understand how and why the law proved so fragile. How did such a supposedly absolute and concrete prohibition prove so delicate? What lessons are to be learned from this, and how might democracies next time avoid this mistake? Ultimately, if a project such as this is to have value, that worth lies in our ability not only to understand but also to change legal structures in an attempt to make such errors less likely in the future. This book, then, is committed to the hope that the world not only outlaws torture but also stops the practice. We may not be able to hold those who committed and facilitated torture strictly accountable through the courts. That may prove politically infeasible, at least for the present. The United States is not prepared to prosecute its own high officials, and the rest of the world is not prepared to directly confront the world's most powerful nation over this issue. We can, however, expose not only what the United States did, with others' help, but we can also analyze the legal, moral, and historical implications of rendition to torture. This examination and contextualization of the jurisprudential and ethical issues is necessary because it may be the closest we can get to approach accountability, and it is necessary because we need to understand the recent past if we are to avoid repetition.

I came to these issues because of the support of my wife and life partner, Laurelyn Whitt, who led me to see these issues anew and who encouraged me to begin this investigation. But for her nudge, I likely would never have started this project.

I would not have come to my understanding of these issues without the support and critique throughout the years of more people than could possibly be mentioned. I am particularly grateful to Craig Scott, my dissertation supervisor at Osgoode Hall Law School, York University, and to Professor Margaret Beare of Osgoode Hall Law School. Those who read and commented on earlier drafts include Marjorie Cohn and Roger S. Clark. I am also grateful to Utah Valley University for providing me with a sabbatical during which I was able to conduct much of the research for this book, and to the UVU library staff for their consistent help with finding source material. Finally, I am grateful to the University of Manitoba Faculty of Law for allowing me to visit as a research associate, and to and their fine reference librarian who ran down hard-to-find references for me.

# ACKNOWLEDGMENTS

Parts of this book have appeared, with substantially updated research and rewriting, in the publications listed below. Their permission is gratefully acknowledged.

"Creating a Torture Culture," *Suffolk Transnational Law Review* 32 (2008).

"De-cloaking Torture: *Boumediene* and the Military Commissions Act," *San Diego International Law Journal* 11 (2009).

"Rendition to Torture: A Critical Legal History," *Rutgers Law Review* 62 (2009).

"U.S. War Crimes: Torture as Official Bush Administration Policy," *National Lawyer's Guild Review* 66 (2009).

# Rendition to Torture

# 1

## Introduction

Universally condemned and everywhere considered illegal, torture goes on and on in liberal Western democracies as well as in dictatorships. Nonetheless, many people were surprised following the terrorist attacks of 9/11 at how easily the United States embraced torture and its pitiless lesser cousin, cruel, inhuman, and degrading treatment. Nothing seemed extreme when it came to questioning real and imagined terrorists.

Extraordinary rendition to nations long counted among the world's worst human rights violators hid the crueler and cruder interrogations while "torture lite" or "torture without marks" became the norm for detainees in U.S. custody. Democratic U.S. allies not only became complicit with renditions to torture but also found their own creative ways to transfer prisoners into the hands of some of the worst human rights violators. In short, as America embraced ever-harsher interrogation techniques, both it and its allies subcontracted the nastiest and most brutal torture.

Democracies claim not to use torture, maintaining that torture is the sole province of dictatorships. Notwithstanding this disclaimer, in times of crisis, democracies employ torture. The fear of violent attack and the need to gain quick intelligence can overwhelm legal structures designed to prevent human rights abuses. Given sufficient violence-induced stress and threats to a frightened civilian population, even the most open democracies sometimes overreach. Torture by democratic governments is not inevitable, but it occurs too often and too pervasively to be dismissed as aberrational or the work of a few rogue agents.

When the question "Would you allow officials to torture a terrorist (or suspected terrorist) in order to save the lives of innocent civilians?" is asked, the answer, at least for democracies, turns on an assessment of whether the practice can be kept secret, or at least characterized as something less than outright torture. Hence, democracies turning to torture need to leave no marks on the body, thus leading to the imaginative creation of ways to enhance human suffering without leaving a visible trace. In this respect, they are the true innovators in an ancient and otherwise primitive practice. Torture has been driven underground, formally forbidden, repeatedly disavowed, and rhetorically recast as something less or other than what it is, but when the stakes are high, it is practiced where plausibly deniable.

In the stress and fear following the terrorist attacks of 9/11, the United States captured thousands of people in its war against terror and used interrogation techniques that any sensible speaker of the English language would call torture. It also knowingly and intentionally kidnapped and then rendered people to such places as Syria, Morocco, and Egypt, where the most brutal forms of torture inevitably followed. Others captured in this war simply disappeared and presumably were killed. While the United States steadfastly denies that it uses torture, or that it renders people to even worse forms of torture and in some cases death, evidence continues to accumulate that it did so knowingly and intentionally, and that some outlawed practices continue into the present. That surprising numbers have proved to be innocent of wrongdoing compounds the problem; even those who think that torture may sometimes be justifiable might hesitate at torturing those who are wholly unconnected to terrorism. Moreover, when one tortures those who are unconnected to terrorism, one risks creating enemies that did not heretofore exist; one thereby compounds the terrorism problem.

Abuse of those who are innocent is not the only instrumental problem. Bad people as well as good will often say whatever it takes to make the pain stop, thus presenting the interrogator with dubious information. For example, false information gleaned from torture was used to justify the Iraq War—adding potency to the charge that the war was illegal under international law and further undercutting assertions that the war was lawful. Moreover, false information obtained by torture has wasted millions of dollars and untold numbers of man-hours in having U.S. officials and agents chase multiple false leads. The cost of either debunking or using bad information is too often underappreciated in evaluating torture's efficacy.

Additionally, torture provides terrorist organizations with an additional recruiting tool. The eminent jurist and counterterrorism expert Arthur Chaskalson points out that torture "tends to be counterproductive. If we are going to address terrorism, we have to find means of dealing with it but if you act in that way, the lesson of history is that you tend to recruit people to the cause, give them reasons to join the cause."[1]

This book explains how the United States came to embrace everharsher interrogation techniques and how both the United States and its allies came to subcontract the nastiest, most brutal torture. It explains the true nature of so-called torture lite interrogation techniques, examines how and why the United States turned to extraordinary rendition and the consequences thereof, and covers the complicity and culpability that European nations and Canada have with the U.S. rendition program. It also tells how Canadian and British military forces engaged in their own unique in-theater renditions, which sent prisoners detained in the war in Afghanistan to be tortured in Afghani prisons. Finally, it outlines the transnational political and legal backlash that may finally constrain torture and renditions to torture under both international and domestic laws.

## Torture Lite and the Creation of a Torture Culture

Building upon earlier harsh intelligence practices developed and refined by the U.S. Central Intelligence Agency (CIA), the United States established a torture culture in response to the "war on terrorism." The Department of Justice's Office of Legal Counsel (OLC) approved so-called harsh or alternative interrogation techniques, and these came to be the accepted practices in the treatment of detainees.[2] Some of the approved techniques included repeatedly drowning people on "waterboards" scientifically designed to maximize suffocation and with personnel trained to intensify distress. This was combined with other abuses, such as stress positions, dietary manipulation, sleep deprivation, wall slamming, and other techniques intended to accentuate and prolong the misery.

The term "torture lite" is a euphemism that attempts to reduce the full horror of these techniques. Imagine being repeatedly drowned and resuscitated while also being deprived of sleep and food and doused with cold water to the point of hypothermia. Imagine that your interrogator waits for you to exhale before dunking you again, then dams the water on your face, forcing you to inhale a saline solution; that before, during, and after these waterboardings you are slammed against a wall, subjected to deafening noises and glaring lights, placed in small boxes and in stress positions for extended periods. Imagine this going on for days upon days, without end and without hope. These are among the interrogation practices that the United States under the Bush administration endorsed, practiced, and attempted to dismiss as either unremarkable torture lite or as not constituting torture at all.[3]

Even skeptics who have doubted the agony caused by waterboarding and have voluntarily subjected themselves to it have recanted and now call it torture. For example, one famous skeptic, the writer and Iraq War advocate Christopher Hitchens questioned the agony caused by waterboarding and initially refused to call it "outright torture." Writing for *Slate* magazine in 2007, he argued for a distinction between the "extreme interrogation," which the United States did do (including waterboarding) and "outright torture," which the United States did not, he asserted, engage in.[4] Allegations that the United States engaged in anything that could be called torture, he said, "besmirch and discredit the United States."[5] As of 2007, it would have been difficult to find a more enthusiastic promoter of administration interrogation policies (including waterboarding suspected terrorists) than Christopher Hitchens.

His critics challenged him to try it.[6] He accepted the challenge; after a few seconds of dunking, he recanted and called it "torture."[7] Similarly, other likeminded skeptics have also been challenged to see for themselves and, upon trying it, have also declared it real drowning and torture.[8]

Hitchens underwent simple waterboarding, without having endured any of the other abuses that U.S. detainees routinely suffer and knowing that it would be stopped immediately upon use of prearranged signal. Unlike suspected terrorists, some of whom have been waterboarded as many as 183 times, he also knew beforehand that he would walk away never again to have to face such abuse.[9] Hitchens writes about his brief flirtation with waterboarding in *Vanity Fair*:

> You may have read by now the official lie about this treatment, which is that it "simulates" the feeling of drowning. This is not the case. You feel that you are drowning because you are drowning—or, rather, being drowned, albeit slowly and under controlled conditions and at the mercy (or otherwise) of those who are applying the pressure. . . . The interrogators would hardly have had time to ask me any questions, and I knew that I would quite readily have agreed to supply any answer. . . . As if detecting my misery and shame, one of my interrogators comfortingly said, "Any time is a long time when you're breathing water." . . . I apply the Abraham Lincoln test for moral casuistry: "If slavery is not wrong, nothing is wrong." Well, then, if waterboarding does not constitute torture, then there is no such thing as torture.[10]

Waterboarding has unquestionably become the best known and most controversial of the so-called harsh interrogation techniques approved by lawyers in the Bush administration for use in interrogating suspected terrorists.[11] However, a too narrow focus on waterboarding inevitably distracts from the other OLC-approved interrogation techniques. Many of these euphemistically misnamed alternative interrogation techniques have equally profound effects on their victims and, as will be demonstrated later, justly deserve the name "torture." For the present, it suffices to say that some victims of U.S. interrogation practices at Guantánamo have become delusional.[12] During interrogation, one detainee was seen chained hand and foot on the floor in the fetal position beside a pile of his hair that he had pulled out over the course of the night.[13] According to one of the leading authorities on the subject, torture lite victims can suffer "depression, excessive anxiety, post-traumatic stress disorder and sometimes full-blown psychosis."[14] These

symptoms can persist for twenty or thirty years and are extremely difficult to treat.[5] Thus, it is important not to make too fine a distinction
between waterboarding and other OLC-approved forms of harsh interrogations. At some point, when used repeatedly and in combination
with other such techniques, many techniques become torture. By any
reasonable definition, virtually all of these interrogation techniques,
at a minimum, constitute cruel, inhuman, and degrading treatment in
direct violation of international law. People vary in their reaction to
these harsh techniques; what one person may tolerate and shrug off as
merely uncomfortable another may find shockingly painful and intoler-
able. Surely, a harsh interrogation technique cannot be justified solely
on the basis that some people exist with sufficient fortitude to resist.

Nonetheless, neither waterboarding nor any of the other enhanced
interrogation techniques used by U.S. forces leaves any visible mark.
This seemingly makes plausible the argument that these practices do
not constitute torture. If the public cannot see it, then it can be denied,
or at least it can be maintained that it was not so bad after all. The same
cannot be said about extraordinary rendition.

Chapter 2 of this book discusses how the United States of America
came to use various no-mark forms of torture within the confines
of territorial United States. This helps one to understand the use of
extraordinary rendition as a way to outsource even more extreme forms
of torture leading up to mutilation, death, and disappearance. We cannot address extraordinary rendition in isolation; first, we must understand the motivation to, and limitations of, using harsh interrogation
techniques by U.S. agents before moving to the practice of rendering
suspected terrorists to third countries where outright, unambiguous
torture is routinely practiced.

## Extraordinary Rendition

The term "extraordinary rendition" arises out of earlier simpler
notions of rendition to justice, in which nations resorted to abduction
to secure the presence of fugitives for trial. The practice was usually
reserved for particularly heinous criminals who had fled to places
where extradition was difficult or impossible. France, for example,

kidnapped the most wanted terrorist of his time, Carlos "the Jackal," and rendered him to France where he was tried, convicted, and sentenced to life imprisonment. The Jackal may have been kidnapped, but he received a fair trial and now spends his days in the relatively humane custody of a French prison.

Extraordinary rendition differs from the rendition of fugitives to face impartial justice in one important respect—instead of taking the kidnapped person back to the home nation for trial, he (or she, but usually he) is taken to a third country where he may be questioned, tried, tortured, or disappeared. Torture and disappearance are undoubtedly the most problematic outcomes. Most awkward is when the nation doing the kidnapping sends the abductees to a nation known for human rights abuses, and knows that torture is likely. Beyond callousness, this practice violates international law and the domestic laws of many nations, including the laws of the United States, Canada, and Great Britain. Needless to say, nations that do engage in this form of rendition find multiple ways either to deny that they have done so or to excuse their conduct: It did not happen; if it did happen, it either was not so bad or the responsible officials did not know that torture would follow; these same officials got assurances against torture; and finally, the "terrorist" deserved it and, moreover, lives were saved as a result. The evidence outlined throughout this book will show these explanations to be dodges.

Once the United States has rendered a person to a third nation with a bad human rights record, he or she falls outside the protections of the U.S. court system. Those so rendered become invisible to the courts, the media, and the public. All constraints disappear. Out of the public's sight, anything—including torture—becomes possible. The person can be beaten and battered, bones can be broken, sharp knives can pierce the skin. The person can be mutilated, disappeared, killed. Despite robust evidence that the United States engages in extraordinary renditions to countries that torture, and that it engages in practices that many consider torture, the Bush administration adamantly denied that it was torturing anyone or was sending people to nations that do. Indeed, President George W. Bush declared that the United States "will always be the world's leader in support of human rights."[16] Despite criticism from international legal scholars, the United States persistently maintains that it follows international law and its treaty obligations.

One might have thought that if the goal was simply to apply pressure sufficient to produce quick interrogation results, the United States had, courtesy of the OLC's permissive legal opinions, all the abusive techniques it would need. Given this, one might ask, what was the need to subcontract out even more extreme forms of torture to such states as Syria, Morocco, and Egypt? Why did the United States resort to rendition? Examining the evidence, which is detailed more fully in the chapters that follow, we find seven reasons:

1. Various international and domestic constraints kept U.S. officials from authorizing the kinds of interrogation practices that are most readily regarded as torture—those techniques that left visible marks; techniques that mutilated, leaving the body battered, scarred, and bloody. Interrogators in some other countries, most notably in the Middle East, were not subject to such constraints and could do far more than anything available to even the most clandestine of the U.S. forces—they had no compunctions about leaving marks and even killing the detainee. In some cases, this was precisely what at least some U.S. officials wanted. Supposed terrorists were both abusively questioned and taken out of action in a way that allowed plausible denials.

2. Early in the war on terror, Guantánamo Bay and the CIA "black sites" had not been set up. Renditions became an easy way to unload prisoners for abusive interrogations when the United States had no place, outside of its own borders, to hold them.

3. The Bush administration became impatient for results, and in some cases gave in to the notion that greater force, applied early on, could yield quick and accurate intelligence.

4. Renditions fall outside of the U.S. justice system; the practice lies beyond the jurisdiction of federal courts. Thus, renditions became a tool to deny detainees the protections of a court system that was seen as an impediment to obtaining actionable intelligence.

5. The sheer numbers of people being captured meant that, even after Guantánamo and other prisons outside U.S. borders were

operational, the United States had to outsource some of the supposed terrorists. Ironically, while in most cases it outsourced the less important terrorists, in the case of Ibn al-Shaykh al-Libi, the United States gave up an important terrorist to be tortured in Egypt in order to get quick results. This was ultimately catastrophic because the information thus obtained turned out to be false.

6. In a few cases, the United States faced the prospect of having to free the suspected terrorist. For example, Maher Arar was a dual citizen of Canada and Syria. Returning him to Canada, which lacked sufficient evidence to detain him, would have resulted in freeing him. Rather than free someone against whom evidence was lacking, the United States simply rendered him to torture in Syria. It turned out that evidence was insufficient precisely because Arar was innocent; although blameless, he was horrifically tortured by the Syrians.

7. Perhaps most importantly, as Craig Scott has persuasively argued, some in the Bush administration held a "security mentality, non-humanist ideology (shared by hawks globally),"[17] which combined with the Kafkaesque power of bureaucracies to deflect and spread out accountability and the ability of civil servants to either help hide or to provide justificatory reasoning for their superiors' actions. It also gave license to a torture culture that could send people abroad to be mutilated and disappeared. Ideological blinders at the top, served by a powerful, desensitized and highly secretive bureaucracy, provided the necessary and perhaps sufficient conditions for extraordinary rendition in aftermath of September 11, 2001.

The United States rendered hundreds, perhaps thousands, to face the most brutal forms of torture, and in some cases those rendered simply disappeared. The false evidence gathered from al-Libi through the use of torture led to the war in Iraq, thus magnifying and supporting the already well-trodden arguments that the war was illegal under international law because it was not within the UN mandates relating to Iraq.

The United States could not have subcontracted torture out without help (and an occasional blind eye) from European nations and Canada. The United States may harbor the greatest measure of culpability;

however, it was not alone in farming out torture, nor could it have sent
so many to torture chambers in Syria, Morocco, and Egypt without help.
Many European nations and Canada aided in this.

As will be detailed in chapter 4, Canada provided misleading information on its own citizen, Maher Arar, to the United States. The United
States then sent him to Syria to be tortured. Many European nations
turned a blind eye by allowing CIA-sponsored flights carrying prisoners the use of airspace and places to land and refuel. Others provided
"black sites" for secret prisons used for harsh interrogations and as
transit points to further rendition.

Despite denials, Spain apparently allowed the CIA to use Spanish
airspace and military bases for transporting detainees from Afghanistan to Guantánamo Bay, Cuba.[18] Italian intelligence agents almost
certainly cooperated with the CIA in abducting Abu Omar and sending
him to Egypt, knowing that he would there face torture.[19] In convicting
twenty-two Americans for the kidnapping and rendition, Judge Oscar
Magi wrote that the ease with which the Americans had operated on
Italian soil "leads to the presumption that such activity was carried out
at least with the knowledge (or maybe with the complicity)" of Italian
intelligence services.[20] Similarly, U.S. rendition flights landed and refueled in Poland, and Poland is alleged to have housed the largest CIA
secret detention facility in Europe.[21] Romania and Lithuania are also
alleged to have housed CIA black site detention facilities, and Sweden
allowed the CIA to render two Egyptians from its soil to Egypt (via a
refueling stop in Scotland) where they were tortured.[22]

Rapporteur Dick Marty reported to the Council of Europe that
"insofar as they did not know, they did not want to know. It is incon-
ceivable that certain operations conducted by American services could
have taken place without the active participation, or at least the collusion, of national intelligence services."[23] While the most active role
unquestionably fell to the United States, it could not have sent so many
people to face torture without the help of others, including nations
with otherwise good human rights records.

Chapters 3, 4, 5, and 6 directly confront the multiple practices of
rendition. Chapter 3 traces the uses of rendition to justice from the rendition of Nazi war criminal Adolf Eichmann to the beginning renditions

to torture under the Clinton administration. Chapter 4 provides sketches of five of the most important extraordinary renditions, those renditions that have caused the greatest legal and political problems for the United States. Chapter 5 compares the way in which state secrets laws in the United States, Canada, and the United Kingdom work to insulate the government from exposure because of civil lawsuits. In all three countries, plaintiffs have used the civil court system to seek redress for their having been rendered to countries that in turned tortured them. Only the United States (which is by far the more culpable government of the three) has completely closed the courthouse doors to such plaintiffs.

## Bad Information, Bad Consequences: The Case of al-Libi

Because of its importance, the rendition of Ibn al-Shaykh al-Libi deserves its own separate discussion. Chapter 6 covers in detail the rendition of al-Libi, whose rendition to and torture in Egypt led to the false claim that Iraq was training al-Qaeda agents in the use of weapons of mass destruction.

At least since Aristotle, informed commentators have questioned the accuracy of information gleaned by using torture. The Roman jurist Ulpian wrote concerning torture that "many persons have such strength of body and soul that they heed pain very little, so that there is no means of obtaining the truth from them. While others are so susceptible to pain that they will tell any lie rather than suffer it."[24] Political scientist Darius Rejali has probably done more empirical and historical research into the problem. Sifting through tens of thousands of records from the Gestapo, the French in Algeria, and the British in Northern Ireland, among others, he concludes that torture simply does not yield accurate information.[25]

The problems with torture-elicited information are multiple.[26] Wholly innocent people will say anything to end the pain. Those with actionable intelligence may lie about what they do know. More importantly, how does one know when a terrorist has spilled all that he knows? No one is immune. Torture spreads from the guilty to the less important to the wholly innocent; it also expands as to any given victim who may reveal yet more under just a bit more torture. The innocent person is most vulnerable. Torturers often suggest that the victim is at fault, and all he or she needs to do is come forward with the truth. But that is a mirage. One can never know whether the person undergoing torture knows anything of value, or if he has told all he knows. How can an innocent person persuade his interrogator that he knows nothing? And how can the person who has told all persuade someone that he has nothing more of value to say? Those who do have important information "can only protect themselves, as torture victims always have, by pretending to be collaborators or innocents, and thereby imperiling the members of these categories."[27]

Sometimes the false information gleaned by torture simply costs money and time. The lie under torture sends investigators out on false leads, spending both money and time that could be better used in fighting the real war on terror. For example, the United States first experimented with its so-called harsh interrogation techniques on the supposed super-terrorist and 9/11 mastermind Abu Zubaydah.[28] It turns out in retrospect that Zubaydah was not a knowledgeable terrorist mastermind but rather a mentally ill, low-level safehouse keeper.[29] U.S. agents, however, thought he knew a great deal and pressed him hard, waterboarding him eighty-three times. He told them just what they wanted to hear. He linked José Padilla to a dirty bomb (that is, a bomb that would spread radioactive materials without undergoing nuclear fission or fusion) plot to destroy an American city. That information turned out to be false. Zubaydah provided multiple leads to other terrorist plots throughout the United States. All turned out to be false. In the meantime, as one former intelligence official put it, "we spent millions of dollars chasing false alarms."[30] Notwithstanding former vice president Dick Cheney's continued claims that waterboarding and other harsh interrogation techniques "worked very, very well," it failed spectacularly precisely in those cases where it would have appeared most promising.[31]

However, false leads, even those that squandered millions of dollars and sent federal agents hither and yon, are not the worst problem caused by information gathered as a product of torture. As will be demonstrated more fully in chapter 6, false information gained through brutal torture helped to justify and arguably led to the war in Iraq. Ibn al-Shaykh al-Libi provided the "evidence" that Saddam Hussein's rogue regime in Iraq was training al-Qaeda terrorists in the use of weapons of mass destruction. Possession of such weapons and the training of terrorists in their use provided the justification for the second Iraq war. For present purposes, the questions are, What sort of pressure caused al-Libi to tell such a monstrous tale? How do we explain false information leading to such disastrous consequences?

According to Human Rights Watch, citing declassified CIA cable records:

> Egyptian interrogators had said they wanted information about al-Qaeda's connections with Iraq, a subject "about which [al-Libi] said he knew nothing and had difficulty even coming up with a story." The cable went on to say that al-Libi indicated that his interrogators did not like his responses and then "placed him in a small box" for approximately 17 hours. When he was let out of the box, the cable states that al-Libi was given a last opportunity to "tell the truth." When al-Libi's answers did not satisfy the interrogator, al-Libi says he "was knocked over with an arm thrust across his chest and he fell on his back" and was then "punched for 15 minutes." It was then that al-Libi told his interrogators that Iraq had trained al-Qaeda operatives in chemical and biological weapons, information that was later used in Colin Powell's speech to the UN Security Council to justify war with Iraq.[32]

Al-Libi, then, had been stuffed into a box measuring approximately twenty inches by twenty inches for seventeen hours and then when taken out, beaten. It is hard to imagine cramming any adult into such a space. It is not surprising that, after that and a right good beating, he told his interlocutors whatever they wished to hear. The important point is not that al-Libi said what he needed to say to end the pain— anyone might well do that. More important by far is that we know about his torture from declassified CIA cables sent contemporaneously with President Bush and Secretary of State Colin Powell's public statements using al-Libi's information to justify the war in Iraq.[33] Thus,

U.S. officials, including the president and his secretary of state, either knew or should have known from contemporaneous CIA cables that the information that they were using to justify the war was gained by using brutal torture. The moral implications of using information acquired through using torture aside, we will see in chapter 6 that these same officials had other reasons to doubt al-Libi's story. This leads to the inference that U.S. justifications for the war were pretextual. Al-Libi's case then raises both moral and legal questions that continue to be relevant in assessing the war in Iraq.

## Conclusion: Complicity and Backlash

Chapter 7 concludes by outlining the complicity of other democracies in U.S. torture practices. Many of the democracies of Europe as well as Canada allowed themselves to become thoroughly enmeshed in U.S. torture practices. Some, like Canada, provided intelligence leading to people (sometimes innocent) being captured and rendered to places in the Middle East with ferocious reputations for torture. Others, such as the United Kingdom, Poland, Romania, Italy, and Lithuania, allowed rendition flights to use their sovereign airspace and allowed CIA rendition planes to land and refuel on their soil without complaint. Secret black site prisons proliferated in Eastern Europe, which served the CIA in its "harsh interrogations" program and as waypoints to fly prisoners to torture chambers in Syria, Morocco, and Egypt. Other countries, such as Sweden and Macedonia, aided in capturing people and turning them over to CIA-run torture flights. Intelligence agencies interposed the state secrets doctrine in an attempt to help the CIA hide its rendition program from public view, although with varying degrees of success. Finally, some allies such as Canada and Great Britain maintained a form of rendition of their own in Afghanistan. Their armed forces turned people captured in that conflict over to Afghan torture chambers. Evidence continues to mount to suggest that this was not the work of a few rogue soldiers but rather stemmed from a conscious willingness at the highest political levels to ignore the consequences of turning people over into the hands of likely torturers.

Thus, while the United States was undoubtedly the most culpable in the return to using torture for interrogation purposes, it was not alone. If the world is to eradicate torture and if it is to end the practice of outsourcing torture, then it must examine the fact that many nations played a role. Those nations are beginning to examine their respective roles, and in this there is hope. As Canada and Europe do what the United States has thus far been reluctant to do—that is, confront the ugly fact of torture and in a few cases begin to provide compensation for those who have been abused—this puts pressure on the United States to improve its record. The record as of this writing is mixed.

# 2

## Cultivating a Torture Culture

QUESTION: Mr. President, I wanted to return to the question of torture. . . . When you say that you want the U.S. to adhere to international and U.S. laws, that's not very comforting. This is a moral question: Is torture ever justified?

PRESIDENT GEORGE W. BUSH: Maybe I can be more clear. The instructions went out to our people to adhere to law. That ought to comfort you. We're a nation of law. We adhere to laws. We have laws on the books. You might look at those laws, and that might provide comfort for you. And those were the instructions out . . . from me to the government!

The United States follows the law; the law prohibits torture; therefore, the United States does not torture. This neat syllogism provides a chilling reminder of how a democratic government can clandestinely inflict pain and suffering while deflecting the moral question: "Is torture ever justified?" President Bush obliquely denied ordering torture and turned to misleading legalisms even while secretly authorizing both torture and rendition to torture.

How and why did the United States turn to torture? Harsh interrogations, so-called torture lite or mark-free torture, and extraordinary rendition have common roots. One cannot fully understand extraordinary rendition without also understanding U.S. use of harsh interrogation techniques that sometimes cross into outright torture.

Even as President Bush sought to obscure actual practices, U.S. agents were, with explicit presidential approval overseen by cabinet-level officers, repeatedly waterboarding and abusing prisoners at U.S. prison sites around the world and rendering people to face torture and disappearance. As early as the fall of 2001 the CIA had rendered a suspected terrorist to a Jordanian prison, where he simply disappeared.[2] The United States increasingly turned to ever more vicious forms of torture even as it repeatedly and vehemently denied its use.

At the time that President Bush made his "we adhere to laws" comment in the summer of 2004, word was leaking out that the Department of Justice, Office of Legal Counsel (OLC) had approved the usage of so-called harsh or alternative interrogation techniques that we have since come to understand included both torture and cruel, inhuman, and degrading treatment of prisoners in the war on terror. More and more information was becoming public about prisoners extraordinarily rendered to nations with some of the worst human rights records imaginable.

## Understanding Why We Torture: Context for U.S. Torture

Psychology teaches that people everywhere are capable of great cruelty just as they are capable of extraordinary kindness. Much turns on the situation, which can bring out the worst in anyone. Institutionalized torture comes about from otherwise ordinary people who, when caught up in situations that seemingly demand it, abuse their fellow humans. As both Stanley Milgram and Phillip Zimbardo's experiments have taught, otherwise normal people can, under the right (or wrong) circumstances, do surprisingly harsh things.[3]

Milgram demonstrated that almost anyone could torture. His experiments at Yale succeeded in persuading ordinary U.S. citizens to deliver supposed electric shocks to strangers, causing grunting, violent screaming, and even what appeared to the test subjects to be fatalities. What the volunteers did not know what that these strangers were actors playing the part of victims and that the shocks were not real. Most people followed orders to the point of delivering what appeared to be severe pain and even death to strangers (or at least rendered the person apparently unconscious or otherwise unable to respond). The finding that ordinary people would so quickly follow such depraved orders from an unknown authority figure surprised Milgram, but shocking as his results seemed, they have been replicated and are now commonly accepted.[4] As David Luban puts it, "Milgram demonstrated that each of us ought to believe three things about ourselves: that we disapprove of destructive obedience, that we think we would never engage in it, and, more likely than not, that we are wrong to think we would never engage in it."[5]

We like to think that horrific human rights abuses are limited to narrow historical circumstances such as those that occurred in the Third Reich, and that normal humans do not act that way. Milgram's experiments teach us that most individuals will do things that they would never have guessed themselves capable. As historian Alfred W. McCoy reports, "one subject, a military veteran . . . recalled feeling like 'an emotional wreck' . . . from the realization 'that somebody could get me to do that stuff.'"[6]

Philip Zimbardo's prison experiments, in which groups of average American students degenerated into extreme abuse after only six days, showed how groups of average people could, when given arbitrary power (and a perceived need), severely abuse others without remorse or thought about the consequences. Zimbardo's experiment adds an understanding of the group dynamic that leads normal people to abuse others. The common theme between Milgram and Zimbardo is how easily both individuals and groups can come to abuse their fellow humans. There is no reason to think that in either experiment the subjects were different in any meaningful way from the rest of us; anyone of us could be the torturer. As Jean-Paul Sartre put it, "when we raise our heads and look into the mirror we see an unfamiliar and hideous reflection: ourselves. . . . Anybody, at any time may equally find himself victim or executioner."[7]

Sociologist Martha Huggins demonstrates a large, real-world application of Milgram and Zimbardo's findings. Her study of police torture in Brazil identifies six conditions that are associated with systemic torture:

1. Unchecked and arbitrary excessive rule;
2. Ideology of war: against evil (or communism, etc.);
3. Secrecy of interrogation locations and procedures;
4. Hidden identities of interrogators and those interrogated;

5. A social control division of labor giving plausible deniability and obscured perpetrator's relationship to the violence; and

6. A public rendered impotent by fear.[8]

Each of these factors has been present to some degree in the war on terror. However, Brazil was, for the period in which many abuses occurred, an authoritarian junta. We know that democracies, also torture. Why?

Political scientist Darius Rejali explains that while democracies are not as bad as totalitarian regimes, they not only engage in torture but also are "the real innovators in 20th century torture. It might make Americans uncomfortable, but the modern repertoire of torture is mainly a democratic innovation." The difference between democratic torture and that of the Gestapo has been the search for "clean" techniques that leave no mark: "as societies have become more open, the art of torture has crept underground and evolved into the chilling new forms—often undetectable—that define torture today." The shift to clean techniques is a response to public pressure. Because the torturer is susceptible to public pressure, "governments that continue to use torture have moved to techniques that leave little trace. . . . Strange as it may seem, torturers and their apologists really do care."[9] Thus, torture can thrive in a democracy if it can be hidden; this depends on a closed system with a lack of accountability and lack of access to courts.

Rejali notes that torture may arise because security bureaucracies overwhelm those assigned to monitor them. Where there is a lack of accountability, democracies will also torture—the main difference is the extent to which they will go to try to hide it.[10]

We are told that the war on terror is a "different kind of war" with "no geographic limitations [and] no end in sight."[11] President Bush said that our enemies are "evil-doers"[12] outside of the law and undeserving of legal protection.[13] We inhabit a world of "us" against "the evil-doers," making those whom we fight less than human, evil, and deserving of no rights or even human sympathy. This was the first step toward a torture culture. Al-Qaeda becomes equated with pirates and slave traders to be dealt with or extirpated at will. As one prominent legal defender of the administration put it, "Why is it so hard for people to understand that there is a category of behavior not covered by the legal system? What were pirates? They weren't fighting on behalf of any nation. What were slave traders? Historically, there were people so bad that they were not given protection of the laws. There were no specific provisions for their trial, or imprisonment. If you were an illegal combatant, you didn't deserve the protection of the laws of war."[14]

In this context, with suspects demonized and placed outside of law, the Bush administration's statements sound uncomfortably similar to Gen. Wilhelm Keitel's Nuremburg testimony: "The main theme [of Hitler's instructions] was that this was the decisive battle between two ideologies, and that this fact made it impossible to use in this war methods as we soldiers knew them and which were considered to be the only correct ones under the International Law. The war could not be carried on by these means. In this case completely different standards had to be applied. This was an entirely new kind of war, based on completely different arguments and principles."[15]

Plainly, Huggins's conditions of a "war against evil," and a "public immobilized by fear," were met in the war on terror. The point is not that the United States came close to becoming another Nazi Germany, whose excesses far outstrip the evils of almost any imagined comparison. However, the reasoning underpinning the abusive practices in the war on terror was very similar to the reasoning underpinning Nazi aggression in Europe. We cannot demonize the enemy and simultaneously raise fears among the public without paying a price. In that respect, the comparison remains apt even if unrelated in other respects.

The teachings of modern psychology, sociology, and history suggest that when faced with systemic, widespread torture and cruel treatment, one should look not to a few bad apples but rather to failures of command and control, failures that go to the top. This suggests that one should be skeptical of the administration's "few bad apples" theory. From this perspective, Abu Ghraib, extraordinary rendition, secret prisons, and the abusive treatment of prisoners at Guantánamo Bay were the foreseeable results of a secret and unaccountable culture.[16] As the legal scholar and ethicist David Luban points out, "American abhorrence to torture now appears to have extraordinarily shallow roots."[17] It is the shallowness of these roots that in part accounts for both domestic use of torture lite to extraordinary rendition and worse.

## U.S. Experiments with Torture

During the Cold War, the CIA and other intelligence services became interested in forceful interrogation tactics that would not leave telltale marks, so-called torture lite or, as Darius Rejali puts it, "clean" torture.[18] Such clean torture, when combined with sensory deprivation and drugs, became the new torture. The methods typically "include sleep deprivation, exposure to heat or cold, the use of drugs to cause confusion, rough treatment (slapping, shoving or shaking), forcing a prisoner to stand for days at a time or sit in uncomfortable positions, and playing on his fears for himself and his family. Although excruciating for the victim, these tactics generally leave no permanent marks and do no lasting physical harm."[19]

In 1994 the *Baltimore Sun* used the Freedom of Information Act to uncover the long-suppressed truth about American use of torture. As a result, the CIA declassified and released two key manuals. Through their efforts, we learned that the United States has been searching since the early 1950s for interrogation techniques that left no physical or emotional mark,[20] resulting, in 1963, in a 128-page how-to manual, called KUBARK.[21] The newspaper also pried loose a 1983 Human Resource Exploitation Manual, which, while based on the earlier KUBARK manual, updated CIA interrogation techniques.

Both manuals explicitly contemplate torture. For example, KUBARK states "the electric current should be known on advance, so that transformers or other modifying devices will be on hand if needed." Under the heading "threats and fear," KUBARK goes on to recommend that, "the threat to inflict pain, for example, can trigger fears more damaging than the immediate sensation of pain. In fact, most people underestimate their capacity to withstand pain." Similarly, KUBARK explains, "threats delivered coldly are more effective." Finally, "resistance is likelier to be sapped by pain which [the person interrogated] seems to inflict upon himself."[22]

The CIA's commitment to permitting and regulating torture is spelled out in the KUBARK section on legal and policy considerations, which, among other things, requires "prior Headquarters approval" before (1) "bodily harm is to be inflicted" or (2) "medical, chemical, or electrical methods or materials are to be used"; the third item on the list requiring headquarters approval is redacted, leaving one to wonder what more an interrogator might do.[23] Plainly, the United States moved toward "clean" torture techniques that leave no mark but leave pain, stress, and extreme discomfort to be the torturer's tools.

The Human Resource Exploitation Manual followed KUBARK twenty years later in 1983. KUBARK and Army field manuals of the 1960s heavily influenced the 1983 manual.[24] After congressional investigators threatened to expose the Human Resource Exploitation Manual, editors hand altered passages "that appeared to advocate coercion and stress techniques," adding that these methods were "prohibited by law" and were "neither authorized nor condoned."[25] These alterations make clear that the government understood the illegal and immoral nature of these practices—practices that continue in today's war on terror. Both of these manuals make clear that much of the torture and torture training that went on in Vietnam, Latin America, Iran, and the Philippines was the result of deliberate U.S. policy.[26]

Spreading the culture of torture requires more than manuals and experimentation. Dissemination of torture techniques requires schools. During the Cold War, the U.S. government sought to understand the communist interrogation techniques in part to see if ways to resist could be developed and taught. As a result, survival, evasion, resistance, and escape (SERE) schools were developed in 1947; within a few years they were, among other things, training military personnel to resist enemy interrogation techniques.[27] Simply by going through SERE training, graduates indirectly learned how to stress and abuse victims without ordinarily causing permanent physical harm. SERE instructors, including psychologists, devised programs that could be "reverse engineered" and then used at Guantánamo Bay.[28]

Torture thus had two paths to leak out into the broader post-9/11 war against terror—through graduates who could improvise interrogations on the spot in war zones, and through SERE instructors who could bring these methods to bear in secret and not-so-secret prisons in Afghanistan, Iraq, and Eastern Europe, and at Guantánamo Bay. Although the United States denied that SERE training tactics were deliberately used in training interrogators, these denials have proven false. Documents obtained by the American Civil Liberties Union quote the former chief interrogator saying, "When I arrived at GTMO my predecessor arranged for SERE instructors to teach their techniques to the interrogators at GTMO. . . . The instructors did give some briefings to the Joint Interrogation Group interrogators." Plainly, SERE instructors were instrumental in transferring the knowledge of "clean" torture to Guantánamo Bay.[29] The introduction of SERE resistance training was deliberately introduced into U.S. interrogation treatment of detainees at Guantánamo and other U.S. offshore prisons. Moreover, as we saw in chapter I, the indignities visited on detainees exceeded in both scope and ferocity that which was visited on volunteer SERE trainees.

A case from earlier in our history serves to demonstrate that the United States uses torture as a matter of official policy: the case of Dan Mitrione, who brought wholesale cruelty to Latin America. Mitrione was an Indiana police chief who became a police advisor for a CIA front organization; his role was "to teach interrogation methods . . . [that] included instructions in torture" first in the Dominican Republic, then Brazil, and finally Uruguay, where he was murdered by Tupamaro guerrillas.[30] Mitrione, who sought to "professionalize" and make torture "scientific," apparently tortured to death innocent beggars during his classroom teaching sessions.[31] His philosophy of interrogation is a chilling reminder of just how far some people will go:

> When you receive a subject, the first thing to do is to determine his physical state, his degree of resistance, through a medical examination. A premature death means a failure by the technician. . . .
>
> Another important thing to know is exactly how far you can go given the political situation and the personality of the prisoner. It is very important to know beforehand whether we have the luxury of letting the subject die. . . .
>
> Before all else, you must be efficient. You must cause only the damage that is strictly necessary, not a bit more. We must control our tempers in any case. You have to act with efficiency and cleanliness of a surgeon and the perfection of an artist.[32]

Mitrione introduced electrified needles manufactured by the CIA and imported in diplomatic pouches. These needles varied in thicknesses and could be inserted in a victim's fingernails and even between teeth.[33] American agents trained both the dreaded Iranian Savak and the torturers of the Philippine military. There is a direct line from past American practices to Abu Ghraib and Guantánamo.

What the administration claims to be lawful interrogation most people would characterize as torture. For example, an unnamed FBI agent observed activities at Guantánamo Bay and reported:

> On a couple of occassions [sic], I entered interview rooms to find a detainee chained hand and foot in a fetal position to the floor, with no chair, food, or water. Most times they had urinated or defacated [sic] on themselves, and had been left there for 18–24 hours or more. On one occassion [sic], the air conditioning had been turned down so far and the temperature was so cold in the room, that the barefooted detainee was shaking with cold. When I asked the MP's what was going on, I was told that interrogators from the day prior had ordered this treatment, and the detainee was not to be moved. On another occassion [sic], the A/C had been turned off, making the temperature in the unventilated room probably well over 100 degrees. The detainee was almost unconcious [sic] on the floor, with a pile of hair next to him. He had apparently been literally pulling out his own hair throughout the night. On another occassion [sic], not only was the temperature unbearably hot, but extremely loud rap music was being played in the room, and had been since the day before, with the detainee chained hand and foot in the fetal position on the tile floor.[34]

In another case, an FBI agent reported that he asked a marine what had caused a detainee at Guantánamo Bay, who was being interrogated, to grimace, "The marine said Sgt. Lacey [the interrogator] had grabbed the detainee's thumbs and bent them backwards and indicated that she also grabbed his genitals. The marine also implied that her treatment of that detainee was less harsh than her treatment of others by indicating that he had seen her treatment of other detainees result in detainees curling into a fetal position on the floor and crying in pain."[35]

Not only has the United States directly tortured detainees, it has also sent captured prisoners to other countries to interrogate them using medieval torture. Binyam Mohamed provides one of many such examples. Picked up in Pakistan, this innocent man was sent by the United States to Morocco where interlocutors broke his bones, sliced his penis with a scalpel, and gave him mind-altering drugs. The United States even attempted to prosecute him for crimes that carry the death penalty long after it was obvious that there was no good case against him because he was, in fact, innocent.[36]

## The President's War Powers: The Road to Torture

Within a week of September 11, 2001, Congress passed by joint resolution the Authorization to Use Military Force (AUMF), giving the president broad powers to prosecute a new kind of war, not solely against a nation but against amorphously defined terrorists and all who helped them, wherever they might be.

Presidential powers included the use of "all necessary and appropriate force against those nations, organizations, or persons he determines planned, authorized, committed, or aided the terrorist attacks." It also provided "specific statutory authorization" under the war powers resolution.[37] The circumstances were extreme. It is, however, difficult to imagine a broader mandate. Congress, overwhelmingly supported by frightened Democrats, voted 420 to 1 to give the president blanket permission.[38] Some scholars maintain that the war on terror is not a true war under the laws of war and argue that, by claiming it to be a war, we give unwarranted legal status to criminal terrorist organizations such as al-Qaeda.[39] Nonetheless, the general assumption has been that President Bush became a wartime president. As the Supreme Court put it, "we assume that the AUMF activated the President's war powers . . . and that those powers include the authority to convene military commissions in appropriate circumstances."[40] These war powers provided the justification for the president's claimed power to suspend legal protections that would otherwise apply in peacetime, and it is this that, in part, allowed the United States to create gaps in the law, which in turn permitted torture and rendition to torture.

## The Torture Lawyers

The story of how the United States came to use torture in the war against terror begins in an otherwise obscure but powerful part of the Department of Justice—its Office of Legal Counsel. No matter what the political operatives in the White House or vice president's office may have wanted, it could not have happened without the OLC's help. The OLC provides opinions as to the legality of proposed actions by the government. In the absence of direct legal precedent, the OLC's opinions become the guiding administrative law to be followed by all governmental agencies. In short, if the OLC says a proposed action is lawful, then governmental agents can carry out those actions without fear of prosecution. The OLC's opinions, then, become a kind of "golden shield" protecting governmental agents in carrying out official policy. While other offices of government may set policy, these policies cannot, as a rule, be implemented unless the OLC approves.

The Bush administration, with the OLC's help, consistently attempted to move the law in the direction of permitting torture, in part by blurring the lines between torture and cruel, inhuman, and degrading treatment. By doing so, they also provided global legal cover for those who have engaged in either torture or cruel, inhuman, or degrading treatment both domestically and through extraordinary rendition. Through a seamless web of opinions the OLC created a legal vacuum that permitted both torture lite and rendition to worse. As Jonathan Hafetz argues, "Since September 11, the Bush Administration has developed an unprecedented global detention system, designed to operate outside any established legal framework or independent oversight. By evading existing constraints on custodial interrogations under domestic and international law, this detention system has undermined the Unites States' longstanding commitment to the prohibition against torture and other abuse."[41]

As Christopher Kutz pointed out, even if the torture lawyers of the OLC fell short of persuading the courts to create a judicial space for torture, the very existence of the torture lawyers' opinions creates an "advice of counsel" defense for senior administration officials.[42] They also create a defense for lower-level operatives—even those who may never have heard of the OLC opinions and who therefore lack any advice of counsel defense. A person merely following orders is not criminally responsible in the absence of a manifestly unlawful command. Thus, as David Luban points out, "skilled legal counsel can point to the Office of Legal Counsel and Department of Defense memos" as evidence that a CIA agent's or a soldier's conduct could not have been manifestly unlawful.[43] Recent revelations make it clear that the National Security Council, with President Bush's explicit approval, micromanaged the interrogation of "high-value" detainees right down to dictating the details of waterboarding, a practice most Americans as well as most other people throughout the world consider a form of torture.[44]

Formerly higher-level officials who generated the orders will undoubtedly argue that they relied in good faith on competent legal counsel. "Advice of counsel" is a defense to the mental state required for some crimes, so the OLC's opinion that certain actions did not constitute torture would have been a partial defense any prosecution.[45]

The lawyers involved argue that they gave good faith advice in conditions of radical uncertainty. One of the primary architects of these controversial opinions and former head of the OLC under President Bush has argued, "We gave our best, honest advice, based on our good-faith analysis of the law."[46] While self-serving, this defense nonetheless carries some weight. In this way, the OLC lawyers protected themselves and their clients. As we will see, however, their good faith was questionable.

The followers of such advice argue good-faith compliance with orders vetted by competent counsel that were not manifestly unlawful. The issue that any court, domestic or foreign, must confront will be whether such orders were so manifestly unlawful as to render the giving or taking of such advice illusory. Plainly, it will be difficult for any court, domestic or foreign, to conclude that orders running from the former president, after relying on legal advice from the Department of Justice, were either in bad faith or manifestly unlawful. This is a political fact rather than a strictly legal conclusion; prosecutions leading to the former U.S. president remain problematic.

The intent and effect of the many OLC legal opinions was to redefine the intentional infliction of suffering that left no physical mark as not rising to the level of being torture. In opinion after opinion, they consistently held that whatever the U.S. government proposed, however painful or disturbing, remained lawful.

## Torture's Roots: The Military Order
## of November 13, 2001

Almost immediately after the September 11 attacks, the Department of Justice began planning to set the legal framework for a new kind of war. Department lawyers were urged to be "forward leaning,"[47] to find ways to justify legally what the administration planned as a "gloves off" war that did "away with all restrictions."[48]

These notions laid the groundwork for an OLC legal opinion arguing that President Bush had the authority to set up military commissions to try terrorists.[49] The president then issued the Military Order of November 13, which authorized indefinite detention of al-Qaeda members (and others connected to al-Qaeda) and created military tribunals to try them. This order could not have been cast more sweepingly—it applied to any noncitizen who "is or was a member of . . . al Qaeda," who "engaged in, aided, or abetted, or conspired" in terrorism or who prepared for such, or who "knowingly harbored" any of the people so broadly described.[50] As written, it could apply to someone who unwittingly gave money to an organization associated with terrorism—even, apparently, a "little old lady in Switzerland who writes checks to what she thinks is a charity that helps orphans in Afghanistan but [what] really is a front to finance al-Qaeda activities."[51] It could apply to the vaguest conspiracy regardless of its stage or ability to accomplish anything consequential. These broad definitions applied to anyone that the president in his sole and unreviewable discretion so determined. If the president claimed someone was somehow connected to terrorism, that person became part of the "worst of the worst," people who would "gnaw through hydraulic lines" to bring an airplane down.[52]

Two things follow from describing people as quintessentially evil. First, to at least some people, it seems easier to justify harsh treatment of people thought to be entirely evil, and it is a short step from abrasive interrogations to torture. In this way, describing detainees as less than human and evil beyond redemption served to inoculate the United States from criticism of its harsh treatment of prisoners in the war against terror. Second, and not surprisingly, this unfettered approach misfired, pulling in people wholly unconnected with terrorism, including people simply fleeing from the conflict and who happened to be in the wrong place at the wrong time.[53]

Excessive breadth was not the order's only problem. Once designated for detention, the new rules stacked the deck in favor of conviction. Punishment, including death, could follow trial based upon any evidence that had "probative value to a reasonable person."[54] Hearsay on hearsay, even hearsay gleaned from torture, might suffice. Moreover, the prisoner might never be able to challenge such evidence. The order also provided for secrecy—cloaking classified or classifiable information. Finally, and most problematically, the order precluded any remedy in any court anywhere. The only appeal ran through the secretary of defense and the president.[55] Thus, the very people who decided to detain the noncitizen would be the ultimate "deciders."

In summary, any non-U.S. citizen deemed by the president to have an amorphous connection to terrorism could be picked up, tried, convicted, and even executed upon secret evidence, including evidence resulting from torture, and double or triple hearsay, without appeal to any neutral forum. Although these tribunals were to be called "military commissions," they were quite unlike earlier U.S. military commissions dating back to the Revolutionary War, which, with exceptions, can be said to have been reasonably fair and justified by the exigencies of war.[56] Contrariwise, the Bush administration argued that military necessity in this new type of war—without temporal or geographic boundaries—required that all alleged terrorists be held incommunicado without access to either lawyers or courts.[57] The president's order barred all court challenges to detention.[58] Initially, until the Supreme Court voided the action, even U.S. citizens José Padilla and Yaser Esam Hamdi, whom the president determined to be enemy combatants, were held incommunicado and without access to lawyers.[59]

## Creating Legal Permission to (Hide) Torture

Two important events followed President Bush's Military Order of November 13, which set up military commissions. First, on December 27, 2001, the administration settled on Guantánamo Bay for detaining what came to be called "unlawful enemy combatants" captured in the "war on terror."[60] By January 11, 2002, the first accused terrorists arrived at the U.S. base at Guantánamo Bay, Cuba.[61]

On December 28, the OLC provided its first legal opinion that attempted to create a legal "black hole," an area outside of oversight by courts or anyone else. That opinion, by Patrick Philbin and John Yoo, argued that Guantánamo Bay, Cuba, lay beyond the jurisdiction of the federal courts; thus, prisoners held there would not be amenable to the writ of habeas corpus. Philbin and Yoo did acknowledge that there was a "non-frivolous argument" that Guantánamo Bay might be "within the territorial jurisdiction of a federal court." Nevertheless, they reasoned—erroneously, as it later turned out—that the better legal conclusion was "that a district court cannot properly entertain an application for a writ of habeas corpus by an enemy alien detained at Guantánamo Bay."[62] Detainees thus would be beyond all legal process.

In retrospect, these two important moves—sending detainees to and justifying a law-free zone at Guantánamo Bay—prepared the way for torture. The administration thought that holding non-U.S. citizens outside of the jurisdictional confines of the United States would eliminate civilian court oversight. This would, it was then thought, protect the CIA and other interrogators from prosecution under the War Crimes Act, the antitorture legislation, or from violating the Foreign Affairs and Restructuring Act of 1998 (which prohibits sending people to places where they may be tortured).[63]

These actions were widely criticized and quickly challenged in the courts. Only a lawyer-free and court-free zone would permit the kind of hyperaggressive legal interpretations that were to set the administrative and legislative branches of government on a collision course with the courts. It was that same drive to create secret zones, free from courts and media, that explains the move toward using extraordinary rendition. Both stem from the same motive, which was to hide torture and cruel, inhuman, and degrading treatment of detainees.

Holding people indefinitely without trial created a firestorm of criticism.[64] Then–White House counsel Alberto Gonzales responded with an op-ed piece in the *New York Times* claiming that the order did not mean what it said and that the courts would remain able to exercise the writ of habeas corpus.[65] That did not keep the administration from fighting to the end to prevent court review.[66] Plainly, the administration sought the appearance of fairness while retaining the power to do whatever it wished with detainees.

Next the OLC wrote a series of opinions advising the president how to avoid the Geneva Conventions regarding either al-Qaeda or the Taliban.[67] This culminated in the president's memorandum declaring that al-Qaeda was not covered by Geneva Conventions; it also held that while the Geneva Conventions technically applied to the Taliban, its detainees were all (without further hearing of any kind) unlawful combatants and not prisoners of war under Article 4 of the Conventions.

This single move arguably not only stripped the protections of the Geneva Conventions from all combatants in Afghanistan, but it also stripped them of any protection under the War Crimes Act, which criminalized grave breaches of the Geneva Conventions as well as violations of Common Article 3 of the Geneva Conventions. The Geneva Conventions generally prohibit torture, cruel, inhuman, and degrading treatment, and sending or turning people over to be tortured. Common Article 3 (so called because it is common to all of the 1949 Conventions) does not have an explicit nonrefoulment clause. (Nonrefoulment is a principle of international law prohibiting returning people to places where they would face such things as death, slavery, or torture. Put another way, this principle prohibits a nation doing by the back door what it could not do directly.) However, as we will see in the last chapter, Common Article 3 regulates the release of prisoners to a safe place. Thus, it too, as a practical matter, prohibits sending people to face torture.

Stripping out the Geneva Conventions would have had the effect (had it worked) of insulating from prosecution those who ordered or carried out torture or who rendered people to torture. In that respect, those caught on the battlefield in Afghanistan would be like the Battling Bastards of Bataan during World War II who quickly learned that Japanese custody meant "no Geneva Convention."[68] Controls against torture slipped in Iraq as well, although there the Geneva Conventions technically continued to apply under the restrictive Bush administration interpretations.

The OLC's method turned on using quirky, ahistorical, and formalistic interpretations of statutory or treaty language that allowed them to find gaps where arguably no law applied. From those gaps they inferred permission. Thus, while U.S. officials do not explicitly defend torture or extraordinary rendition, "they imply that the practice is legal by pointing to what they claim are lacunae in the relevant legal frameworks" where "prohibitions give way to permission," and "territories outside the United States are conceptualized as locations where the U.S. may act as it pleases."[69]

The administration failed to recognize or ignored the fact that their legal reasoning closely mirrored that of Nazi lawyers more than sixty years ago who likewise argued that the Geneva Conventions were obsolete in a war against a barbarous enemy that engaged in terrorist practices. Indeed, the Nazis thought that international humanitarian law was "the relic of a chivalrous notion"[70] while U.S. Attorney General Alberto Gonzales thought the Geneva Conventions "quaint" and "obsolete."[71] Although some legal scholars argue that these government lawyers should be prosecuted as Nazi lawyers and judges were prosecuted at Nuremburg, the point here is not that the United States and its lawyers can be fairly compared with Nazi Germany's lawyers—they cannot.[72] The enormity of the Holocaust beggars any such comparison. However, the fact that their legal reasoning so closely mirrored that of Nazi lawyers and judges helps explain how the United States so easily slipped into torture lite and rendition to torture. History teaches that demonization of the enemy is a first step, a necessary but by itself insufficient condition toward abusive behavior.

The administration also sought to change the rules by narrowing the definitional scope upon which any prosecution or lawsuit might act. By far the most controversial move to strip out all protections and oversight came with the infamous "torture memo" from James Bybee to

Gonzales.[73] Legal scholars labeled it a "laughingstock" and "a stunning failure of lawyerly craft."[74]

That memo contained such a perversely narrow definition of torture that it deserves quotation at length:

> We conclude that torture . . . covers only extreme acts. . . . Where the pain is physical, it must be of an intensity akin to that which accompanies *serious physical injury such as death or organ failure.* Severe mental pain requires suffering not just at the moment of infliction but it also requires lasting psychological harm, such as seen in mental disorders like post-traumatic stress disorder. . . . Because the acts inflicting torture are extreme, *there is significant range of acts that though they might constitute cruel, inhuman or degrading treatment or punishment fail to rise to the level of torture.*[75]

The goal was plain. Having deprived the detainees court oversight, a narrow definition restricting torture to things that cause death or organ failure, had it been successful, would have permitted the administration to say that it did not allow torture while encouraging interrogators—with impunity and without oversight—to engage in practices that most people would consider torture. The goal was to simultaneously evade and obfuscate.

This narrowing of the definition of torture expanded the kinds of harsh interrogation techniques that plausibly can be claimed as lawful thereby reducing the chances a given interrogation practice might be found to have been "manifestly unlawful." It also had implications for extraordinary rendition in that it became easier to argue that the person extraordinarily rendered was not actually tortured, that whatever abuses they underwent did not rise to the level of torture. While the Convention against Torture prohibited the infliction of both torture and cruel, inhuman, and degrading treatment, its nonrefoulment clause only prohibited sending someone to face a substantial risk of torture. This change in definition mattered because the CAT did not prohibit sending a person to face cruel, inhuman, and degrading treatment, only outright torture. Narrowing the definition of torture to nearly the vanishing point automatically expanded the ambit for cruel, inhuman, and degrading treatment. The CAT prohibits sending people to other nations where they risk being tortured, but it does not prohibit sending people to places where cruel, inhuman, and degrading treatment is practiced. Redefining and narrowing torture while increasing the ambit for cruel, inhuman, and degrading treatment increases the opportunity to render someone without admitting a purpose to inflict torture by proxy. Thus, the OLC's narrow definition of torture helped create another gap in the law, facilitating not only extremely abusive interrogation practices but also extraordinary rendition.

That this definition of torture met with such a storm of controversy that it had to be withdrawn does not detract from the basic point that the administration sought, primarily through opinions from its OLC, to change the legal landscape both to permit and to hide torture.[76] The critical point is that by setting up such a "torture culture" (as David Luban puts it)[77] torture became inevitable. Later, when the courts failed to go along, the game shifted to legislation to protect what had been done. Intent is often difficult to prove and, with institutions and governments, it is generally unnecessary. However, intent here seems quite clear. One does not so radically change a definition otherwise.

The Bybee torture memorandum (as well as other OLC memos) did much more than redefine torture.[78] In addition to creating a vanishingly narrow definition of torture, this memorandum also provided a definition of specific intent that claimed that one could not torture unless one specifically intended to harm or cause pain. This suggested (without explicitly endorsing) that an interrogator would be free to cause even intense pain so long as the intent was interrogation and not the intentional infliction of suffering.[79] Plainly foreseeable pain might not count if one sought information.[80] The Bybee memorandum also posits (as do other OLC memos from the Bush administration) that Congress lacks the power to prohibit torture if performed under the direction of the president. (This, of course, renders the distinction between torture and cruel, inhuman, and degrading treatment irrelevant—at least insofar as this argument ultimately prevails). These parts of the Bybee memorandum remained intact, allowing the Bush administration to move grudgingly to head off the worst criticism without materially changing course.

The important point is that the administration sought to screen its actions from both legislative and judicial oversight (as well as public view) and sought to create a permissive regime that would allow torture and cruel interrogation practices. The administration also deployed, among other legal theories, the state secrets privilege in order to prevent civil suits alleging torture or extraordinary rendition from going forward—even to the discovery stage. We will discuss the renditions to torture of three wholly innocent people, Binyam Mohamed, Maher Arar, and Khalid El-Masri, in chapter 4. Each sued the United States and lost.[81] The administration thus avoided, until *Boumediene*, detailed judicial or legislative oversight.[82]

## Critiquing the OLC's Opinions

Many thoughtful legal scholars have since condemned the "torture memos" issued by the "torture lawyers" of the OLC during the Bush administration. These legal opinions, informed critics argued, were manifestly erroneous and in bad faith and created by out-of-control, rogue operators. The critics called for prosecution or, failing that, disbarment or termination from employment.[83] Justice Department lawyers, they argued, consciously sought to distort the law to justify the unjustifiable: out-and-out torture and its pitiless lesser cousin cruel, inhuman and degrading interrogation. Until recently, however, proof seemed debatable; it remained for *The Torture Memos: Rationalizing the Unthinkable*, by David Cole, to fill that gap.[84]

Cole's book makes the case more persuasively than any other that the OLC was, at least for a time, a rogue institution, its lawyers acting not as legal advisors but rather as the facilitators of torture and cruel, inhuman, and degrading treatment. He makes the strongest case yet that these administration lawyers conspired to justify the manifestly unlawful, that the most important legal office in the land acted in bad faith. It is a stunning indictment.

As Cole points out, these torture lawyers continued to distort the law in the direction of permitting torture long after the immediate panic of the attacks of 9/11 had worn off. More importantly, these secret opinions continued to rationalize torture long after the "law in public appeared to tighten its standards to prohibit these tactics."[85] Indeed, the torture lawyers deliberately mislead the public in that they withdrew some of the more controversial early opinions even while preserving the bottom line by approving every single one of the CIA's abusive interrogation techniques. Not only were OLC lawyers acting in bad faith, they also deceived both the Congress and the public into thinking that interrogation practices had changed when they had not.

The OLC subscribed to a sliding-scale test for evaluating whether particular interrogation practices, such as waterboarding and sleep deprivation, used either singly, repeatedly, or in combination, would "shock the conscience" thereby violating due process. They opined that the greater the government's interest in, and need for, information, the less likely the conduct would be considered either torture or, cruel, inhuman, or degrading treatment. In discussing the "shocks the conscience" test, Stephen G. Bradbury, principal deputy assistant attorney general, argues, "Far from being constitutionally arbitrary, the interrogation techniques at issue here are employed by the CIA only as reasonably deemed necessary to protect against grave threats to United States interests." His memorandum concludes: "Given that the CIA interrogation program is carefully limited to further the Government's paramount interest in protecting the Nation while avoiding unnecessary or serious harm, we conclude that the interrogation program cannot 'be said to shock the contemporary conscience' when considered in light of 'traditional executive behavior' and 'contemporary practice.'"[86]

The OLC concluded that because the perceived need was great, a host of harsh interrogation techniques (including waterboarding) were neither torture nor cruel, inhuman, and degrading treatment. They also concluded that the use of such techniques did not shock the conscience even when used repeatedly and in combination with any or all of such OLC-approved techniques on a single subject over a thirty-day period. Nor did the OLC think that use of these techniques could be characterized as causing severe pain.[87] Among other things, the OLC looked to the training of U.S. soldiers in its SERE training, which allowed, among other things, waterboarding. However, their conclusion seems at odds not only with Christopher Hitchen's experience outlined in chapter 1 but also with what at least some SERE graduates say. One graduate describes being waterboarded as "real drowning that simulates death." He continued:

The questions (What is your unit? Where are you from?) were asked by one man. But we were not supposed to talk. I remember that the blindfold was heavy and completely covered my face. As the two men held me down, one on each side, someone began pouring water onto the blindfold, and suddenly I was drowning. The water streamed into my nose and then into my mouth when I gasped for breath. I couldn't stop it. All I could breathe was water, and it was terrifying. I think I began to lose consciousness. I felt my lungs begin to fill with burning liquid. Pulling out my fingernails or even cutting off a finger would have been preferable. At least if someone had attacked my hands, I would have had to simply tolerate pain. But drowning is another matter.[88]

Similarly, former director of national intelligence Mike McConnell has said, "If I had water draining in my nose, oh God, I just can't imagine how painful."[89] It is this along with other harsh techniques such as stress positions, wall slamming, placement in small boxes, and the like that the OLC balances on its sliding scale to determine if the need for the information renders the practice "not torture."

Is the OLC's interpretation of the "shocks the conscience" test a fair reading of Supreme Court precedent? Cole convincingly demonstrates that the OLC's reading of the law is plainly erroneous. He argues, "The case law is clear that any intentional infliction of pain for interrogation purposes violates due process. And the Court has recognized no sliding scale that would permit the infliction of pain if the government's reason is good enough. . . . The court has repeatedly found its conscience shocked where the government acted with wholly legitimate interests."[90] Indeed, the OLC's approach is not simply wrong. Cole shows that when all of the newly disclosed memoranda are read together, it becomes apparent that they were not written in good faith. "Precisely because the questions were so difficult . . . one would expect a good-faith analysis to reach a nuanced conclusion, perhaps approving some measures while definitely prohibiting others. Yet on every question, no matter how much the law had to be stretched, the OLC lawyers reached the same result—The CIA could do whatever it had proposed to do."[91]

In *Chavez v. Martinez*, a case cited by the OLC, interrogators continued the interrogation of a man who had been shot and who was apparently in intense pain.[92] They did not, however, initiate or cause the pain. The Supreme Court remanded to the lower courts to determine whether due process had been violated. In dissent, even Justice Clarence Thomas, who did not think that due process had been violated on the facts of the case, concluded that "the deliberate infliction of pain on an individual to compel him to talk would shock the conscience."[93] Thus, even one of the most conservative Supreme Court justices, while not being shocked by an interrogation of a man apparently in excruciating pain, would halt at the deliberate infliction of pain.[94] Contrary to the views of Justice Thomas, the majority opinion on the Court was that "any use of pain to compel a suspect to talk violated due process."[95] If *any use* of pain shocks the conscience, then the argument is even stronger as to the deliberate and repeated use of painful interrogation techniques, used in combination, and over as many as thirty days at a time.

Given the revelation of these formerly secret memoranda, it is no longer possible to see the OLC's position as plausible. And if not plausible, then the good faith of the OLC lawyers is placed squarely in question. Cole accurately describes the Bush administration's misreading of the law (articulated publicly by Vice President Cheney, Senator John McCain, and former attorney general Mukasey)[96] and then deconstructs the attempted justification for practices that, under any sensible understanding of the English language, count as torture.

As Cole puts it, "When considered as a whole, the [torture] memos read not as an objective assessment of what the law permits or precludes, but as a strained effort to rationalize a predetermined—and illegal—result. Rather than demand that the CIA conform its conduct to the law, the lawyers contorted the law to conform it to the CIA's desires."[97]

## The World Understands that
## Torture Lite Is Real Torture

Polls show that overwhelming majorities of Americans believe that the United States uses torture in its war on terror, and similar majorities believe that the United States resorts to rendition. Polls are split on whether Americans believe that torture can be justified. The United States admits to waterboarding suspects, and a "majority of Americans consider waterboarding a form of torture."[98]

Former Bush administration officials stoutly deny using torture and claim that everything done by the administration was lawful. Notwithstanding these denials, robust evidence points to an intentional policy reinstituting torture as an interrogation technique. The issue is a hot one, prompting domestic and international astonishment at the claimed lawfulness of such practices.[99] Manfred Nowak, who is both a law processor and the UN special rapporteur on torture, said, "I'm not willing any more to discuss these questions with the U.S. government, when they say this [waterboarding] is allowed. It's not allowed."[100]

Prior to the Bush administration, American courts and other tribunals consistently branded waterboarding "torture." The United States prosecuted members of the Japanese armed forces after World War II in part because they used waterboarding as a form of torture. Moreover, U.S. courts have called waterboarding torture when used by domestic law enforcement. The United States even court-martialed at least one of its own military officers for employing waterboarding during the occupation of the Philippines at the beginning of the twentieth century.[101] The United States, during the eight years of the Bush administration, was virtually alone in arguing that waterboarding does not constitute torture, much less cruel, inhuman, and degrading treatment. If waterboarding is not torture, it is only because the United States has succeeded in redefining the term.

While waterboarding may be the most obvious example of a practice constituting torture, it is not the sole technique; torture encompasses a range of physically and mentally debilitating practices. Many of the authorized alternative interrogation techniques are ill disguised by the euphemisms currently in vogue. The Bush administration chose coercive techniques in addition to waterboarding that would conventionally be thought of as straightforwardly torturous: false burial, "Palestinian hanging" (where the prisoner is suspended by his arms, which are manacled behind his back), leaving a prisoner naked in a cold cell and doused with cold water, and making a prisoner stand for forty hours while shackled to a cell floor.[102]

As we saw in chapter I, torture lite victims can suffer "depression, excessive anxiety, post-traumatic stress disorder and sometimes
full-blown psychosis,"[103]and symptoms can persist for many years.
According to a study of nearly three hundred persons from the former Yugoslavia, the degree of stress reported by those who suffered
"clean" torture did not differ from that of those subjected to psychic
torture. Both groups showed "equally high levels of post-traumatic
stress disorder. . . . 'Clean' methods of interrogation might appear
more sanitized and therefore more acceptable than those that leave
physical scars. But don't be fooled. They are just as brutal, crude—and
pointless—as ever."[104]

Finally, regardless of whether the U.S. government counts these
techniques as torture, others do. For example, a Spanish judge dropped
extradition requests of the United Kingdom for two alleged members of
al-Qaeda. Both were determined incompetent to stand trial because of
severe mental and physical stress caused by detention at Guantánamo
and in Afghanistan.[105]

Torture and its near cousin, rendition to torture, are war crimes
practiced by the United States as a matter of official policy. However,
these practices are strongly contested internationally, and this in turn
imposes significant costs on the United States. International human
rights norms generally and international laws more specifically inform
the backlash against the United States' use of torture and cruel, inhuman, and degrading interrogation techniques, and this criticism by the
international community works to curtail the practice.


## How High Did the Torture Culture Reach?

Toward the end of his eight years in office in 2008, we learned that President Bush personally approved his cabinet secretary's micromanage-
ment of high-value detainee interrogations, which included the use of
torture, and that the White House had formally approved waterboarding for al-Qaeda suspects. At that time, we learned that two classified
memos sent from the Bush administration to the CIA in 2003 and 2004
explicitly sanctioned the use of waterboarding.[106] Open admission of
White House approval of waterboarding radically changed the torture

debate![107] Given that approvals came from the highest possible level within the U.S. government, prosecution of anyone within the United States became politically inconvenient and virtually impossible as a practical matter. Exercise of universal jurisdiction by foreign governments also became much harder. It seems reasonable that the admissions were not inadvertent but were a determined effort to staunch the calls for investigation into and prosecution of abusive interrogation at the hands of the CIA.

Almost from the beginning the public knew that former secretary of defense Donald Rumsfeld was directly involved with torture; that he set down techniques, including chaining to the floor, stripping, hooding, and the use of dogs at Guantánamo and Abu Ghraib; and that he was personally involved in Mohammed al-Qahtani's case,[108] where "interrogators subjected him to eighteen to twenty hours per day of aggressive interrogation for forty-eight days over a fifty-four day period. During this time, his body temperature fell to ninety-five degrees on two occasions, and his pulse dropped to a life-threatening thirty-five beats per minute."[109]

Al-Qahtani's treatment has been well documented using an official interrogation log obtained by *Time* magazine, so unlike the treatment of some of the other detainees, it is not a matter of taking the word of the victim over official denials.[110] The administration could not plausibly respond in al-Qahtani's case (as it so often did) that members of al-Qaeda are trained to claim that they have been tortured and, therefore, those claims are not believable.

What we did not know until *ABC News* broke the story in 2008 was just how far into the White House the orders to torture went; we now know that the authorization to torture al-Qaeda suspects reached the highest levels of the White House![111] According to *ABC News*'s report, senior administration officials held dozens of meetings in the White House Situation Room specifically to approve the precise techniques used against individual detainees. Chaired by then National Security Advisor Condoleezza Rice, a meeting including Vice President Dick Cheney, Defense Secretary Rumsfeld, Secretary of State Colin Powell, CIA Director George Tenet, and Attorney General John Ashcroft decided the minutiae of torture down to the specific number of times that CIA agents could use a specific tactic such as pushing, slapping, sleep deprivation, or waterboarding.

President Bush knew that these officials were meeting to discuss these interrogations, and he approved. According to an *ABC News* report on April 11, 2008, President Bush said, "Well, we started to connect the dots in order to protect the American people. . . . Yes, I'm aware our national security team met on this issue. And I approved."[112] Thus, we now know what was previously only suspected—that orders to torture went all the way to the top.

At the time, only John Ashcroft expressed reservations—not to the wisdom of the policy of aggressive interrogations but rather about whether "White House advisors should . . . be involved in the grim details," asking, "why are we talking about this in the White House? History will not judge this kindly." These meetings continued after the withdrawal of the infamous Bybee torture memo. Even as Secretary Powell expressed concerns that the program was hurting the United States' image abroad, National Security Advisor Rice told the CIA: "This is your baby. Go do it."[113]

The reason for making decisions on the minute details of interrogations at such a high level stemmed from the CIA's need for protection. Civilian political masters do not usually give explicit orders that, if later exposed, may cause embarrassment. Here, however, the usual situation became reversed. Older CIA agents recalled the agency's public tarring after the exposure of its Phoenix Program, which involved torturing and killing thousands of Viet Cong and their sympathizers.[114] Field agents worried about potential prosecution and exposure to civil suits. For example, agents have bought insurance to protect themselves from litigation costs and liability arising from the use of harsh interrogation techniques.[115] To protect individual agents from being later scapegoated should the program be exposed, explicit orders needed to come from the highest level of government, and these orders needed to be provable, preferably in writing. Because of this, the political superiors lost their usual plausible deniability and gave the orders for harsh interrogations including waterboarding.

Could the officials who ordered the use of torture be prosecuted under the War Crimes Act?[116] Law professor Jack Balkin points out that sections 8 and 6(b) of the Military Commission Act of 2006 "[insulate] these officials from liability for many of the violations of the War Crimes Act," and Marty Lederman points out that the Justice Department would not likely prosecute persons who reasonably relied on a prior Justice Department opinion.[117] The political cost to any succeeding administration would likely be too high—such prosecutions would likely sour any attempt to pursue bipartisan legislation. Prosecution would have to come from another country exercising universal jurisdiction over a former official who happened to travel to that country.

Any trial of a former administration official would lead directly to a former president of the United States. Any domestic prosecution of U.S. agents or officers would have to surmount the practical hurdle that the president of the United States authorized these interrogations. While it is true that Nuremburg put an end to the "just following orders" defense, it would be difficult for a U.S. court to find orders approved by a sitting president with support of the entire National Security Council, including the attorney general, to be so "manifestly unlawful" that a person following them would be criminally liable under the War Crimes Act or any other law. This is because a person following orders is not responsible, even if the orders prove unlawful, so long as they are not "manifestly unlawful." The Nuremburg principle is not a trap for the unwary but is rather a rule that one cannot commit an obviously criminal act and then claim that one was merely following orders.[118] Thus, it is no surprise that the Obama administration refused to prosecute any former officials of the Bush administration while limiting its investigations to those CIA agents who went demonstrably beyond the former administration's official directives. It is no surprise that foreign attempts to exercise universal jurisdiction have sputtered.

The Bush administration may have achieved what it set out to do from the beginning—insulate both itself and lower-level officials from criminal prosecution for torture. However, public knowledge that the United States engaged in torture and sending people to other countries to face torture is now a part of the Bush administration's legacy. Anthony Lewis says that for him, George W. Bush will always be "the Torture President."[119]

## The Supreme Court Strikes Back

In the period following the attacks on the World Trade Center and the Pentagon, Congress and the executive branch were unusually united. Overwhelming majorities in both houses of Congress, determined to demonstrate a tough response, consistently ceded power to the president. The Supreme Court rarely confronts such united and consistent opposition. As we will see, each time the Supreme Court curbed the administration's most extravagant claims in narrowly crafted opinions, Congress passed laws designed to undercut those decisions. The Court struck back each time in measured tones. In doing so, the Court engaged in constitutional dialogue with the other branches of government, preserving the institutional power of the Court and, more importantly, preserving the constitutional right of habeas corpus. The story of how the courts, Congress, and the president dueled over court access for detainees at Guantánamo Bay is an important one that indirectly affected renditions as well.

The Supreme Court decided three cases involving detainees in 2004. These cases and the reaction of both Congress and the president are important not only for what they say about the institutional powers of the three branches of government but also for the way in which they led up to the final constitutional battles that opened up the court process to detainees, which in turn exposed the U.S. use of torture in the war on terror and for rendition to torture.

### *Rumsfeld v. Padilla*

The first of the three cases involved a U.S. citizen, José Padilla, who was arrested on U.S. soil.[120] The Supreme Court's ruling that a petition for a writ of habeas corpus could only be filed in South Carolina rather than New York is of lesser importance to most detainees in the war on terror who were being denied access to any court at all; for them the issue was not which court had venue but rather whether any court could or would hear their claims. Most detainees were noncitizens found on foreign shores and transported to Guantánamo Bay, Cuba. They were fighting in the courts for civil court access in the first instance and, unlike Padilla, were not fighting about the narrower issue of where the writ might properly be filed.

Nonetheless, Padilla's case does have important connections to rendition and torture. Padilla was tried in 2007 in Federal District Court in Miami and, along with two others, was convicted of conspiring to murder in Chechnya, Afghanistan, Bosnia, and elsewhere. On January 23, 2008, he was sentenced to serve seventeen years in prison. The government denied Padilla's allegations of torture, but the judge in the case agreed that he was subjected to "harsh conditions" and "extreme stresses."[121]

The government's original charge, that Padilla plotted to detonate a radioactive "dirty bomb," never surfaced and is presumably without foundation and forever gone. While one cannot know with assurance why this charge was dropped, it seems virtually certain that the prosecution would not have dropped such a serious charge if it had sufficient evidence to proceed. Moreover the judge in the case ruled that "there is no evidence that these defendants personally maimed, kidnapped, or killed anyone in the United States or elsewhere."[122] The government's most incendiary charges were never proved.

More importantly, we also know that some of the evidence against him came from the rendition and "savage medieval torture" of an innocent man, Binyam Mohamed, whose case will be discussed more fully in chapter 4.[123] Mohamed was tortured and subjected to a mock execution while in U.S. and Pakistani custody. Later he was rendered to Morocco, where, among other things, his chest and penis were repeatedly sliced with a scalpel. His interrogators provided Mohamed with enough information that he knew what they wanted—and under extreme torture, it is not surprising that he told his interrogators what they wanted to hear. "American intelligence agencies were 'obsessed' with the possibility that Al Qaeda might have acquired nuclear fissile material. 'Every interrogator would ask questions about it.'"[124]

Under this pressure and given that he had been told enough to know what he what he needed to say to stop the torture, Binyam Mohamed also falsely confessed to conspiring with José Padilla and 9/11 mastermind Khalid Sheikh Mohammed to blow up gas tankers, spray people with cyanide, blow up apartment buildings, and, most sinister of all, to construct and detonate an improvised radioactive dirty bomb.[125] Thus, José Padilla, who was also subjected to "harsh conditions" and "extreme stresses," at a minimum, became entangled in the almost certainly fanciful dirty bomb plot via the "confession" of a man rendered to the most brutal torture imaginable. As we will see repeatedly, torture has led to false confessions that in turn have consequences beyond the individuals subjected to torture. It also illustrates the multiple overlapping lines and common roots between torture lite and rendition to torture.

One troubling aspect of this ruling is not discussed in any of the justices' opinions. Not only did the government resort to a secret ex parte proceeding to spirit Padilla out of New York and into South Carolina, it did so in order to gain a clear tactical advantage. First, the Southern District of New York and the Second Circuit Court of Appeals would ordinarily be a more hospitable forum for Padilla than the more conservative federal courts with jurisdiction in South Carolina. Unquestionably, Padilla would also have been more able in New York to procure a timely hearing on the merits and create a record than he would have in South Carolina. Second, in New York, Padilla was not in the custody of the Department of Defense, whereas in the naval brig in South Carolina he was held incommunicado for a time. This materially affected interrogation techniques and the harsh treatment he suffered as well as his access to counsel. The government engaged in forum shopping and got away with it. The immediate goals were time, a more sympathetic court, and, most importantly, the ability to coercively interrogate Padilla without interference from civilian lawyers. Among other things, this case demonstrates the lengths to which the government was prepared to go to maintain secrecy about its interrogation policies—a fact that pervaded both domestic harsh interrogations sometimes yielding to torture and extraordinary renditions almost certainly resulting in torture.

### Hamdi v. Rumsfeld

Yaser Esam Hamdi was a dual U.S. and Saudi citizen picked up in Afghanistan by the Northern Alliance in 2001 and turned over to the Americans. He was declared an "illegal enemy combatant" and transported to

Guantánamo Bay, Cuba. Upon discovery that he was a U.S. citizen, the government transferred him to the naval brig in South Carolina.

*Hamdi* raises an interesting question about the rights of a U.S. citizen abroad. Unlike Padilla, who was arrested in Chicago, Hamdi was captured in Afghanistan and was alleged to have been fighting alongside of the Taliban militia![26] However, the fact that he was turned over by the Northern Alliance suggests that bounty money may have had more to do with his capture than any actual guilt in fighting against the United States, and Hamdi steadfastly denied that he ever took up arms against the United States or its allies![27]

*Hamdi* held that a citizen, even if picked up on a foreign battlefield, could not be held indefinitely without charges![28] At a minimum, he had a right to notice of the charges against him and a hearing of some ill-defined sort. This access to process entailed the right for someone who has been declared an enemy combatant to "receive notice of the factual basis for his classification, and a fair opportunity to rebut the Government's factual assertions before a neutral decision-maker."[129] Writing for the plurality, Justice Sandra O'Connor said, "We have long since made clear that a state of war is not a blank check for the President when it comes to the rights of the Nation's citizens."[130] This case breached the administration's most extravagant claim: that the president could declare anyone at anytime an enemy combatant and could hold that person without any process whatsoever.

*Hamdi*'s grant of access to a hearing seems to have had disastrous consequences for the U.S. position. Rather than try him for his alleged crimes, the United States reached an agreement with him and deported him to Saudi Arabia. Hamdi, who was never charged with any crime, spent more than two years in captivity before surrendering U.S. citizenship![31]

This is the troubling aspect of this case. Had the government possessed truly persuasive evidence that Hamdi was a dangerous person who might return to the battle against the United States, it surely would have made some effort to prove a case against him or found some other basis for holding him. While it is possible that the evidence against him was so secret that it could not be disclosed, the fact that he was turned over by the Northern Alliance, presumably for a bounty, suggests otherwise. Hamdi may have been one more innocent person swept up and sent wrongly to Guantánamo. At the least, he does not seem to have been a dangerous terrorist as initially claimed.

This pattern recurred repeatedly. The United States made the most serious of charges, then claimed that the person seized was a conspirator to the most dangerous and vicious terrorist plots against the United States and its allies (one cannot get much worse than a plot to detonate a radioactive dirty bomb in a large city). Evidence then gleaned from torture or from cruel, inhuman, or degrading interrogations repeatedly turned out to be untrustworthy, and the charges then either collapsed entirely, or, as with the case of José Padilla, were extravagantly overstated. The public was left to wonder at the extent to which innocent people were tortured, held for years without trial, and then either released or disappeared. And we are left to wonder how many of the others were, like Padilla, only guilty of lesser offenses and were, far from being the worst of the worst, simply low-level operatives who happened to be caught.

The war against terror again proves what other similar wars (such as the Vietnam War) have demonstrated—that torture devolves to the lowest-level enemies and to the innocent as well as those few who remain truly dangerous. It is estimated that as many as 80 percent of those tortured in the Vietnam War were either innocent people in the wrong place at the wrong time or just low-level Viet Cong without useful information.[132]

There is no reason to think that this war has been any different. Indeed, as of 2010, long after most of the easy cases were disposed of and the majority of Guantánamo inmates had been released or returned to their home countries, the Guantánamo Review Task Force found that fewer than 10 percent of the remaining 240 detainees were "'leaders, operatives and facilitators involved in plots against the United States' but a majority were low-level fighters."[133] In short, even after many of the easiest releases of detainees, some of whom were wholly innocent of any connection to terrorism, the remaining detainees were mostly low-level with a few yet who could not be categorized. The report recommended holding only forty-eight under the laws of war.[134]

Of the 775 of detainees held over time at Guantánamo Bay, approximately 445 have been released without charge as of this writing.[135] Many were, as UN special rapporteur on torture and other cruel, inhuman, or degrading treatment of punishment Manfred Nowak says, "in the wrong place at the wrong time" and posed no security risk.[136]

The appalling incidence of innocent persons wrongfully convicted after otherwise fair trials should give pause to those who think our intelligence services, acting on incomplete and often speculative information, always focus only on the guilty.[137] Moreover, torture is complicated. Not only do we torture the innocent, but we also glean evidence from torture to implicate the innocent as well as the guilty, thus continuing and exacerbating the cycle. One should also be skeptical of the claim that our intelligence services only single out the worst of the worst.

### Rasul v. Rumsfeld

*Rasul* was the third, last, most difficult, and most significant of the terrorism cases decided during the Supreme Court's 2004 term.[138] The petitioners were noncitizens held at Guantánamo Bay, Cuba, and therefore outside the territorial United States. The Court decided the case on the narrowest possible ground, holding that the statutory writ of habeas corpus applied to noncitizens detained at the Guantánamo Bay naval base.[139] The case turned on the fact that, notwithstanding Cuba's ultimate sovereignty over the area, the U.S. naval base there was subject to the United States' exclusive jurisdiction. Cuban law had no application, so a different ruling would have left Guantánamo Bay wholly outside of any effective law. This ruling, however, had the potential of wiping out the administration's entire strategy of creating a law-free zone where alleged terrorists could be held and, more importantly, interrogated without judicial oversight.

By deciding the case on statutory grounds, the Supreme Court avoided deciding a more difficult constitutional question. The U.S. Constitution provides that "the privilege of the Writ of Habeas Corpus shall not be suspended, unless when in Cases of Rebellion or Invasion the public Safety may require it."[140] This is the only human right specified in the original Constitution, and arguably the most important.

The narrow basis for the Court's decision left open the possibility that Congress might change the law adversely to the detainees. It also

left open the possibility, later addressed in *Boumediene*, that congressional action could be trumped if constitutional habeas corpus applied
to executive detention of noncitizens outside of the United States.
Congress may alter a statute at any time, but, absent constitutional
amendment, Congress cannot change the Supreme Court's interpretation of the Constitution.[41]

## The Executive and Legislative Response
## to the Supreme Court

*Padilla*, *Hamdi*, and *Rasul* are important for the executive branch and
legislative branch reactions they triggered in a scramble to save the
administration's carefully constructed law-free interrogation zone. First,
the Department of Defense narrowly interpreted the scope of the (admittedly ill-defined) hearings required by *Rasul* by setting up Combatant
Status Review Tribunals (CSRTs). These tribunals featured restrictive
rules that, among other things, failed to provide a detainee with sufficient information to defend himself, gave an overly vague definition
of "enemy combatant," and failed to adequately handle accusations
of torture. The CSRTs allowed for secret evidence, hearings outside of
the presence of defense counsel, the use of hearsay upon hearsay, and
a vague and overbroad definition of "enemy combatant."[142] The CSRTs
simply ignored evidence that cleared detainees. A detainee's innocence
of any crime, it seems, was irrelevant. Indeed, the record and findings
of the hearings were in some cases kept from the detainee, and the
material was classified and thereby effectively hidden from the public.

The press reported that the military possessed in 2002 compelling evidence that would clear a detainee named Murat Kurnaz. The
evidence seemed sufficiently clear by then that a German intelligence
officer wrote that the United States considered his "innocence proven"
and predicted his quick release. Nonetheless, Kurnaz languished in
Guantánamo until 2006. Even after his release, he had to sue to compel
release of the classified documents in his case. Even more damaging
to the U.S. position, a U.S. district court judge ruled in 2005 that he
did not receive a "fair opportunity to contest the material allegations

against him."[143] The best summary description of the CSRTs comes an *amici* brief filed with the Supreme Court in *Boumediene*:

> The CSRTs consist of panels of three military officers who are "not bound by the rules of evidence such as would apply in a court of law" and may consider any information—including classified, hearsay, and coerced information—in making their determination as to whether, by a "preponderance of the evidence" the detainee is "properly detained as an enemy combatant." The detainee is not entitled to legal counsel and is not entitled to have access to or know the details of any classified evidence used against him. There is a presumption that the Government Information submitted to the CSRT in support of the detainee's classification as an "enemy combatant" is "genuine and accurate."[144]

It is difficult to avoid the conclusion that the CSRT process was set up in order to evade to the maximum extent possible *Hamdi*'s fair hearing requirement. The goal seems to have been to continue to hide the government's treatment of detainees.

Next Congress rushed through the Detainee Treatment Act of 2005, which, among other things, gave congressional blessing to the CSRT process, purported to strip the federal courts of habeas jurisdiction, and provided rules that facilitated convictions rather than a just process. Neither the president nor Congress appears to have been anxious to have the courts inquire into the Guantánamo detainee's cases.

Most importantly, notwithstanding the act's ban on torture, the president's signing statement said that the law shall be construed "in a manner consistent with the constitutional authority of the President to supervise the unitary executive branch and as Commander in Chief and consistent with the constitutional limitations on judicial power."[145] With this statement President Bush implicitly but clearly declared that, notwithstanding the Detainee Treatment Act (DTA), he had the power to continue to order interrogations that included torture. As professor Martin Lederman put it, "Translation: I reserve the constitutional right to waterboard when it will 'assist' in protecting the American people from terrorist attacks."[146] Thus, even though the DTA claimed to prohibit torture and cruel, inhuman, and degrading treatment, the president claimed the right to continue the practice.

## The Supreme Court Reasserts Itself

The jurisdiction-stripping provisions of the Detainee Treatment Act of 2005 were aimed directly at *Rasul*'s holding that detainees at Guantánamo Bay were entitled to statutory habeas review. In a complex and narrow opinion, a bare majority in *Hamdan v. Rumsfeld*, decided a year later, concluded that the DTA applied prospectively.[147] Thus, all of the detainees at Guantánamo as of the effective date of the DTA could still maintain petitions for writs of habeas corpus. The Court also held that the procedures set forth in the DTA violated the Uniform Code of Military Justice, which had incorporated the laws of war and thus incorporated the Geneva Conventions into domestic law. This meant that Common Article Three of the Geneva Conventions, with its proscription of torture and cruel, degrading, and inhumane treatment, applied to the detainees, and that a federal habeas court could inquire into both their continued detention and their treatment.

However, the Court in *Hamdan* avoided the two major questions. First, does constitutional habeas corpus apply to Guantánamo's detainees (as opposed to statutory habeas corpus, which Congress can change)? Second, *Hamdan* left open the question of whether the Geneva Conventions are self-executing. Do the Geneva Conventions apply to the detainees irrespective of the Uniform Code of Military Justice (which Congress can also change)? Thus there remained room for Congress and president to stage yet another end-run on the Court. The Bush administration, it seemed, was determined to keep detainees away from civilian courts, which would, by providing a fair process, expose the administration's detention policies to the world.

## The Military Commissions Act of 2006: Another Way to Hide Torture

Congress responded to *Hamdan* with the Military Commissions Act of 2006, which attempted to again cut off all civilian court review for

Guantánamo detainees. As one scholar put it, "With the adoption of the DTA and MCA [Military Commissions Act], Congress has now given the President virtually all that he sought with respect to detention and trial of enemy combatants."[148] If upheld, these two pieces of legislation would have returned detainees to roughly their original position under President Bush's original military commissions system.

The rules of evidence under the Military Commissions Act paved the way for hiding torture, including the use of secret evidence from which the detainee and his lawyer are excluded; hearsay evidence, including hearsay within hearsay; the use of evidence stemming from coercive interrogation techniques; and the use of nontestimonial evidence stemming from torture, including the use of such to validate or render reliable statements obtained through coercion. Even evidence obtained using torture, although formally prohibited, provided a back door into evidence.[149]

Both the CSRTs and the military commissions, staffed completely by the military, became so politicized that the chief prosecutor, Col. Morris Davis, resigned, complaining about "political interference with the independence of his office" and saying, "as things stand right now, I think it's a disgrace to call it a military commission—it's a political commission."[150] Under these circumstances, it is reasonable to ask how independent these tribunals could ever be and how likely they would exercise discretion in favor of a detainee.[151]

## *Boumediene* Changes the Legal Framework

Justice Anthony Kennedy's majority opinion in *Boumediene* features a modestly limited holding that purports to invalidate a single subsection of one law—the habeas jurisdiction-stripping portions of the MCA.[152] However, the ramifications of providing the Great Writ, habeas corpus, to alien detainees held outside U.S. territory reaches far more broadly than this unassuming claim suggests. Not only does independent review by civilian courts give detainees a better (and quicker) opportunity for release, it also creates a greater likelihood of forcing disclosure of torture or cruel, inhuman, or degrading treatment. Moreover, it undermines the authority granted the president to make unreviewable legal determinations about the legal scope of the Geneva Conventions, the War Crimes Act, and, through it, the Convention against Torture. It added to the pressure to close the detention facility at Guantánamo Bay. Finally, and perhaps most importantly, by bringing the United States closer to compliance with international human rights norms, it will almost certainly lessen the level of criticism directed at the United States internationally.

In *Boumediene*, noncitizen aliens captured abroad in Afghanistan and elsewhere in the war on terror had been detained at Guantánamo Bay for up to six years (since 2002) as enemy combatants. Recall that the Court in *Hamdi v. Rumsfeld* held that alleged enemy combatants were entitled to minimum due process requirements. The Department of Justice created CSRTs to attempt to comply with this holding. All detainees then held by the Department of Justice were thereafter designated enemy combatants under these newly created CSRTs. None had review applications heard on the merits, each denied that he is a member of al-Qaeda or the Taliban, and none were citizens of a nation at war with the United States.

The U.S. Supreme Court held that the constitutional writ of habeas corpus (as opposed to the statutory writ addressed in *Rasul*) applies to aliens captured abroad and held at Guantánamo Bay, Cuba, an area where the U.S. exercises complete control, Cuban courts having no jurisdiction. It reasoned that the MCA does not purport to suspend the writ, and the protections of the Constitution's Suspension Clause do operate on noncitizens captured abroad and detained as enemy combatants in a place where the United States lacks formal sovereignty but has complete jurisdiction and control. The MCA acts as an unconstitutional suspension of the writ. The Court only struck down a narrow (but crucially important) slice of the law.

Second, Congress had passed, and the administration had signed into law, alternative remedies. Were they an adequate substitute remedy for the writ of habeas corpus? The Court answered no. The majority found many deficiencies in the CSRT process, including the inability to consider after-acquired evidence of innocence that led to the conclusion that the DTA is not an adequate substitute for habeas corpus. The majority said, "Procedural protections afforded to the detainees in the CSRT hearings . . . fall well short of the procedures and adversarial mechanisms that would eliminate the need for habeas corpus review."[153]

Do these prisoners have to exhaust their remedies before seeking habeas corpus? Again, the Court held, no. These detainees had been held for as many as six years without meaningful hearings and "the costs of delay can no longer be borne by those who are held in custody. The detainees in these cases are entitled to a prompt habeas corpus hearing."[154]

The implications of this decision are far-reaching. They include the following six points, the last in the form of a remaining question:

1. *Torture will be harder to hide.*
Habeas courts are far more likely than military commissions to hear allegations and to consider evidence that detainees were tortured, and such evidence is more likely to become a matter of public record.[155] *Boumediene*'s extension of the writ of habeas corpus to these detainees makes it unlikely that the military commissions, even those reformed under the new administration, would operate in the same way as previously. Thus, *Boumediene* changed how detainees' trials or commissions could proceed, and it gave detainees access to federal courts through the writ of habeas corpus.

The habeas cases thus far suggest that habeas will result in the release of Guantánamo detainees; as of June 2010, detainees had won thirty-six of forty-nine habeas cases in the federal district court, for a winning percentage of 73 percent.[156] Habeas courts already appear to provide a more hospitable forum for detainees, and they have already proved to be more open to allegations that a detainee's evidence was tainted by torture. Finally, habeas courts will publish at least parts of their opinions (even as they may redact sensitive or classified material), which will make it easier for journalists, historians, legal scholars, and others to access and evaluate that evidence. Habeas courts cannot help but to open up, speed up, and make more transparent a previously opaque, glacial process.

2. *Some detainees will be released from detention.*
Because a habeas court will not be bound by the MCA's rules of evidence and can create its own record, it will be easier for a detainee to

establish innocence and secure release. The decision will likely spur the administration to find some way to release those whom it no longer considers dangerous. Habeas courts are already releasing some detainees, and the new administration is scrambling to try to find ways to deal with the rest.[57]

*3. The president lost sole power to interpret Geneva Conventions.*
The MCA purported to give the president the final authority to determine the meaning and application of the Geneva Conventions. Had it held, this would have excluded courts from what had been a quintessential legal question—the meaning and application of a particular kind of law—treaty law.[58]

The Supreme Court has, since *Marbury v. Madison* in 1803, consistently held that it is the province of the courts to say what the law is.[59] Indeed, the majority in *Boumediene* mentioned this well-established principle.[60] The rule that the courts are the final arbiters of what the law is applies to construction of treaties.[61] The courts are therefore unlikely to cede the sole power of treaty interpretation in the case of an important treaty such as the Geneva Conventions. The availability of habeas corpus gives the courts a mechanism by which a question concerning the construction of the Geneva Conventions could potentially come before the courts.

In a proper case, a federal habeas court could review the president's determination of the meaning or application as a matter of law of the Geneva Conventions, and that issue could percolate on to the appellate courts and finally the Supreme Court. Notwithstanding the *Boumediene* Court's statement that it was only overruling the habeas stripping portions of the MCA, the opinion calls into question and arguably overrules *sub silentio* the grant of exclusive authority on the part of the president to determine the meaning and application of the Geneva Conventions. By reinstating adherence to Common Article 3 of the Geneva Conventions, the administration avoids a potential confrontation with the courts.

Because of *Boumediene*, any president will be less likely to provide aggressive interpretations of the Geneva Conventions. If *Boumediene* acts as a deterrent to odd or overly restrictive interpretations of these international treaties, it may have succeeded in bringing the United

States into line with international opinion without any confrontation with the courts.

*4. The president lost the exclusive power to define torture.*

The MCA also gave the president the unilateral and unreviewable power to establish interrogation methods. As pointed out earlier, under the DTA the president can effectively define, by negative inference, what constitutes torture. *Boumediene* calls this into question. Is what constitutes torture a legal question? The War Crimes Act presumably makes this a legal question, and if this is true, then presumably a court could hold, in an appropriate case, that presidentially approved inter-rogation methods constitute torture as a matter of law, thus rendering evidence or a confession inadmissible. Granted, a court would give great weight to presidential determination, but that determination would not be dispositive.[162] *Boumediene*, then, without mentioning the issue, potentially negates this part of the MCA. This again is likely to result in mollifying world opinion that, for the most part, has reacted negatively to United States' use of torture in the war on terror.[163] It also plainly provides additional political cover to the decision to abjure tor-ture in favor of more humane interrogation techniques.

*5. The case is important internationally.*

Even before *Boumediene*, international pressure had already embar-rassed the United States and made Guantánamo's closure desirable. Now the reason for its existence is gone. Contrary to the OLC's argu-ments, it is not a law-free zone devoid of the U.S. Constitution, the pri-mary reason for sending alien "enemy combatants" to a place beyond the reach of U.S. courts has evaporated. Its closure will do much to mute international criticism and will bring the United States closer to international consensus on international human rights law and international humanitarian law. International opinion played a role in Bush's political weakness because many Americans are aware of world opinion and the problems that this creates for the United States. This in turn undercut the impetus for many of the positions advocated by the Bush administration and arguably hurt his case. International pres-sure may have played an unacknowledged role in *Boumediene*.

Furthermore, international legal opinion played a role in *Boume-diene*. Many international scholars participated in amicus briefs, some of which appeared to be highly influential. The majority opinion specifically mentions the Brief of Legal Historians (which includes international scholars), saying their "expertise in legal history the Court has relied upon in the past." Like it or not (and there are some that bridle at any international influence on U.S. law), international legal scholarship is likely to play an increasingly important role in U.S. jurisprudence.

While this case did not go so far as to address the issue of whether the Geneva Conventions are self-executing, it does have the effect of avoiding the necessity of determining that issue. It leaves in place *Rasul*'s holding that the Geneva Conventions apply to Guantánamo detainees through the Uniform Military Code of Justice. Although international law was not mentioned in the majority opinion, it is increasingly playing a background role in Justice Kennedy's thinking.[164] *Boumediene* neatly obviates the necessity for determining whether the Geneva Conventions are self-executing while undercutting the president's ability to define its protections away. Thus, *Rasul*'s holding that the Geneva Conventions apply continues unless expressly overridden by Congress, and the extension of the writ of habeas corpus gives the courts the opportunity to police those issues. This returns the United States to potentially full compliance with international law. Given Justice Kennedy's well-known sensitivity to these sorts of issues, it seems plausible that international law played an unacknowledged role in Boumediene.[165]

*6. Does* Boumediene *apply more broadly than Guantánamo Bay, Cuba?*
On April 2, 2009, District Judge John D. Bates ruled in *Maqaleh v. Gates* that *Boumediene* applies to at least some detainees in U.S. custody at Bagram Air Force Base in Afghanistan.[166] He concluded that the Constitution's suspension clause applied to those detainees at Bagram who did not have Afghan citizenship or who were not captured there. The judge felt that the record was insufficiently developed to determine whether the fourth petitioner—an Afghan citizen—might also be entitled to the remedy of habeas corpus on other grounds. The Court of Appeals for the D.C. Circuit has reversed, on the ground that Afghanistan, unlike Guantánamo Bay remains an active battle zone,

thus rendering *Boumediene* inapplicable.[167] However, this decision by the Court of Appeals may not be the final word, as the Supreme Court could come to a different decision.[168] The Court of Appeals left a small crack in the jurisdictional door, acknowledging that "the United States chose the place of detention" and might be able "to evade judicial review of Executive detention decisions by transferring detainees into active conflict zones, thereby granting the Executive the power to switch the Constitution on or off at will."[169] This suggests that even under the Court of Appeals decision there may be habeas jurisdiction in the federal courts for detainees held around the world. If it turns out that detainees have limited rights to constitutional habeas corpus anywhere in the world, then *Boumediene* becomes even more important as it then potentially affects future conflicts.

## Conclusion

The CIA has destroyed ninety-two videotapes of interrogations, possibly to avoid prosecution for torture.[170] We know what coerced statements "not rising to the level of torture" look like to the CIA and even to the U.S. military. Most importantly, we can now see that rendition and torture lite arise from the policy of secrecy. Both provide different ways toward the same goal—to use a continuum spanning from harsh interrogation techniques to outright torture while keeping the entire process as secret as possible. When considering the fate of an individual detainee, the options were to send that person to a U.S. military base such as Guantánamo or Bagram Air Force base, to a black site, to some other host country, or to render them to a nation such as Egypt, Syria, or Morocco. While each individual decision rested on a variety of factors in the end, there is no bright line between harsh interrogation practices to torture lite to torture and extraordinary rendition to torture.

# 3

---

# From Eichmann and
# Carlos "the Jackal" to
# Reagan and Clinton

If any principle of international law seemed certain prior to the September 11, 2001, attacks on the World Trade Center and Pentagon, it was that no nation could lawfully send people to places where they would face torture. Given then-president George W. Bush's longstanding rhetorical posture against torture and his attempts to eliminate torture worldwide, the United States might have seemed a most unlikely candidate to abduct people and send them to third countries for interrogations using torture as well as cruel, inhumane, and degrading interrogations! President Bush told high school seniors designated Presidential Scholars (one from each state) that "the United States does not torture and that we value human rights."[2] He also said, "I want to be absolutely clear. . . . The United States does not torture. It's against our laws, and it's against our values. I have not authorized it—and I will not authorize it."[3]

Even though the United States resorted to torture throughout the twentieth century, many were nonetheless surprised at the extent and viciousness of the U.S. turn to torture after 9/11.[4] Given this disjuncture between official rhetoric and actual U.S. practice, one might ask how the irregular renditions to justice became renditions to torture, mutilation, and disappearance. This chapter sets out the international and domestic precedents for extraordinary rendition to torture.

## International Laws Affecting Rendition to Torture

The Convention against Torture (CAT), which the United States ratified in 1994 (albeit with reservations, understandings, and declarations) appears unambiguous: "No State Party shall expel, return ('refouler') or extradite a person to another State where there are substantial grounds for believing that he would be in danger of being subjected to torture."[5] The International Covenant on Civil and Political Rights (ICCPR), also ratified by the United States, contains a nonderogable prohibition against torture as well as cruel, inhuman, or degrading treatment.[6] In international law, a nonderogable term in a treaty is such that a country cannot lawfully make exceptions. Once the treaty has been ratified, a nation must comply strictly with all nonderogable terms. Thus, a nonderogable treaty clause prohibiting torture prevents a nation that has bound itself to its terms from reserving the later right to use any form of torture during war, civil strife, or even in the face of the so-called ticking bomb. No reservation, understanding, or declaration, no matter how dire the situation, suffices to avoid a nonderogable treaty term.

While the ICCPR does not explicitly address the issue of non-refoulement, the United Nations Human Rights Committee has authoritatively interpreted the treaty's prohibition against torture as including a prohibition against sending people to places "where there are substantial grounds for believing that there is a real risk of irreparable harm," which includes torture.[7] The term "nonrefoulement" is a principle in international law prohibiting the sending of persons to countries or places where fundamental freedoms (such as the freedom from torture, slavery, or genocide) are in jeopardy. International law thus prohibits end-runs around the prohibition on torture; one cannot avoid its proscription by sending people to countries where torture is commonly practiced.

While the ICCPR does not, strictly speaking, apply to war, its provisions prohibiting torture cannot be limited in any way, even during times of emergency or war. Thus, while much of the ICCPR's formal application to the war on terror depends on whether it is a "real" war as opposed to a metaphor, like the "war on drugs," its proscription against torture remains applicable regardless of how it is formally classified. Moreover, there is substantial disagreement as to whether the "war on terror" constitutes a war at all.[8] The ICCPR and CAT are thus part of the broader sweep of international human rights law that is usually thought to have primary application during peacetime but that has important application to war and civil strife, particularly where treaty terms are made nonderogable.

International humanitarian law (the laws of war), including the Geneva Conventions, also prohibits torture as well as "outrages upon personal dignity."[9] Both international human rights law and international humanitarian law combine to provide what was thought by many international legal scholars to be a seamless norm prohibiting torture under all circumstances, including the sending of anyone anywhere to face torture.[10]

Even those few scholars who disagree and find gaps in the treaties concede, at a minimum, that international law, as developed since Nuremberg, absolutely prohibits torture. One skeptic who argues that the Geneva Conventions do not apply to terrorists, and that the nonrefoulement clauses of the CAT do not apply to extraordinary renditions because "the United States is not 'expelling' or 'returning' persons under this scheme," nonetheless argues that the United States' attempt to relieve itself of obligations under international law by overemphasizing territoriality fails because it "ignores the fact that the procedure might be illegal under international law."[11]

The rules seemed plain and appeared not to admit loopholes. The treaties prohibiting torture not only codified international customary law but also stated principles that are considered *jus cogens*, permitting no derogation and constituting the highest order of international norms, which nation-states cannot (lawfully) modify either by state practice or as a matter of domestic law.[12] The prohibitions against slavery, genocide, and torture admit of no exceptions "even when the 'survival of the nation is at stake.'"[13] As a famous U.S. case states: "the torturer has become like the pirate and the slave trader before him *hostis humani generis*, an enemy of all mankind."[14] Scholars agree that the norms prohibiting torture have become absolute, as has the International Court for the Former Yugoslavia and the courts of the United Kingdom.[15]

Breaches of these norms are "punishable by international individual criminal responsibility," including, in the case of Augusto Pinochet
of Chile, the loss of head-of-state immunity.[16] This last point suggests
that, at least in legal theory, some American officials, up to the president of the United States, could potentially face criminal liability for
its extraordinary rendition program. The practical and political costs of
confronting (and affronting) the world's most powerful nation militar-
ily probably preclude such a prosecution in any international or transnational forum. Nonetheless, some Bush administration officials may
have cause to worry because respected legal scholars citing the *Pinochet*
precedent have argued that some Bush administration officials "may
be in danger of facing charges at the International Criminal Court in
The Hague or from a court in another country."[17] Thus, the charge that
U.S. officials violated international proscription of torture is more than
academic. As we will see in chapter 4, the threat of international prosecution has very real consequences in circumscribing both individuals
and agencies ability to act and travel freely.

Like the earlier prohibitions on slavery and genocide, the prohibitions against torture and against sending people to places that torture
trended toward absolute.[18] Scholars only varied on the theory underlying the conclusion that torture is always prohibited, but the conclusion remains sound. Attempts to circumvent the prohibition are thus
unsound as a matter of international law, as domestic law may not be
distorted to accommodate or legitimate torture.

The United States, during the George W. Bush administration,
swept this aside with formalistic if not fallacious reasoning.[19] First, the
United States relied on empty assurances from the receiving nations
that they would not use torture. In addition, the CAT prohibits sending persons to countries where there is a substantial risk that they will
be tortured. In ratifying the CAT, the United States narrowly construed
article 3's "substantial grounds for believing that he would be subjected
to torture" as only requiring nonrefoulement where "the United States
determines whether it is more likely than not that a person would be
tortured," thus rejecting the the Committee's more restrictive view that
it should not send anyone to an nation where "a person faces a 'real
risk' of torture."[20] Moreover, the United States, "with very little in the

way of support for its view" disputes the Human Rights Committee's view that the Convention has extraterritorial effect, applying wherever a state party has effective control.[21] This allows the United States to avoid application of the torture convention to its forces operating overseas; put another way, under this anomalous interpretation the convention would only apply on U.S. soil and not to anything it did abroad.

While a nation is prohibited from treating its prisoners in a cruel, inhuman, and degrading manner (not rising to the level of outright torture), it is not prohibited from sending a person to another country where they face such treatment. Article 3, Section I of CAT specifically states that "no State Party shall expel, return ('refouler') or extradite a person to another State where there are substantial grounds for believing that he would be in danger of being subjected to torture." However, the torture convention contains no language prohibiting sending people to places where they might face cruel, inhuman, or degrading treatment.

By restrictively defining torture, the United States increased the scope for lesser cruel treatments, which has allowed the United States to claim that so long as it was not sending a person to face outright torture, the United States' actions remained legal. Put simply, the United States attempted to create a loophole in the law—so long as it could claim that rendition did not result in outright torture, only cruel or harsh treatment (as redefined and expanded by the U.S. restrictive definition of torture), then the rendition remained (barely) lawful. This is the bureaucratic equivalent of saying "it is OK to render someone to a Syrian prison because all that will happen is cruelty, not torture."[22]

Nonetheless, administration apologists have continued to insist that the United States could send people to places such as Syria because there was no restriction against sending people to places that were only cruel, not torturous. For example, former CIA lawyer John Radsan has argued that "article Three of the CAT is most relevant to irregular rendition. This article requires that no country 'expel, return ("refouler") or extradite a person to another State where there are substantial grounds for believing that he would be in danger of being subjected to torture.' It is significant that CID is not mentioned in this article and that a parallel provision related to CID does not exist under the Convention. As such, the definition on which the legality of irregular rendition turns is only the likelihood of torture."[23]

The argument that the United States is not sending people to be tortured, only to "harsh" interrogations, also implicitly eliminates the second section of article 3 of the torture convention, which enjoined nations to "take into account . . . the existence in the State concerned of a consistent pattern of gross, flagrant or mass violations of human rights." One can hardly doubt that Syria, Morocco, or Egypt have historically participated in "gross, flagrant or mass violations of human rights." Only by ignoring these nations' historically poor human rights records could one plausibly (even after redefining torture) pretend that all the rendered person faced were harsh yet nontorturous interrogations.

By relying on demonstrably untrustworthy assurances from nations with poor human rights records that the receiving nation would not torture, by restrictively construing the test for determining whether a person actually faced torture, and by restrictively defining torture, the United States enabled itself to ignore both international law and its moral obligation to avoid complicity in torture. The United States could pretend that torture after rendition to places such as Egypt, Syria, and Morocco was something that it could not reasonably foresee; that once given assurances against torture, it was not responsible for another nation's duplicity (even though it knew or should have known better). In short, it could attempt to justify the unjustifiable—rendition to torture.

## Rendition's International Roots

The term "extraordinary rendition" arises out of earlier simpler notions of rendition, in which nations resorted to abduction to secure the presence of fugitives for trial. At least at first, rendition usually meant snatching a fugitive found in a place where extradition was difficult or even impossible—thus lending quasi-legitimacy to an otherwise legally murky process. This chapter traces the evolution of this process of abduction from arguably legitimate or "just" reasons to a process in the war on terror meant to evade any semblance of lawful process. This chapter tells the story of how rendition became extraordinary, of how rendition and "harsh interrogations" became euphemisms for torture.

Rendition has always been controversial in part because it meant violating another nations laws as well as the law of nations (international law). The phrase, "rendition to justice" reflects the fact that the process began as an extralegal way to bring people to justice—to an otherwise fair trial where, if convicted, only lawful penal sanctions followed. Frowned upon but tolerated, it became a way to outsource torture—a way to kidnap people for harsh interrogations in countries that did not observe the legal niceties found in international human rights instruments.[24]

Both renditions to justice and its metastasized successor, extraordinary rendition, begin with governmentally sanctioned abduction. Without resorting to extradition, deportation, or any internationally recognized process, a person who is wanted by one country is snatched from another without that country's formal consent and often in violation of the aggrieved second nation's domestic law. Sometimes, however, the nation seeking the "snatch" carries it out with implicit or overt consent by local or national officials in the nation where the kidnapping occurs. In some cases local law enforcement assists in the "arrest." In any event, there are cases in which the supposedly injured nation makes little or no protest. Irregular rendition can be seen as a matter of degree, with some violations of international law being seen as more egregious than others, and some seemingly following the "no harm, no foul" rule of playground basketball.

Rendition can implicate prickly issues of national sovereignty and pride. One nation cannot normally (or at least openly) kidnap persons from within another nation without consequence. Even the most benign example of rendition—bringing a truly bad person to face relatively impartial justice—can cause wounded pride, protest, and retaliation by the offended nation.

## The Eichmann Precedent

The twentieth century's most famous rendition involved the notorious Nazi war criminal Adolf Eichmann, who was abducted from Argentina by Israeli agents in 1960. At first, Israel contended that volunteers who acted independently of the government of Israel had captured Eichmann. Argentina countered, "Israel's express approval of the acts of the volunteers and intent to place Eichmann on trial resulted in the imputation of legal responsibility to the Jewish State."[25] History records that Israel's intelligence service, the Mossad, tracked Eichmann to Argentina and forcibly abducted him, leaving little doubt that his abduction was the result of official Israeli governmental action.[26]

Eichmann, one of the architects of Hitler's final solution, "was a bureaucratic mass murderer" who organized and coordinated the details of identifying Jews, then assembling and transporting them to the concentration camps, without, however, directly participating in their genocide.[27] He seems to have been the quintessential bureaucratic functionary. In his words, "it was a job I had. It wasn't anything I'd planned, nor anything I'd have chosen." He continued, saying that toward the end, "Himmler himself wanted me to stop. He thought we could save our skins. But I pressed on. If a man has an assignment to perform, he does not stop until it is done." In his own mind he was neither a "murderer nor a mass murderer. . . . I carried out with a clear conscience and faithful heart the duty imposed upon me." His last words to the Israeli court were: "I had to obey the rules of war and my flag. I am ready."[28]

Eichmann provides a historical example of Stanley Milgram's experimental test results that demonstrate how an ordinary person can follow authority to commit utterly depraved things, how ordinary people can torture, murder, enslave, and commit genocide. While Eichmann's case is important as one of the most famous and controversial of twentieth-century renditions, it also serves as an example of the larger point about how and why American military and intelligence officers could also obey orders to both torture adversaries and render them to places where even greater evils were visited upon them. Eichmann proved to be a sort of everyman, obeying orders just as many of Milgram's test subjects did, without remorse or understanding of the evil wrought by following those orders.

Eichmann escaped the Nuremberg war crimes trials by fleeing to Argentina where he and his wife "made no sustained effort to conceal their identity."[29] In a mid-1950s recording Eichmann recalled, "If it has to be . . . I will gladly jump into my grave in the knowledge that five million enemies of the Reich have already died like animals." There is little doubt that Eichmann qualified as a war criminal even if he was not "the central, demonic figure." David Cesarani concludes:

> That he committed atrocities before then is beyond doubt, and there is no disputing the fact that he became an accomplice to a widening circle of mass murder that he helped to sustain with all his might. What makes his crimes so chilling is that they were not preordained by any evident pathology or inbuilt racism. Eichmann learned to hate, and to hate in a controlled and impersonal way.
>
> He applied business methods to the handling of human beings who, once they had been dehumanised, could be treated no differently from cargoes of kerosene. In his mind there was little difference between setting up a petrol station or a death camp.[30]

Israel never attempted to extradite Eichmann and then, ignoring Argentine protests, refused to return him, perhaps because they doubted that formal extradition would be effective. They would not risk losing him.

Eichmann's abduction was considered at the time to have violated Argentine sovereignty and international law.[31] Israel apologized to Argentina, and Argentina, recognizing that Israel was not going to return him, arguably acquiesced. Israel proceeded to try, convict, sentence, and, on June 1, 1962, hanged Adolf Eichmann. In retrospect, many might feel that the violation of international law was justified in this case. Strong evidence directly linked Eichmann to some of the worst excesses of the Holocaust; few people, then or now, regret that he faced the only measure of justice that the world had then to offer. Had Israel not kidnapped and tried Eichmann, he would likely have lived out his life without facing any consequence greater than emigration. Israel's apology combined with Argentina's apparent acquiescence mitigated this violation of international law.

Had renditions remained limited to such extraordinary circumstances as bringing a genocidal murderer to justice, the process might not have fallen into disrepute. Renditions and, later, renditions to justice laid the intellectual, political, and legal basis for the far more controversial and less justifiable post-9/11 extraordinary renditions. Eichmann and the increasingly less compelling cases that followed made the post-9/11 extraordinary renditions to torture seem less radical and, at least arguably, justifiable extensions of precedent.

## Carlos "the Jackal": Rhetorical Support for Later U.S. Practice

In 1994 French intelligence agents of the Direction de la Surveillance du Territoire (DST), with help from Sudanese officials, abducted, hand-cuffed, and hooded the notorious terrorist Ilich Ramirez Sánchez, aka Carlos "the Jackal," from Sudan and rendered him to France for trial.[32] According to one of his lawyers, "there was no procedure or extradition. It was kidnapping."[33] Notwithstanding the lack of formal process, the Sudanese government willingly cooperated in the kidnapping, and "he was betrayed by the Sudanese guards charged with his protection, bound, drugged and put on board a French plane. There, agents of the DST (French counterintelligence agency) awaited him."[34]

Few besides Carlos himself protested this rendering to justice. He was wanted by many nations, and implicated in the murder of eight Israeli athletes at the Munich Olympics in 1972, the kidnapping of OPEC ministers from a meeting in Vienna, and the explosion of a French express train that killed six people; many people applauded his capture.[35] It is unlikely that Carlos was guilty of all that had been alleged, "but these attributions greatly enhanced his mystique."[36] At one time, before Osama bin Laden became synonymous with terrorism, Carlos the Jackal was considered the "world's most wanted terror chief."[37] It was said that "the DST had a personal vendetta against . . . [the Jackal] who killed two of its agents in 1975."[38] He was convicted in 1997 for the murder of the two intelligence officers and sentenced to life in prison. But evidence of his many crimes continues to surface, and in 2007 he was ordered to stand trial for a series of other crimes committed during the early 1980s.[39]

The Jackal contested the legality of his abduction, but, partly because of Sudan's complicity in his capture, the European Commission of Human Rights "ruled that the circumstances of his arrest and transfer to France did not violate the European Convention on Human Rights."[40] He was "effectively under the authority, and therefore the jurisdiction of France" as soon as he was handed over to French authorities in Sudan.[41] Service of the otherwise lawful arrest warrant in France was therefore proper under French law and did not otherwise violate the European Convention on Human Rights.[42] In summary, his detention by Sudanese authorities and transfer to French authorities in Sudan pursuant to a valid domestic French arrest warrant but without an international warrant and without formal extradition proceedings did not violate the European Convention for the Protection of Human Rights and Fundamental Freedoms.[43]

Another factor may have animated the Human Rights Commission's decision. Carlos the Jackal complained that there had been a violation of the prohibition under article 3 of the Convention to be free from "torture or to inhuman or degrading treatment or punishment." However, he apparently presented no evidence in support of this claim and failed to raise it before the French courts.[44] One can only speculate how the decision might have gone had there been evidence of mistreatment in his capture and transfer to French authorities. As it was, the case was limited to whether his liberty interests were improperly violated when the French bypassed formal extradition procedures. Even the most formalistic legal technician might balk at allowing a plainly dangerous terrorist to escape justice on such grounds.

Carlos was tried, convicted, and is now serving a life sentence, much of it in solitary confinement, in France. He remains unrepentant, refusing to "express any remorse for his crimes to the victims on the grounds that there were 'no innocent victims'"; French prison authorities consider him a continuing danger.[45]

U.S. secretary of state Condoleezza Rice cited the Jackal's case as precedent for extraordinary renditions under George W. Bush, claiming that "for decades, the United States and other countries have used 'renditions' to transport terrorist suspects from the country where they were captured to their home country or to other countries where they can be questioned, held, or brought to justice."[46] While there had long been renditions to justice, Rice's suggestion by implication that European nations had rendered people solely for interrogations remained questionable (although, as we will see, there was precedent from the Clinton administration for the practice). Despite accumulating evidence to the contrary, Rice continued to advance the administration's line that the United States did not render people to torture.

Terry Davis, secretary general of the Council of Europe, vigorously disputed Rice's characterization, calling it "obfuscation," and distinguished the case from post-9/11 U.S. extraordinary rendition by pointing out that

> Carlos did not disappear, nor did he end up in some Caribbean gulag. He was taken to Paris and brought before a judge, with the right to a lawyer and a fair trial. This was because he was arrested on the basis of a valid arrest warrant, issued before his capture on the basis of his alleged involvement in a car-bomb attack which killed two people and injured 70 people in Paris. An arrest warrant is a piece of paper signed by a judge. This may not seem much, but it makes all the difference. This is the stuff our freedom is made of.[47]

Given Sudanese governmental complicity in his capture; the presence of a valid, preexisting warrant; the rendering to a fair trial in France; and his undeniable guilt of heinous crimes, it is not surprising that French and European authorities continue to defend Carlos the Jackal's irregular rendering to justice while castigating U.S. kidnappings as a way to outsource torture.

Despite the Council of Europe's protestations to the contrary, one can easily see how this type of rendition provided plausible (if plainly distinguishable) justification for U.S. use of extraordinary rendition. The administration did not need to persuade everyone; it also did not need an airtight legal defense. What it needed was legal and political cover, sufficient to quiet formal governmental protest, and Rice's explanation provided that. Many European nations were quietly complicit in the CIA's extraordinary rendition program and were in no position to vigorously protest. Condoleezza Rice rather bluntly reminded the Europeans of that complicity saying: "The intelligence so gathered has stopped terrorist attacks and saved innocent lives—in Europe as well as in the United States and other countries. The United States has fully respected the sovereignty of other countries that cooperate in these matters."[48] Legal scholar Louis Fisher commented that this was "a very shrewd sentence. It implies that abusive interrogations helped gather intelligence that thwarted terrorist plots, helped protect Europe, and reminded some countries that they cooperated in the CIA flights and were fully complicit in what was done."[49]

Besides an implied threat to expose European complicity in illegal renditions, Rice's statement put most European governments in an awkward position in that future terrorist attacks could be blamed on them if they ceased cooperation with the United States. Rice's statement to the Europeans combined both threat of exposure and threat of blame in the event things went wrong. From a diplomatic perspective, Rice performed masterfully in muting official European protest.

At least regarding human rights matters, the United States does not submit to the jurisdiction of the World Court or any other international judicial or quasi-judicial body (such as the United Nations Human Rights Committee).[50] As the UN Committee against Torture put it, "the United States does not see itself bound to satisfy anyone's interpretation of international law but its own."[51] It thus arrogates to itself the determination of the legality of its compliance with international human rights treaties. This allows the United States to violate those same treaties "without effective redress, because of peculiar but dominant contemporary views of treaties held by domestic authorities responsible for their implementation."[52] It only needed a plausible analogy to bolster its case, to provide surface plausibility to its assertions of legality in order to make the larger political point. Rice, then, succeeded in the short run in deflecting European criticism.

## Additional Historical Context

Other renditions seem less controversial and provide less persuasive cover for U.S. expansion of the concept. Nonetheless, they remain important as part of the intellectual backdrop that the United States appeals to in justifying its use of rendition. They also demonstrate the baseless and misleading nature of U.S. justifications for extraordinary rendition, revealing them to be, at best, thin political cover.

For example, the European Court of Human Rights has consistently found no legal impediment under the European Convention for the Protection of Human Rights and Fundamental Freedoms for a country to omit formal extradition proceedings when the rendering state cooperates by making the arrest and turning a fugitive over to authorities of the prosecuting state. In one early case the European Human Rights Commission ruled that the Convention was not violated where Costa Rican police arrested a fugitive from Italy and then turned him over (without formal legal process) to Italian authorities for transport to Italy to face charges.[53]

Similarly, Klaus Barbie's somewhat irregular return to France with Bolivia's cooperation was deemed lawful.[54] During World War II Barbie was aptly called "the Butcher of Lyon," where, as Gestapo chief, he was thought to have been responsible for the deaths of more than 7,500 people (4,000 of them Jews).[55] The fact that Barbie had been hidden and protected by U.S. intelligence services caused the U.S. Department of Justice to issue a formal apology to France for "delaying justice in Lyon." This apology, combined with Bolivian assistance in his arrest and expulsion to France, mitigates the lack of formal extradition procedures in this unusual case.[56]

Europe's famously pro–human rights sensibilities are not offended by minor legal irregularities in a fugitive's rendition to justice, particularly where the crime is heinous and the fugitive is otherwise difficult to capture when relying solely on formal processes. One important difference in the European cases dealt with here is that in each case the local government either assisted with, or was complicit in, the rendition of the fugitive to justice. In this respect, unlike the Eichmann rendition to Israel, and unlike many of the U.S. renditions, the sovereignty of the nation from which the fugitive was seized was not seen as violated.

This, however, is a dangerous distinction. U.S. authorities seeking to justify their own more audacious extraordinary renditions might well point out that the complicity of certain officials in the nation to which the fugitive is found is not the same thing as receiving formal legal permission via extradition procedures. Except for a few authoritarian regimes, it is rare that any one person or group of persons can be said to speak authoritatively for a country such that its sovereignty has not been compromised by such irregular renditions. Ironically, the Council of Europe recognizes this problem. The European Commission for Democracy through Law (an advisory body to the Council of Europe) issued an opinion on its legal obligations, that said, among other things: "The responsibility of the Council of Europe member States in engaged also in the case that some section of its public authorities (police, security forces etc.) has co-operated with the foreign authorities or has not prevented an arrest without government knowledge. This situation raises the question of governmental control over the security/police services, and possibly, if the applicable national law so foresees, of parliamentary control over the government."[57]

Indeed, the cynic might point out that often it is only in weak countries without a strong judiciary and without strong control over intelligence services that such irregular renditions frequently occur. But that argument can be turned on its head, for it is often the weak governments that cannot extradite and from which it remains difficult or impossible to capture the fugitive absent irregular rendition.

National sovereignty is seen as important in these cases because the kidnapping by one nation of a person on another nation's soil can lead to a breach of the peace between nations. The United Nations Security Council Resolution 38 stated during the Eichmann affair that his kidnapping both "violated the sovereignty of a Member State" and involved "a breach of the principles upon which international order is founded, creating an atmosphere of insecurity and distrust incompatible with the preservation of peace."[58] The Security Council ruled that "acts such as [the Eichmann kidnapping] . . . which affect the sovereignty of a Member State and therefore cause international friction may, if repeated endanger international peace and security." Put simply, kidnappings and renderings of a fugitive to justice violate international law because they risk bruising domestic feelings and can lead to international friction and even breaches of the peace.[59] However, despite these risks, failing to use proper legal channels to extradite a person can be seen as less offensive and perhaps dispensable when both the sending and receiving nations cooperate in the irregular rendition, and when the fugitive is seen to receive a fair trial.

The United States ignored this legal nicety in many of its renditions, thus violating both the other nation's sovereignty and, according to most legal authorities, international law. It appears that the nation with the world's most powerful military is not as concerned with the possibility that its actions might lead to a breach of "harmonious coexistence."

One can readily see why courts would not wish to free someone merely because of minor irregularities attending the capture of a particularly wicked and elusive fugitive. One can also see how these barely lawful European irregular renditions became precedents for more audacious and problematic renditions developed in response to post-9/11 terrorism. The question remains whether these far more severe breaches of national sovereignty are somehow less illegal simply because no other nation would dare make war with the nation with the world's most powerful military.

### Early U.S. Precedents—Reagan to Clinton: Nineteenth- and Twentieth-Century Roots

Although sometimes attributed to policies beginning under the Clinton administration, extrajudicial kidnappings by the United States had earlier legal roots—albeit limited to bringing people to U.S. justice rather than taking them to third countries for trial or questioning.[60] The roots for rendition to torture, however, trace to earlier renditions to justice. Indeed some scholars trace the practice back to U.S. fugitive slave laws that permitted the summary rendition of a slave back into the hand of his master.[61] The problem is partly one of nomenclature. Some scholars begin with domestic nineteenth-century precedents. Others, without always clearly making the distinction, look to Clinton administration policies that expanded the notion by rendering people to other nations where, despite assurances that they would not be tortured, torture was apparently practiced, a practice that was greatly expanded during the Bush administration.

Both views are in their own way correct, but distinctions in the object and methods are sometimes overlooked. Nineteenth-century U.S. renditions included both the return of fugitive slaves and irregular renditions to justice of ordinary criminal fugitives who had fled to another country. The U.S. line of precedents cannot be viewed in isolation from international precedents, such as the cases of Eichmann and Carlos the Jackal.

One can find precedents going back for almost as long as there have been international laws governing the affairs of nations. Early English precedents provide a tenuous but arguable line to U.S. law on the subject.[62] For example, during the reign of Queen Elizabeth I, the captain of an English vessel tricked the English papist, former member of parliament, and secretary of state Dr. John Story into boarding his vessel, and thereupon kidnapped him and "brought him clear away out of Flanders into England."[63] He was imprisoned, tried, convicted, and in 1571 hanged for the crime of treason. Story refused to plead claiming, that he "was not the queen's subject, . . . but was the subject of the most catholic and mighty prince king Philip, king of Spain."[64] This argument failed, with the court ruling that he was born an Englishman and "no man can shake off his country wherein hee is borne, nor abjure his native soyle, or his prince at his pleasure."[65] It followed that he was "subject to the laws of this realm, and should be so to our queen."[66] Story's abduction "was a gross violation of the rights of the King of Spain," whose ambassador protested.[67] His case may be viewed as one of the earlier known rendition cases considered to have violated international law at a time when modern notions of state sovereignty had not fully developed and issues surrounding international law generally, and extradition more specifically, were in their infancy.[68] One prominent nineteenth-century international legal scholar says of this irregular rendition, "the carelessness of territorial rights involved in Story's seizure can only be dismissed as characteristic of a day of religious fanaticism."[69]

The force of such early precedents for understanding modern renditions is attenuated by time and circumstance. However, the case does demonstrate that kidnappings that impinge on another nation's sovereignty have long been thought to violate international law as well as tending toward breaches of international peace. It also stands as precedent for the somewhat contrary proposition that a subject could be tried and punished under English law notwithstanding the circumstances of how he or she might be brought before that country's courts.[70] As we will see with later U.S. cases that also involve abductions to bring a person to trial, Dr. Story's case provides an early instance where international and domestic law were at odds, if not outright contradictory. The major difference is that modern international law—particularly human rights law since World War II—carries far more weight now than it did in the sixteenth century, and the consequences for openly opposing it (even for an exceptionalist nation such as the United States) are greater.

Early U.S. precedents in lower courts involving abductions to justice culminated in the nineteenth-century Supreme Court case of *Ker v. Illinois*, which provides a useful starting point for understanding how the United States came to its position on extraordinary rendition.[71] This case supplied the precedent in the nation's highest court, which was used to justify later renditions to justice and which still later was used to justify extraordinary rendition.

In *Ker*, Henry G. Julien, a private citizen working for the Pinkerton Company, a private agency "hired to retrieve prisoners from extraditing countries,"[72] was pursuing Ker on behalf of the government. Despite an extradition treaty and without higher-level authorization, Julien ignored a formal extradition warrant, kidnapped the defendant, and then rendered him to face American justice.[73] The Supreme Court held that "such forcible abduction is no sufficient reason why the party should not answer when brought within the jurisdiction of the court which has the right to try him for such an offense, and presents no valid objection to his trial in such court." The Court pointed out that there was "no language in this treaty . . . which says in terms that a party fleeing from the United States to escape punishment for crime becomes thereby entitled to an asylum in the country to which he has fled."[74] It remained open for treaty language to expressly prohibit such abductions, but in the absence of such language, it would not matter how the fugitive was brought to trial.

In 1952 *Frisbie v. Collins* held that forcible abduction from one state to another within the United States does not impair a court's power to try a person.[75] The domestic legal basis for renditions to justice was laid in the nineteenth century and upheld long before the practice became common.

## Renditions under Presidents
## Ronald Reagan and George H. W. Bush

The modern concept of rendition (at least for the United States) begins with congressional passage in 1984 of extraterritorial laws aimed at combating terrorism, which were expanded in 1986.[76] During hearings before the Judiciary Committee and the Appropriations Subcommittee on Foreign Operations in 1985, Senator Arlen Specter urged law enforcement officials to apply the *Ker-Frisbie* doctrine to capture and try terrorists abroad.[77] In 1986 President Ronald Reagan approved by secret executive order a more aggressive use of renditions.[78]

As a result of the new law, and armed with the authority of Reagan's executive order, in 1987 the FBI lured Fawaz Yunis out of Beirut, Lebanon, and into international waters off the coast of Cyprus with promises of a drug deal; they then brought him to face U.S. justice.[79] Yunis had been the leader of the terrorist group associated with Lebanon's Amal Militia that hijacked a Royal Jordanian airline flight in which two hostages were United States citizens.[80] The Court of Appeals, citing *Frisbie v. Collins* and *Ker v. Illinois*, rejected Yunis's complaint that jurisdiction should have been declined because of the government's outrageous conduct.[81]

There was little question that Yunis was a dangerous terrorist (although, since no one died in this hijacking, he was certainly not of the same level of infamy or culpability as Carlos the Jackal). However, deception rather than force animated and thereby partially justified this particular rendition. Unlike Eichmann or Carlos the Jackal, Yunis's capture in international waters did not so directly aggrieve another nation as it might have if it had occurred on another nation's soil, waters, or airspace. While international customary law unequivocally prohibits abductions that violate another nation's sovereignty, luring a fugitive onto international waters to capture him occupies a murkier status under the law. In that instance, a nation might still protest the abduction of one of its citizens or nationals. However, U.S. long-arm jurisdiction over Yunis was predicated upon the fact that two of his hostages were American, and international law recognizes that a nation may prosecute a noncitizen under the "passive personal principle" where "the state has a particularly strong interest in the crime."[82] The United States had a strong interest in prosecuting Yunis that arguably mitigated any harm under international customary law. Yunis was born in Lebanon, which plainly had an interest in its citizen and would have been the only nation with standing to protest; it did not.

The Court of Appeals held that the Convention for the Suppression of Unlawful Seizure of Aircraft (the Hague Convention) required the United States to prosecute hijackers "present" in their territory.[83] The Antihijacking Act of 1974 was enacted to conform to this convention, and its language was construed to require the United States to prosecute Yunis however he came to be present within the United States and without the "voluntariness limitation urged by Yunis." Thus, the court construed international treaty law to require Yunis's prosecution regardless of the circumstances of his capture.[84]

In Yunis's case, the violation of customary international law could be seen as a technical violation. That country's justice minister, Nabih Berri, called the arrest "an aggression against the dignity of Lebanon" and "an act close to piracy."[85] However, Berri was the head of the Amal Militia in Lebanon. According to Yunis's testimony at sentencing, the Amal Militia ordered the hijacking.[86] As a result, Berri was not entirely without self-interest in the matter and, in any event, this seems to have been the extent of the denunciation, which carried little weight under international law and no weight whatsoever under U.S. domestic law.[87]

Although Yunis's abduction might possibly be argued to have violated customary international law, it did not violate the express terms of any treaty. According to the court that tried him, Congress's enactment of the Hostage Taking Act "reflects an unmistakable congressional intent, consistent with treaty obligations of the United States, to authorize prosecution of those who take Americans hostage abroad no matter where the offense occurs or where the offender is found."[88] It remains clear under U.S. law that while courts will always attempt to construe congressional legislation consistently with international law, Congress retains the power, if it makes its intent clear, to supersede customary international law.[89] Yunis was the first person rendered under these new laws, and his rendition became the direct precedent for later, more audacious renditions.[90]

In December 1989 President George H. W. Bush ordered the invasion of Panama, initiating one of the more controversial early rendition
cases. In part, the goal was to bring cocaine-smuggling dictator and
self-appointed general Manuel Noriega to justice. Mounting evidence
of massive drug smuggling and money laundering using Panama as a
safe haven inevitably caused Noriega to come into conflict with the
United States. Furthermore, General Noriega's dictatorship threatened
the Panama Canal's neutrality, and he had threatened the lives of U.S.
citizens living there. On January 3, 1990, U.S. forces captured Noriega
and rendered him to the United States for trial.

Noriega vigorously protested, arguing that his arrest, capture, and
forcible removal to the United States was illegal and "shocking to the
conscience and in violation of the laws and norms of humanity," and
that the invasion of Panama violated both the Constitution and international law. The successor government in Panama led by Guillermo
Endara (installed by the United States after Endara's earlier election
had been nullified by Noriega) did not protest the irregular rendition
to the United States.[91]

The Federal District Court for the Southern District of Florida
rejected all of Noriega's claims under international law and responded:
"It is well settled that the manner by which a defendant is brought
before the court normally does not affect the ability of the government
to try him. The *Ker-Frisbie* doctrine, as this rule has come to be known,
provides that a court is not deprived of jurisdiction to try a defendant
on the ground that the defendant's presence before the court was procured by unlawful means."[92]

Noriega, who came to power in a military coup, was never considered the legitimate head of state and was not successful in his attempt
to assert head-of-state immunity. Such a defense, had it been available to him, might have worked in 1989. A decade later the law had
changed and head-of-state immunity became more difficult to assert,
at least insofar as crimes against humanity are involved. The first case
to directly confront (and reject) the defense of head-of-state immunity
for crimes against humanity was that of the extradition of Chilean
president Augusto Pinochet before the British House of Lords.[93] And
even that decision, involving Pinochet's extradition from the United

Kingdom to Spain, was limited to cases involving torture committed after ratification of CAT by both the United Kingdom and Chile. The head-of-state defense might have posed a closer question had Noriega qualified as a legitimate head of state. Even then it is not certain which way it might have gone given the development of the law at the time, which even then might have denied a former head of state immunity "for private criminal acts."[94]

The important thing to notice is how the "ends justify the means" argument has changed. Eichmann's abduction for genocide seems more than justifiable; the crime was against humanity itself and involved the loss of millions of lives. The Jackal's capture seems only slightly less compelling; while it did not involve the staggering numbers of the Holocaust, his brand of international terrorism likewise involved the killing of large numbers of innocent people. Yunis was also a terrorist, but his case does not appear to have violated international law in any meaningful respect.

Noriega's case, however, included starting a war with the foreseeable killing and displacement of large numbers of innocents. It also involved ending large-scale drug smuggling, and stopping a criminal dictatorship. The loss of lives and disruption for others was horrific. As Human Rights Watch reported in 1991,

> We remain skeptical about larger numbers. . . . They reveal that the "surgical operation" by American forces inflicted a toll in civilian lives that was at least four-and-a-half times higher than military causalities in the enemy, and twelve or thirteen times higher than the casualties suffered by U.S. troops. By themselves these ratios suggest that the rule of proportionality and the duty to minimize harm to civilians, where doing so would not compromise a legitimate military objective, were not faithfully observed by the invading U.S. forces. For us, the controversy over the number of civilian casualties should not obscure the important debate on the manner in which those people died.[95]

Note the shift and expansion of rendition's logic. From constituting the rare exception, renditions to justice were becoming accepted as an increasingly important if also murkily illicit policy tool. Powerful nations—particularly the United States—overlooked the illegality of kidnapping under international law; norms seemed to be shifting (prematurely and erroneously, as it has turned out) in favor of an ambiguous, neither quite legal nor demonstrably illegal status for renditions to justice. In any event, as demonstrated in the case of *Alvarez-Machain*, discussed in the following, the United States seemed prepared to weather the criticism of illegality.[96] The rules were changing, at least for an exceptionalist nation such as the United States, both in the degree of force that could be brought to bear and in toleration of increasingly lesser purposes animating renditions.

In 1990, in a case that ultimately reached the U.S. Supreme Court, the United States government authorized the abduction of a medical doctor, Humberto Álvarez-Machain, who was accused of participating in the torture-murder of a U.S. drug enforcement agent in Mexico.[97] The case differed from *Ker* in two respects. First, Mexico vigorously protested the kidnapping, sending a diplomatic note to the United States demanding Dr. Álvarez's return and claiming that such abductions on Mexican soil violated the extradition treaty with the United States. This provided Dr. Álvarez with derivative standing to contest his abduction.[98] Second, unlike *Ker*, the U.S. government explicitly authorized Álvarez-Machain's abduction.[99] This direct governmental involvement hurt Mexican sensitivities, informed as they were by a long history of U.S. meddling in Mexico's internal affairs.[100] Long before this case, the diplomatic tensions stemming from that interference had directly and adversely affected extradition between the two countries. Mexicans have long been of the view "that the United States tramples on its sovereignty and violates its law."[101]

A six-vote majority on the U.S. Supreme Court held that, notwithstanding Mexico's protest and notwithstanding the violation of international law, the treaty did not explicitly prohibit such abductions. Thus, the *Ker-Frisbie* doctrine applied and the trial court was not divested of jurisdiction. Writing for the majority, Justice William Rehnquist wrote,

> Respondent and his amici may be correct that respondent's abduction was "shocking," and that it may be in violation of general international law principles. Mexico has protested the

abduction of respondent through diplomatic notes, and the decision of whether respondent should be returned to Mexico, as a
matter outside of the Treaty, is a matter for the Executive Branch.
We conclude, however, that respondent's abduction was not in
violation of the Extradition Treaty between the United States and
Mexico, and therefore the rule of *Ker v. Illinois* is fully applicable
to this case. The fact of respondent's forcible abduction does not
therefore prohibit his trial in a court in the United States for
violations of the criminal laws of the United States.[102]

In his dissent in *United States v. Alvarez-Machain*, Justice John Paul Stevens (joined by justices David Souter and Harry Blackmun) responded
by pointing out the distinction between kidnappings by private citizens (such as occurred in *Ker*), which do not implicate much less violate extradition treaty obligations, and cases such as this, where the
abduction was expressly authorized by the government, arguing that "a
critical flaw pervades the Court's entire opinion. It fails to differenti-
ate between the conduct of private citizens, which does not violate any
treaty obligation, and conduct expressly authorized by the Executive
Branch of the Government, which unquestionably constitutes a flagrant
violation of international law, and in my opinion, also constitutes a
breach of our treaty obligations."[103]

Álvarez-Machain was acquitted at trial, and he then sued those
responsible for his abduction. The Supreme Court again heard his case,
this time ruling, among other things, that his abduction, brief illegal
detention, and rendering to justice in the United States did not violate
a well-defined norm of customary law, thus leaving him without civil
remedy for his abduction from Mexico.[104]

By this point, rendition to justice had expanded to include garden
varieties of serious crime. However heinous Álvarez-Machain's alleged
crime may have been, it was neither a war crime nor terrorism, as those
crimes are conventionally understood. More importantly, although
this rendition was deemed lawful by the Supreme Court, some scholars
have pointed out that the Supreme Court "provided no support for
its extraordinary conclusion," which "is mistaken." They have further
argued that the United States' actions with respect to Álvarez-Machain

were plainly illegal under international law. Most commentators argue that the violation of another nation's sovereignty by abducting one of its citizens is a clear violation of international customary law.[105]

U.S. actions also constituted a flagrant, prosecutable violation of Mexican law.[106] This violation of another nation's domestic law by American agents should not be overlooked. As we will see with the case of extraordinary rendition, the threat of international prosecution of U.S. agents remains substantial. Even if the United States refuses to extradite its officials to face kidnapping charges, those officials are then hampered by the mere fact of an international warrant for their arrest.

The *Alvarez-Machain* expansion of the rendition to justice concept was not without other immediate consequence. It was inevitable that once renditions to justice became more common, wholly innocent persons as well as those only marginally connected to terrorism would be snatched and tortured. This problem could only increase as more people were kidnapped on what would sometimes prove shaky intelligence. Both the United States and Canada have had great difficulty with wrongful convictions of persons even after fair trials.[107] All of our procedural trial protections cannot suffice to prevent unsettling numbers or erroneous convictions. At least in Álvarez-Machain's case there was an arrest warrant preceding the kidnapping and a fair trial afterward. One can easily see how the innocence problem might become much greater in extraordinary rendition cases, when those constraints were removed. As we will see, an astonishing number of persons rendered for torture were innocent of any provable connection to terrorism.

The fact that the trial court acquitted Álvarez-Machain should serve as an important reminder of the need for due process protections; a reminder of the fact that our law enforcement and intelligence agencies do not inevitably get it right; a reminder that we can only protect the innocent by providing a fair process to everyone, including the guilty. This fact of innocence, however, should not deflect one from inquiry concerning those who were guilty of terrorist acts. As we saw in chapter 2 and will see in chapter 4 and 5 in the cases of those who were rendered to torture, there are both instrumental and moral reasons for avoiding torture for the guilty as well as the innocent.

The *Alvarez-Machain* case also demonstrates that even before the extraordinary renditions of the George W. Bush administration, the international community was becoming increasingly hostile to these "abductions to justice" violations of international law and national sovereignty.[108] Two years later, the House of Lords (at the time the highest appellate court in the United Kingdom) directly repudiated both *Alvarez-Machain*'s reasoning and result, calling the majority opinion in *Alvarez-Machain* "monstrous" while endorsing Justice Stevens's dissent.

> Whatever differences there may be between the legal systems of South Africa, the United States, New Zealand and this country, many of the basic principles to which they seek to give effect stem from common roots. There is, I think, no principle more basic to any proper system of law than the maintenance of the rule of law itself. When it is shown that the law enforcement agency responsible for bringing a prosecution has only been enabled to do so by participating in violations of international law and of the laws of another state in order to secure the presence of the accused within the territorial jurisdiction of the court, I think that respect for the rule of law demands that the court take cognisance of that circumstance. To hold that the court may turn a blind eye to executive lawlessness beyond the frontiers of its own jurisdiction is, to my mind, an insular and unacceptable view. Having then taken cognisance of the lawlessness it would again appear to me to be a wholly inadequate response for the court to hold that the only remedy lies in civil proceedings at the suit of the defendant or in disciplinary or criminal.[109]

It is hard to imagine a more thorough rebuke by a national court of similar stature to the U.S. Supreme Court. Its tone demonstrates the dissatisfaction that much of the international community holds toward the U.S. position.

Álvarez-Machain's rendition to justice provoked Mexican outrage, a flurry of scholarly criticism, and a "storm of international protest." In the end, the United States was forced to modify its behavior toward Mexico.[110] Among other things, the United States has now signed a new treaty with Mexico prohibiting transborder abductions, and while the

Senate has yet to ratify this agreement, the United States has since assured Mexico that it will no longer carry out abductions from Mexico.[111] The Council of Europe, which legally binds forty-six nation-states in Europe, now unequivocally prohibits such abductions to render someone to justice.[112]

The *Alvarez-Machain* case illustrates the way in which the precedent for forcible abductions to justice expanded both in number and in kind. More importantly, with this case, we begin to see the world community react forcibly and effectively against renditions to justice. In this sense then, *Alvarez-Machain* provided the legal, political, and moral arguments for and against the yet-to-come expansion into extraordinary rendition.

Proponents argue that *Alvarez-Machain* declared rendition lawful and constitutes a salutary step in dealing with the intractable problem of putting fugitive international terrorists out of action. For example, Daniel Benjamin of the Brookings Institution argues in favor of the extraordinary rendition program and points out that there have been numerous supporting precedents, including *Alvarez-Machain*.

> President George H. W. Bush approved the kidnapping in 1990 of Mexican physician Humberto Alvarez Machain, who was believed to be involved in the torture and killing of a Drug Enforcement Administration official. Nothing says that renditions can involve only suspected terrorists; Israel's abduction of Nazi war criminal Adolf Eichmann in Argentina in 1960 could be called a rendition, though the term was not yet in use. . . . According to former CIA director George J. Tenet, about 70 renditions were carried out before Sept. 11, 2001, most of them during the Clinton years.[113]

To proponents, extraordinary renditions are the logical and helpful extension of *Alvarez-Machain*, a way to demonstrate that terrorists have no safe haven anywhere in the world.

Opponents of rendition emphasize the almost universal nation-by-nation backlash to *Alvarez-Machain*, its violation of evolving international norms, and transnational case law undercutting its authority. To them *Alvarez-Machain* is an outlier precedent, a throwback to an earlier age. To them all types of rendition must end, or at least be limited to European-style renditions, such as that of Carlos the Jackal, that are done with the implicit cooperation with the host country and are irregular only in the sense that formal extradition is not resorted to.

In this way, the *Alvarez-Machain* cases (criminal and civil) were the most important international rendition precedents since Eichmann. Nonetheless, regardless of international disapproval, U.S. law continues to permit abductions to justice, and government regulations allow them so long as prosecutors secure approval from the Department of Justice.[114]

## Clinton and the First Renditions to Torture

Renditions continued to move toward the modifier "extraordinary." Two things facilitated this change: the 1984 passage of laws giving extraterritorial reach to certain terrorist crimes, and the 1995 executive order signed by President Bill Clinton that expanded the CIA's ability to render terrorists from abroad.[115] Although much of this order remains classified, it was a part of the basis for greater flexibility in carrying out renditions and particularly in renditions from one country to another outside of the United States. According to former CIA counterterrorism expert Michael Scheuer, Clinton's extraordinary rendition program was "was begun in desperation" to capture terrorists and take them to a third party such as Egypt. The CIA was "wary of granting terrorism suspects the due process afforded by American law" because of fear of divulging "secrets about its intelligence sources and methods."[116]

At first the administration followed the familiar path of simply snatching a suspected terrorist for trial. Legal scholar Margaret Satterthwaite points out that "when it was first approved, rendition to justice involved the apprehension of suspected terrorists by U.S. agents in (1) countries in which no government exercised effective control (i.e., 'failed states' or states in chaos because of civil war or other massive unrest); (2) countries known to plan and support international terrorism; or (3) international waters or airspace."[117] Thus, at first these renditions could be justified instrumentally even though one might question their legality under international customary law.

For example, in 1995 the United States captured Ramzi Yousef for his role in the 1993 World Trade Center bombing as well as other

conspiracies to commit terrorist acts. U.S. agents rendered him from
Pakistan to the United States for trial where he was convicted for his
role in the first World Trade Center bombing and sentenced to life
imprisonment.[118] Yousef's rendition arguably could be justified by the
need to bring international terrorists to justice from countries that
could not or would not extradite.[119] Pakistani authorities assisted in
Yousef's arrest in Islamabad, thus making his rendition more like
that of Carlos the Jackal and arguably lawful even under more restrictive European views on the subject.[120] In any event, the courts rejected
Yousef's jurisdictional challenges, including arguments that his capture and arrest violated international law.[121]

Soon thereafter the Clinton administration began to render persons
to third countries such as Egypt, but even this required some semblance
of legal process before rendering a suspected terrorist—there had to be a
warrant, indictment, or other lawful process directed toward the person
to be rendered.[122] However, once the United States began renditions to
third countries (at least in part for the purpose of interrogation) such as
Egypt, Jordan, or Syria, the person so rendered lost the protections that
would have been present in a U.S. Federal District Court. Plainly, the
original safeguards of trial in the United States were being relaxed. The
suspects who were to be rendered had generally been tried in absentia in
the country to which they were to be transferred, and the CIA prepared
the equivalent of a rap sheet, thus reducing the possibility of rendering
an innocent person.[123] Michael Scheuer points out that "what was clever
was that some of the senior people in Al Qaeda were Egyptian," therefore, "it served American purposes to get these people arrested, and
Egyptian purposes to get these people back, where they could be interrogated."[124] Despite precautions, this step more than any other opened
the process to torture as well as the rendition of innocent people.

Under Clinton, the person being rendered, even if sent to a third
country, was not supposed to be sent to a country where there was a
likelihood of torture.[125] Nonetheless, the Clinton administration was
the first to render people to countries such as Egypt, where torture
of prisoners remains common.[126] The U.S. Department of State, in its
annual human rights report, points out that Egypt has been in a state
of emergency "almost continuously since 1967." Its "respect for human

rights remained poor," and the report recounted many instances of torture. According to Human Rights Watch, "Torture is a widespread and persistent phenomenon" in Egypt and has "become epidemic."[127] "Egypt has a consistent history of mistreating political prisoners, often in the name of fighting terrorism."[128] With that record, it is hard to credit Clinton administration claims that it did not know that people rendered to Egypt would likely be tortured.

The CIA agent tasked with implementing Clinton's rendition policy has been quoted publicly and inconsistently on whether the government received assurances that the person being rendered would not be tortured.[129] According to press reports some were tortured and have disappeared:

> The first known rendition by the U.S. government to a third country with a record of torture occurred in 1995 when an Egyptian Islamist, Talaat Fouad Qassem, went missing while visiting Croatia. Mr. Qassem, the leader of a banned Islamic group in Egypt, had been sentenced to death in absentia three years earlier by a military tribunal. The Croatian authorities had originally apprehended Mr. Qassem on an immigration charge, but his transport to Egypt was arranged by the U.S. and he was interrogated by Americans on board a ship in the Adriatic before sending him to Cairo's torturers.
>
> Three years later, following reports that an Egyptian terrorist cell based in Albania were planning to attack U.S. embassies in the region, a CIA paramilitary team arranged the arrest and rendition of a further six Islamic militants to Egypt. Many of them, including Mr. Qassem, have not been heard of since. Those who have say they were tortured horrendously.
>
> But it was after the terror attacks on New York and Washington on 9 September 2001, when "the gloves came off," that the phenomenon exploded. As Cofer Black, onetime director of the CIA's counterterrorist unit, put it: "There was a before-9/11 and an after-9/11."[130]

It appears likely that Qassem was executed without trial by Egypt.[131] Although the publically disclosed details appear somewhat murky, the

Clinton administration apparently rendered five Egyptian al-Qaeda suspects from Albania to Egypt in 1998; all were tortured and two hanged.[132] Given Egypt's well-known, longstanding, and widespread use of torture, U.S. officials at the time almost surely knew they were sending people to be tortured.[133] To be fair, the Clinton administration eventually ceased cooperation with Egypt's intelligence services because of its use of torture.[134] But the concept had again expanded and now allowed renditions to third countries. All that remained for this metastasizing concept was to use the practice while turning a blind eye to violations of the assurances; to wink and nod while sending people to torture; to expand the program from a handful of cases to perhaps thousands, or at least to a number that reaches into the hundreds.[135]

Because assurances that torture would not be employed had failed during the Clinton administration and had been abandoned, the George W. Bush administration knew, or should have known, that similar assurances given to it would likewise be unsuccessful. Some of our most important allies have since recognized that assurances from nations that regularly torture can be meaningless. This skepticism about assurances combined with legal liability issues may lead to close allies not being able to trust assurances by the United States.[136] Thus, the Clinton administration set the precedent for the abusive renditions of the Bush administration.

# 4

# Significant U.S. Renditions
to Torture

It seems easy for those not immediately affected to forget the fear and anger following the terrible events of September 11, 2001, and to fail to appreciate the pressure put on the Bush administration, the public's enthusiastic approval of that administration's robust response, and the general trust in the government's approach to the war on terror.[1] Plainly, the Bush administration had a broad mandate from a frightened American public to "bring [the] terrorists to justice,"[2] and it did so by, among other things, promulgating a secret order that allowed the CIA to establish "secret detention facilities outside the United States, and to question those held in them with unprecedented harshness."[3]

This, along with other policy decisions, opened the door to expanding and transforming the country's rendition program. It allowed the creation of a massive, worldwide torture culture that included, among other things, kidnapping large numbers of people and then sending them to places where they would face torture and cruel, inhuman, and degrading interrogations.[4] This section explores one manifestation of that culture—extraordinary rendition.

The Bush administration's aggressive policy expanded the rendition process sending hundreds or, by some estimates, thousands of people into a legal no-man's land to face torture and disappearance.[5] What we know, despite the many books and articles by investigative journalists written on the subject, remains fragmentary and incomplete because much remains secret.[6] However, the program has resulted in intense scrutiny from the European Union, the Council of Europe, numerous European states, and Canada and has drawn the attention of investigative reporters. Despite the secrecy, it is possible to piece together the process, at least in broad outline.

## Key Cases: The Human Side of Extraordinary Rendition

Given the numbers of cases of extraordinary rendition and the secrecy that continues to shroud the process, it will not be possible to provide even a short summary of all such cases. However, some renditions have created immense legal difficulties while others have seemingly disappeared from view, leaving fewer consequential legal issues. It is also helpful to put a human face on the issue, to always remember that real, flesh-and-blood people are part of and play a role within these legal concepts and conflicts. We must heed Felix S. Cohen's warning against the "divorce of legal reasoning from questions of social fact and ethical value."[7] In this chapter, we will outline the better-known and significant cases, those that drive legal and policy debates.

## Beginnings: Jamil Qasim Saeed Mohammed

Within weeks after the September 11 attacks, the CIA ramped up attempts to take suspected terrorists out of action. On October 24, 2001, Pakistani intelligence operatives, at U.S. request, arrested in Karachi a Yemeni microbiology student named Jamil Qassim Saeed Mohammed, who was suspected of being a member of al-Qaeda and of involvement in the 1998 bombing of the USS *Cole* off the coast of Aden. Bypassing formal extradition or deportation procedures, he was handed over to CIA agents, who blindfolded and shackled him and put him on a Gulfstream V jet owned by a CIA front company. The plane dropped off Mohammed in Jordan where he disappeared.[8] Amnesty International has asked the Jordanian government for information on his whereabouts but has received no answer.[9] This appears to have been the first reported case after 9/11 of extraordinary rendition, but, of course, we have no way of knowing whether it was in fact the first rendition to a country where torture is practiced.[10]

The story received very little notice at the time. Americans, like most of the world, remained unaware that the United States was using rendition to make people disappear in violation of its obligations under international human rights law.[11] Shortly thereafter, another rendition received slightly more attention in a first-page article in the *Washington Post*, which informed the American public that the United States had "secretly transported dozens of people suspected of links to terrorists . . . bypassing extradition procedures and legal formalities . . . to countries, including Egypt and Jordan, . . . where they can be subjected to interrogation tactics—including torture and threats to families—that are illegal in the United States, the sources said. . . . U.S. intelligence agents remain closely involved in the interrogation."[12] Yet, despite allegations that by then there had been dozens of such renditions to countries that practiced torture, the issue remained largely quiescent with "little interest in what the consequences of a policy of rendition might be."[13]

The case raises several questions. Most obviously, what happened to Mohammed in Jordanian hands? Was he tortured? If so, did the Bush administration know or have reason to know that he would likely face torture? More importantly, should the American public have known that people were tortured by and on behalf of the United States? Just five days after the attacks on the World Trade Center and the Pentagon, Vice President Dick Cheney said on NBC's *Meet the Press*, "We also have to work, though, sort of the dark side, if you will. We've got to spend time in the shadows in the intelligence world."[14] At about the same time, the *Washington Post* quoted anonymous U.S. diplomat is quoted as saying: "After September 11, these sorts of movements have been occurring all the time. . . . It allows us to get information from terrorists in a way we can't do on U.S. soil."[15] What could the Jordanians do in conducting an interrogation that the Americans could not, unless it included torture? Where were the protests?

Perhaps just as important, what evidence has been lost as a result of his disappearance? If Jamil Qasim Saeed Mohammed was involved in the conspiracy to bomb the *Cole* (seventeen U.S. sailors were killed in that incident), one would think that it would have been important to bring him to trial so that the survivors and their families could see that justice was done. Did we sacrifice closure on the *Cole* incident in our hurry to remove a suspected terrorist?

## Torture's Truth: Binyam Mohamed

Binyam Mohamed's rendition to torture tied the legal systems of two countries, the United Kingdom and the United States, in knots, and it caused friction between both nations' intelligence services.[16] President Barak Obama and Prime Minister Gordon Brown scrambled to argue (despite defeats in the courts) that court-ordered disclosure of the facts surrounding Binyam Mohamed's rendition and subsequent torture would irreparably harm both countries' national security.[17]

The United States threatened to curb intelligence cooperation between the two nations if the classified details were publically disclosed.[18] Any case that captures the attention of both the United States' and the United Kingdom's legal systems, their respective executive branches, and both nations' intelligence services merits attention.

Ethiopian-born U.K. resident Binyam Mohamed traveled to Afghanistan in June 2001 to rid himself of a drug habit and, as he put it, "to take the journey to Afghanistan as any 21-year-old would do, just go and see part of the world and learn about what's happening over there." He had converted to Islam and said, "I was trying to understand Islam and I was told that Afghanistan was where the real Islam was."[19] The United States, however, alleged a far more sinister motive. At least until the cases fell apart, the United States argued that Mohamed received terrorist training from al-Qaeda while in Afghanistan; went to the frontline to participate in combat against the Northern Alliance; and conspired with José Padilla and the infamous Khalid Sheikh Mohammed (the top al-Qaeda operative and Guantánamo detainee who planned the 9/11 attacks, thought also to have been the architect of the 1993 attempt on the World Trade Center, the attacks on the U.S. embassies in Kenya and Tanzania in 1998, and the Cole bombing in Yemen in 2000) on the construction and detonation of a radioactive dirty bomb in the United States.[20] If Binyam Mohammed had in fact been responsible for even a fraction of what he was accused of, he would have been one of the more important persons captured in the war on terror, and his charges carried a potential death penalty under the Military Commissions Act of 2006.[21] The conflict between the United States and United Kingdom arose out of the tortuous path leading through these conflicting stories.

The United States, along with coalition allies, responded to the attacks of September 11 by launching Operation Enduring Freedom, the war in Afghanistan to dislodge the Taliban and al-Qaeda. Binyam Mohamed left Afghanistan shortly after the war began, traveling to Karachi, Pakistan. On April 10, 2002, he made his second attempt to board an airplane, intending to return to the United Kingdom. Using the false passport of a British national, he was arrested by Pakistani agents on immigration charges, held incommunicado without legal representation, and turned over to American agents without judicial process. The Americans questioned him and allowed British intelligence agents question him as well, and it is here that the case became hotly contested. Mohamed claimed (as we will see, his claims have since been proven) that he was tortured both by Pakistani and American agents, that the torture temporarily stopped when visited by a British agent, and that his subsequent confessions were false and nothing more than the product of years of torture and brutal treatment by Pakistani, American, and Moroccan agents.[22]

What is not seriously contested is that he was secretly sent to Morocco, a nation with a checkered human rights record, and in which there have been "credible reports of torture and mistreatment of [terrorist] suspects."[23] There Mohamed was repeatedly and brutally tortured, including having his penis sliced with a scalpel, and being threatened with having it severed. He says he was "beaten . . . given mind-altering drugs and subjected to extremely loud rock music." He also claims that after his rendition to Morocco, an agent known only as informant A told him that the torture would stop if he cooperated with British intelligence.[24] The British strongly denied this last allegation.[25] Regardless, as we will see in chapter 5 covering the state secrets privilege, it turns out that the British were indeed complicit in his torture.

For years the United States and Great Britain vigorously contested Mohamed's claims of medieval slicing of the body and bone-breaking torture, claiming that they were no more than the lies of a terrorist.[26] Only slowly and reluctantly did they yield to evidence corroborating his claims. For years he languished at Guantánamo Bay facing capital charges while the public in both nations was seemingly left with one more irresolvable and contested claim of torture. What makes Binyam Mohamed's case interesting, and where chronology becomes important, is that it demonstrates not only that there was sufficient evidence at the time to conclude that his allegations were true but also that the United States was fully prepared to try, convict, and sentence a man to death on evidence that officials either knew or should have known to have been false. Because so much even now remains classified and shrouded in secrecy, we must look to inferences requiring attention to detail and timing. However, as we will see, the facts as they ultimately played out suggest that Mohamed's account is nearer the truth than U.S. denials. We will go through the evidence as it developed before outlining the evidence that demonstrates the truth of his story. We do this not because there is any doubt that he was tortured by and on behalf of the United States with British complicity but to demonstrate that the United States held and was prepared to try, convict, and execute a man on evidence that its officials knew or should have known to be false. This is an appalling revelation, and it takes careful consideration of the public, nonsecret evidence to see the strength of it.

Binyam Mohamed was transferred back from Morocco to U.S. custody—first to a CIA black site secret prison in Afghanistan (where he alleges further torture), then to the prison at Bagram, Afghanistan, and finally to Guantánamo Bay, Cuba. He "confessed" to the dirty bomb conspiracy (with, as we saw in chapter 2, José Padilla and Khalid Sheikh Mohamed) in statements made both in Afghanistan and again at Guantánamo Bay.[27] It is these confessions that become important. Were they the unreliable product of years of torture, beginning with Pakistan and moving to Morocco and finally Afghanistan? Or were they the true story of a sinister plot?

As to the torture, his lawyer, Clive Stafford Smith claimed that "through diligent investigation we know when the CIA took pictures

. . . we know the identity of the CIA agents who were present including the person who took the pictures (we know both their false identities and their true names), and we know what those pictures show."[28] Smith was trying to obtain those pictures along with other evidence in the hands of the CIA and British intelligence to show both the fact of Binyam Mohamed's torture and British complicity therein.[29] Evidence was in the possession of both governments, which neither would give up, each claiming the overriding necessity of protecting national security. One might wonder how pictures of Binyam Mohamed's body, including his genitalia, harms the national security of either the United Kingdom or the United States.[30] What sources, methods, or other valuable intelligence were protected by this state secret?

The legal effort to secure evidence of Binyam Mohamed's rendition and torture took two legal paths, one in the United States and one in the United Kingdom. Of the two, the case in the United States is the easier to understand and the less probative on the issue of whether Mohamed was tortured. The U.S. case involved five men, all of whom had been the subject of extraordinary renditions that they alleged had been facilitated by a private contractor, Jeppesen Dataplan, Inc. The contractor allegedly flew Binyam Mohamed and the other plaintiffs to countries where they would be interrogated and tortured. Management officials at Jeppesen Dataplan apparently knew that these were "torture flights."[31]

Plaintiffs filed suit against Jeppesen under the Alien Tort Statute. The United States intervened both in the Federal District Court and on appeal, seeking dismissal on the grounds of the state secrets doctrine. (We explain the state secrets doctrine and this case in detail in chapter 5. It suffices for now that the state secrets privilege in U.S. law is a judge-made principle that protects state secrets from disclosure in court proceedings.) The district court dismissed the complaint, citing state secrets. This ruling was initially reversed by a three-judge panel, which held that the case should return to the trial court to see if it could fairly be tried without the use of materials found to be state secrets. However, the Ninth Circuit Court of Appeals en banc (the entire court, not just a panel of three judges) ultimately upheld the district court and dismissed the case in its entirety without trial on the merits.[32]

This case by itself does not prove that anyone was in fact tortured, or that it was done with the knowledge of U.S. officials. It only points in that direction; rendition to torture is certainly one possible secret that the government would likely wish to protect. The evidence becomes much stronger when considered along with the British High Court case, *R (on the application of Mohamed) v. Secretary of State for Foreign and Commonwealth Affairs.*[33] It is this case and its aftermath that, more than anything else, suggests that U.S. officials dissembled when they denied Binyam Mohamed's claims, and suggests that they were willing to withhold evidence of innocence in a capital case.

In August 2007 Britain asked the United States to return five of its residents, including Binyam Mohamed, from detention at Guantánamo Bay.[34] Three had been released and another was slated for release by May 2008,[35] when Mohamed, the remaining detainee, filed suit in the United Kingdom seeking evidence in the government's hands that allegedly showed that he had been the victim of an extraordinary rendition and that he had been tortured into falsely confessing.[36]

It is here that timing becomes part of the reason for concluding that U.S. officials likely knew they rendered him to torture. The relevant events include the following:

1. May 28, 2008: Binyam Mohamed was charged under MCA 2006 with serious crimes *potentially carrying a death penalty* (and involving an alleged conspiracy to detonate a radioactive dirty bomb in the United States).

2. Summer 2008: The United States sent a letter to the United Kingdom stating that Binyam Mohamed's allegations that he was tortured and that his confessions were the product of that torture were "not credible" and "could be disproved and that BM knew his claims were demonstrably false."[37]

3. August 21, 2008: British High Court, citing classified as well as open evidence, ruled that the U.K. government must produce exculpatory evidence in its hands essential to Mohamed's defense and tending to support his account.[38]

4. Fall 2008: Prosecutors offer Binyam Mohamed a highly restrictive plea agreement, including one more year to serve and an

agreement not to take any kind of legal action and to sign a document saying that he had not been tortured. He rejects the offer.

5. October 21, 2008: Charges against Binyam Mohamed are dropped.

6. February 23, 2009: Binyam Mohamed was released from Guantánamo Bay and returned to Great Britain a free man. No charges of
any kind were brought in either nation.

7. May 2009: The Obama administration reiterates the position of the
former Bush administration admonishing the British government
that release of its secret evidence by the High Court could jeopar-
dize intelligence sharing between the two countries.

One might reasonably ask how it is that a man who has allegedly
confessed to conspiring to detonate a radioactive bomb in the United
States could simply be let go without trial and without any further consequence in either the United States or Great Britain. One might also
ask how it is that the official position of the United States could move
from saying Mohamed's allegation that his confession was the product of torture was "not credible" to judging his allegation sufficiently
credible to release him unconditionally. We can be reasonably certain
that the evidence in the hands of the United States and the United
Kingdom and its High Court did not radically change in this short time.
What seems to have changed is the calculation by U.S. officials about
the likelihood that evidence of torture might be made available to the
defense and ultimately the military commission (and somewhat less
likely—the public).

Seen from this perspective, the prosecution's end-of-game attempt
to secure a plea agreement appears more likely to have been a last-
ditch effort at saving face rather than a serious attempt to do justice;
the point was to obscure evidence of torture rather than protection of
the American public. Mohamed's radioactive bomb conspiracy, if even
plausibly true, surely made him exceptionally dangerous. Prosecutors
do deal away weaker cases, but not generally if it means allowing someone who is monumentally dangerous back into society. Good prosecutors ordinarily take their chances at trial before doing that. Prosecutors
do not usually do multiple backflips quite so quickly. Within a matter
of months, Binyam Mohamed went from being "not credible" and

enormously dangerous, to meriting a plea agreement that combined a statement denying torture and a little more prison time, to going completely and unequivocally free. This particular series of flip-flops is unusual. Plainly, the prosecution did not accurately present Binyam Mohamed's situation.

This does not mean that the secret evidence, had it been disclosed to the defense lawyers, would necessarily have been made publically available—the rules of evidence under the Military Commissions Act of 2006 allow for the use of classified evidence without public disclosure.[39] It is reasonable to conclude that once the British had disclosed the evidence to defense counsel, this would have led to an embarrassing exoneration before a guilt-prone military commission. We now know that Binyam Mohamed's confession was in fact the product of torture and was emphatically false. But the rapid series of events leading to his release makes it clear that the United States covered its mistake up until it became impossible to continue to do so. As his lawyer, Clive Stafford Smith said at the time, "the U.S. Government has consistently tried to cover up the truth of Binyam Mohamed's torture. Gradually, the truth is leaking out, and the governments on both sides of the Atlantic should pause to consider whether they should continue to fight to keep this torture evidence secret."[40]

The United States has neither tried nor released other dangerous persons such as Khalid Sheikh Mohammed.[41] The United States is prepared to keep imprisoned at least some dangerous people even if it cannot effectively try them without evidence untainted by torture. Binyam Mohamed was not released on a mere technicality; he was not dangerous and not guilty of any serious crime. Thus, even at the time it appeared from the publically available evidence that the United States tortured an innocent man and then and rendered him to even more extreme forms of torture.

A bit more detail about the British High Court decision is needed to appreciate the force of this argument. We noted that, based partly on classified evidence available to the court but not made public, the court felt that the evidence acquired from the CIA was essential to Binyam Mohamed's defense, should a military commission have been convened for him. It was essential precisely because it undermined his confessions and tended to support his account that they were procured by torture. Based on this same confidential evidence, the High Court also concluded that "the unreasoned dismissal by the United States Government of BM's allegations as 'not credible' as recorded in the letter of 22 July 2008 is, in our view, untenable, as it was made after consideration of almost all the material provided to us."[42]

These are strong words, and it cannot be supposed that the judges of the Queen's Bench are any less circumspect than are American judges of similar rank. Finally, even the United Kingdom's foreign secretary conceded to the court that Binyam Mohamed had established an arguable case that

i)   After being subject to torture and cruel, inhuman or degrading treatment in Pakistan, he was unlawfully rendered from Pakistan to Morocco by the United States authorities.

ii)  Whilst in Morocco he was subject to unlawful incommunicado detention and torture during his interrogation there by or on behalf of the United States authorities.

iii) He was unlawfully rendered by the United States authorities from Morocco to Afghanistan on 21 or 22 January 2004.

iv)  He was detained unlawfully and incommunicado at the "Dark Prison" near Kabul and thereafter at the United States Air Force base at Bagram.

v)   He was tortured or subject to cruel, inhuman or degrading treatment by or on behalf of the United States authorities in the "Dark Prison."[43]

Thus, the U.K. foreign secretary at the time, David Miliband, who was charged with defending these U.S.-provided secrets before the High Court, conceded that, if publicly disclosed, they would show an arguable case that the United States both tortured Mohamed and rendered him to further, more brutal torture. If the agency charged with defending the secrecy of this evidence felt forced to concede "an arguable case" of torture and rendition, then it should not surprise that the neutral judges described this same evidence as "essential" to a fair trial, and described the U.S. attack on Mohamed's credibility as "unreasoned."[44]

The judges must have thought it at least plausible that a U.S. military commission, acting under the Military Commissions Act of 2006, would not provide this material to the defense on its own, even though it was "essential" to a fair trial in a case carrying a potential death penalty. The British foreign secretary had originally taken the position before the court that the United States would provide the evidence to the defense to be used under the rules of the High Court for the use of such classified materials.[45] However, the court had a basis for questioning whether that was so.[46] The thought that the defendant in a serious capital case might not be allowed access to serious exculpatory evidence must have added urgency to the court's opinion.

The Obama administration continued to attempt to keep this matter secret with its letter to the British government. Most significant from the American perspective, this case is not alone among major international court rulings forcing disclosure of sensitive materials affecting U.S. intelligence. The Supreme Court of Canada ordered the release of classified information compiled by Canadian intelligence officials following interviews with one of its citizens detained by the United States as an alleged terrorist at Guantánamo Bay.[47] The Federal Court of Canada wrote in implementing the Supreme Court order, "Canada cannot now object to the disclosure of this information. The information is relevant to the applicant's complaints of mistreatment while in detention. While it may cause some harm to Canada-U.S. relations, that effect will be minimized by the fact that the use of such interrogation techniques by the U.S. military at Guantánamo is now a matter of public record and debate. In any event, I am satisfied that the public interest in disclosure of this information outweighs the public interest in non-disclosure."[48] Plainly, like the U.K. High Court, the Federal Court of Canada considered the arguments concerning the potential harm to Canada's relationship to the United States and decided that the evidence of mistreatment outweighed that risk.

The Canadian *Khadr* case and Binyam Mohamed's U.K. case are distinguishable. Khadr was a Canadian citizen, and Canada has not extended the right to such confidential information to noncitizen permanent residents or landed immigrants, as was Binyam Mohamed in the United Kingdom.[49] In that respect, the U.K. High Court ruling is broader. Unlike the *Khadr* case, Binyam Mohamed's did not reach the nation's court of last resort (the House of Lords) and so cannot be said to be the final word on the subject. Nonetheless, it is rare for a court of any nation to resist its own executive branch on a sensitive matter of national security; particularly when that security matter adversely affects its relationship with a close ally. Such court-ordered disclosures are rarer yet when the complaining ally remains the world's sole super-power. It may seem like a small thing, but these cases present another constraint on the U.S. war on terror. Unlike Binyam Mohamed, Omar Khadr has now pled guilty before a U.S. military commission at Guantá-namo Bay.[50] One problem with torture is that it not only inculpates the innocent but also greatly complicates prosecution of the guilty.

We now know that Binyam Mohamed was innocent and was bru-tally tortured by the United States with British complicity. The burden of this section has only been to show that U.S. officials knew or should have known that they were fully prepared to try, convict, and execute an innocent man.

## Is the Bureaucratic Outsourcing of Torture Legal? Maher Arar

> So the minute that the executive raises the specter of foreign policy, national security, it is the government's position that is a license to torture anyone?
>
> Judge Sonia Sotomayor, Court of Appeals for the
> Second Circuit (now Justice Sotomayor of the Supreme Court)[51]

Maher Arar's rendition from New York's JFK airport to Syria undoubt-edly remains the best-known—some might say most infamous—post-9/11 rendition. It was also arguably not even a rendition but rather a complex matter of immigration law.[52] In any event, it differed from other well-known renditions in that it began on U.S., not foreign, soil and was implemented not by CIA agents but domestic law enforce-ment officials. The basic issue, at least for the United States, turns on whether rendering someone to another country against his will to face interrogation by torture violates U.S. law. Or is there, as Judge Soto-mayor vividly put it, a "license to torture"?[53] If there is such license, is it embedded in bureaucracies' ability to deflect blame onto the victim? These are two important questions raised by Maher Arar's rendition to torture by the United States to Syria.

Maher Arar, a dual citizen of Canada and Syria, had lived in Canada since he was a teenager. He obtained a bachelor's degree from McGill University and a master's degree in telecommunications from the University of Quebec, and in 2002 was working as a telecommunications engineer. In June of that year, he went on a family vacation to Tunisia but returned alone in September for a business meeting in Montreal.[54] It is at this point that both Canadian and U.S. bureaucracies turned Arar's transitory stop at JFK International Airport in New York City into a juridical nightmare that "would beggar the imagination of Franz Kafka."[55]

The Royal Canadian Mounted Police (RCMP) turned its attention to Arar as a "person of interest" when he was seen having coffee with Abullah Almalki, "the primary target of a national security investigation."[56] He also attended the same Mosque with Almalki and had cosigned as guarantor on a residential lease with him.[57] Based on nothing more than thin guilt-by-association with someone suspected of having terrorist links, the RCMP then exaggerated his role to U.S. authorities, "indicating that he was probably connected to Al Qaeda when, in fact, they had no information to that effect."[58]

The RCMP exaggerations continued to magnify. When Arar arrived at JFK, he had become to U.S. immigration authorities "the subject of a . . . lookout as being a member of a known terrorist organization," and by the time he was handed over to Syria via Jordan, he had become "'clearly and unequivocally' a member of al Qaeda and, therefore, 'clearly and unequivocally inadmissible to the United States.'"[59]

Did the United States have powerful evidence to add to the RCMP's exaggerations? While the United States continues to claim Arar is or was a terrorist, maintaining him on its "no-fly" list, the publically available evidence suggests instead that the United States is simply saving face with those claims but lacks evidential support.[60] Two sources into Canadian and U.S. secret evidence allow such inference. First, the Canadian government (unlike the United States) conducted an exhaustive formal inquiry into the matter, which assessed the information in the hands of the Canadian government. The highly respected Justice Dennis O'Connor, associate chief justice of Ontario, concluded that there "is no evidence to indicate that Mr. Arar has committed any offence or that his activities constitute a threat to the security of Canada."[61] Second, several U.S. congressional representatives and senators who have access to classified U.S. information came to the same conclusion—that no evidence exists linking Arar to terrorism in any way.[62]

Arar has never been charged with any crime, and the person he had briefly associated with continues to reside in Canada and has likewise not been charged.[63] The public cannot view the classified evidence for itself, nor can journalists and scholars do it for them. But given the integrity and competency of the people in both countries who have carefully reviewed these documents, it is reasonable to conclude that the United States sent Arar to Syria without more than the exaggerated RCMP information as further magnified by later U.S. immigration authorities, and that the information was "inaccurate or false."[64]

It is also reasonable to assume that the United States sent Arar to Syria rather than Canada precisely because they knew that he would be tortured in Syria. Arar has testified that "I clearly and repeatedly told them that I was afraid I would be tortured there. I told [American officials] I would be tortured because I was being wrongly accused of being a member of al Qaeda. I also conveyed to them my fear of returning to Syria, given that I had not fulfilled my compulsory military service."[65]

"Syria is renowned for using torture."[66] U.S. State Department reports repeatedly confirm continuing abuses.[67] Canadian intelligence officials were aware that the United States sent Arar to Syria to face torture. The deputy director of the Canadian Security Intelligence Service said in an e-mail that the United States was sending Arar to the Syrians so that they "could have their way with him."[68] The assurances against torture sought and received by the United States were at a low level, ambiguous, and worthless.[69] As Jules Lobel asks, "what other purpose could the U.S. government possibly have for sending Arar to Syria, and not Canada, except its interest in obtaining information through tactics such as detention without charges and coercive interrogation?"[70]

Thus, the United States, accepting uncritically exaggerated intelligence from Canada, and then magnifying it for its own reasons or incompetence, sent Arar to face torture in Syria. What happened is best told in Arar's own words:

> My pleas fell on deaf ears. On October 8th at 3:00 in the morning I was awakened and told that they had decided to remove me to Syria. When I told them again about my fears of being tortured, they told me they were not the office; that this was the torture convention.
>
> By then it was becoming more and more clear to me that I was being sent to Syria for the purpose of being tortured. I was put on a private jet and flown to Jordan, then driven to Syria, and eventually ended up at the Palestine branch of the Syria military intelligence October 9th.
>
> There I was put in a dark underground cell that was more like a grave. It was three feet wide, six feet deep, and seven feet high. Life in that cell was hell. I spent 10 months and 10 days in that grave.
>
> During the early days of my detention, I was interrogated and physically tortured. I was beaten with an electrical cable and threatened with a metal chair, a tire and electric shocks. I was forced to falsely confess that I had been to Afghanistan.
>
> When I was not being beaten, I was put in a waiting room so that I could hear the screams of other prisoners. The cries of the women still haunt me the most.
>
> Over the next 10 months, the only time I left my cell was to be interrogated or for meetings with the Canadian consul. I was allowed to meet with  the consul seven times, but only in the controlled presence of Syrian officials. I was warned prior to those meetings not to say how I was being treated.
>
> During the last visit, however, I burst out yelling about the beatings and the horrible conditions I had been living in. After 374 days of torture and wrongful detention, I was finally released to Canadian embassy.[71]

He remained in a Syrian torture chamber for nearly a year until Canadian consular services secured his freedom and returned him to Canada. Neither nation's bureaucracies were through. Even while Arar languished in Syria, Canadian intelligence officials lobbied to prevent his return, and after his return "the same officials engaged in a smear campaign to undermine public support for him and his demands for a public inquiry."[72] Even while he was still held in Syria "unnamed government officials began to mark a campaign of disinformation regarding Mr. Arar" including leaking to the media that Arar had received training from al-Qaeda in Afghanistan, that he had not been tortured. These disinformation leaks continued even after the Commission of Inquiry had begun its work.[73]

American officials continue to claim that their actions were based on reliable intelligence.[74] Neither Syria nor the United States cooperated with the Canadian Commission of Inquiry, but neither has ever offered any credible evidence that Arar was implicated in any wrongdoing.

Arar's case demonstrates that the bureaucracies of even stable democracies are self-protective and defensive in the face of even their most egregious mistakes. Law enforcement agencies, intelligence agencies and the courts are susceptible to extreme indifference and outright resistance when confronted with their own errors, even when they result in the torture or death of a citizen. In this respect Kafka's Joseph K., arrested without apparent cause, wound through an unhearing and impenetrable judicial system to be "killed like a dog" provides a literary example of a much larger truth about power and innocence.[75]

Bureaucracies resist in part because they can get away with it. It is not just that they have power. They also have great credibility with the citizenry that can be manipulated to their advantage. Many citizens (and certainly most of the university students I teach) seem to think that some sort of self-correcting mechanism works to fix extreme abuses, and that, if law enforcement and courts really go after someone to an unusual extent, there must be something there. The person must "have done something wrong." They are surprised at those who are completely innocent yet convicted of capital crimes and sentenced to death. Often one hears that claims of innocence must surely be some sort of technicality and not true innocence, that despite the evidence, the person must have some guilt somewhere. Yet, both in Canada and in the United States, surprising numbers of wholly innocent people turn up.[76] In many of these cases, those innocent people (sometimes on death row, in the United States at least) find that law enforcement agencies and even the courts resist to the utmost, claiming against all reason that the innocent person was somehow complicit in the original crime or otherwise should not be released. Arar provides a nearly unique example of how a wholly innocent person can find himself in the crosshairs of the bureaucracies of two nations, traduced, sentenced without trial, and tortured with both bureaucracies' combined force arrayed against him, and maintaining that stance even in the face of overwhelming evidence of innocence.

Given the history of law enforcement agencies in both nations resisting efforts to expose those who are innocent yet nonetheless convicted and incarcerated (and, in the United Sates, executed) we should not be overly surprised at Arar's ordeal. If police can frame an innocent man, put him on death row, and then resist all efforts to expose the fraud, they can also mistakenly send a man to torture in Syria.[77] Seen in this light, Arar is not unusual. Law enforcement bureaucracies are under great pressure to solve and prevent crime. Similarly, both Canadian and U.S. law enforcement and intelligence services were under great pressure to prevent another catastrophic terrorist attack. This enormous pressure in both systems led to each casting a wider and wider net, thus leading to greater probability of error. The instinct to hide the inevitable mistakes, such as evidenced by Arar, is no different from the pressures leading to error in serious criminal cases.

Scholar Samuel R. Gross summarizes the problem in the capital case context:

> The basic cause for the comparatively large number of errors in capital cases is a natural and laudable human impulse: We want murderers to be caught and punished. In some cases that impulse drives police and prosecutors to lie and cheat, but more often it simply motivates them to work harder to catch killers and to convict them. It works: More cases are cleared, more murderers are convicted. But harder cases are more likely to produce errors. . . . If there were some general method for identifying the errors, we wouldn't have this problem in the first place. But of course, there isn't. Instead, the errors that we do discover advertise the existence of others that we don't. What are the

odds that an innocent prisoner will run into a movie producer who is struck by his story? What if the real killer is killed in a car crash, or dies from a drug overdose, or is never arrested, or never confesses?[78]

Arar's case then serves to advertise the innocence problem transferred to the war on terror. It leads one to ask how many other innocent people have been caught up and sent to torture. How many cases are left in this "war" to be discovered? How many others like Maher Arar languish undiscovered? So, "mistakes were made" and then hidden for pretty much the usual reasons, magnified by the workings of bureaucracies on both sides of the border.[79] How many innocent people were wrongfully rendered to torture? We do not, and cannot, know the magnitude of the problem.

The Canadian justice system, on average, has done a better job at uncovering innocent people who were nonetheless convicted and incarcerated than has the United States. Canadian courts provide greater appellate scrutiny and greater liberal access to civil courts in liability actions for police misconduct. The Canadian system of establishing commissions of inquiry provides a systematic quasi-judicial, fact-finding procedure for uncovering truth in the face of governmental wrongdoing.[80]

Not surprisingly, the Canadian system of justice has responded differently to Arar's ordeal than has the justice system of the United States. The Commission of Inquiry headed by Justice O'Connor thoroughly investigated and exposed the facts of the case, and the Canadian government settled with Arar and gave him an official public apology.[81]

The U.S. court system, regrettably, has thus far been complicit in the wrong. In *Arar v. Ashcroft,* both the District Court and the Court of Appeals have held Arar remediless for rendition to torture.[82] This, too, is not wholly surprising, as the victims of rendition have thus far not received much traction in U.S. courts.[83] Courts in the United States, with few exceptions, have been part of a larger bureaucracy determined to keep as much hidden as possible, notwithstanding the greater openness shown by Canadian courts. Arar has sought unsuccessfully to appeal to the Supreme Court and has received support from one unlikely source—Canadian foreign minister Lawrence Cannon, who has

written in a letter filed with the U.S. Supreme Court that "the government of Canada confirms that it does not have reason to believe that
Mr. Arar's civil suit in the United States would risk harming relations
between Canada and the United States."[84]

Arar reinforces Kafka's notion of the oppressive power of bureaucracy, but his case also speaks of the ability of some courts to provide a
counterweight. Just as the United States might learn from the Canadian
court system in its effort to uncover wrongful convictions, it might also
learn from Canada's handling of cases like Arar's.

## State Secrets and Rendition: El-Masri

The rendition of German citizen Khalid El-Masri shares many features
with the renditions of Maher Arar and Binyam Mohamed.[85] El-Masri is
a German citizen of Lebanese descent. He was stopped at the border
attempting to enter Macedonia in December 2003 and turned over
to the CIA, who in turn flew him to Afghanistan where he was sent to
a prison known as "the Salt Pit," allegedly beaten, deprived of food,
injected with drugs, and held without charge in a filthy cell for five
months.[86] Eventually the CIA realized that it had made a mistake and
released him in the middle of the night on dark road in Albania where
he was met by others and flown back to Germany. This reasonably simple case, possibly of mistaken identity, led to the interposition of the
state secrets doctrine, which scuttled cases in both Germany and the
United States. The most definitive official report detailing El-Masri's
kidnapping by the CIA and ordeal at their hands has concluded that
"it is now undisputed . . . that Mr. El-Masri's account of his ordeal is
true."[87] Moreover, former secretary of state Condoleezza Rice directly
intervened in his case, ordering him released once she learned that
CIA officials had "concluded he was the victim of mistaken identity."[88]
However, Dick Marty concludes that the detailed knowledge of El-
Masri's real life by his interrogators "rules out the theory that Mr. El-
Masri was the victim of mere mistaken identity."[89] Rice later officially
apologized on behalf of the U.S. government to the German govern-
ment (although not to El-Masri), thus lending additional credence to
El-Masri's account.[90]

In January 2007 German prosecutors sought arrest warrants for thirteen alleged CIA agents linked to Khalid El-Masri's kidnapping from Macedonia in 2003 and his January 2004 rendition to Afghanistan.[91] Within six months the press was reporting that the German prosecution of CIA agents was straining relations between the two countries, splitting the German cabinet even as it was reported that the United States would not likely comply with any extradition request.[92] The German government acceded to U.S. pressure and refused the prosecution's request for formal extradition warrants for the Americans.[93] The core problem with bringing CIA kidnappers to justice in Germany appears to be state invocation of the state secrets doctrine, which, in addition to the inability to extradite from the United States or to try the kidnappers in absentia, has thwarted the prosecution in Germany. Members of the German Bundestag's parliamentary committee of inquiry have sought to inquire into the truth of El-Masri's abduction but have thus far been frustrated by executive invocation of official secrecy.[94] The state secrets doctrine was used by the executive in Germany to block all further inquiry into El-Masri's kidnapping and alleged torture at the hands of the CIA. Little doubt exists that this is a result of U.S. diplomatic pressure to limit the damage.[95]

The state secrets doctrine also stymied El-Masri's civil attempt to pursue for damages in the courts of the United States those who had kidnapped him.[96] El-Masri's botched case also demonstrates a lack of accountability at the CIA. The agent who pressed the agency to capture and render him to Afghanistan has never been disciplined—on the contrary, that agent has been promoted. Neither the courts nor the agency itself has imposed any form of accountability on anyone arising out of this "diplomatic embarrassment."[97] This case is a reminder of how easy it seems to be for innocent people to find themselves swept up into the torture gulag without recourse of any kind.

## A Demoralized CIA? Abu Omar

During the Bush administration, U.S. intelligence agents became increasingly demoralized. They feared and to some extent had good reason to fear domestic criminal prosecution. While there have been no domestic prosecutions (and none are likely), unlikely is not the same as impossible; thus, at least some agents have reason to wonder whether they will ever be free from potential prosecution. It has been alleged that the CIA destroyed videotapes of waterboarding and use of harsh interrogation techniques out of fear that public disclosure of these tapes could expose agents to federal prosecution.[98] Despite resistance, there have been continued calls for such prosecutions.[99] Moreover, there have been foreign prosecutions, attempts to prosecute CIA agents, and civil lawsuits (albeit unsuccessful in the United States to date). Agents have responded to the fear of prosecution and civil lawsuits by purchasing private insurance.[100] Agents are also finding their careers stymied by the inability to go abroad because of the threat of criminal prosecution for renditions and have been forced to "choose between . . . family overseas and . . . employment" with the U.S. government.[101] Agents who think that they might someday be targeted by foreign prosecutions may ask whether this problem will follow even into retirement. If so, where, outside of the United States, can they safely travel? Agents face EUROPOL warrants for their arrests and cannot safely travel anywhere in the world where those warrants might be honored either directly or as a result of an extradition treaty, for as long as those warrants remain outstanding. Because agents may have to report their prosecution (and in some cases conviction) in employment applications, even employment outside of the CIA may be compromised. Plainly, many agents face multiple adverse consequences for their participation in these programs, notwithstanding the inability of other countries to secure their presence at trial by means of extradition.[102]

Many Americans may not see a problem. After all, if the United States never allows extradition of its agents and they remain safe within the confines of U.S. sovereignty, have not they and the CIA succeeded without major consequence? This view fails to recognize that the CIA operates primarily abroad. Agents who cannot serve overseas may find promotions more difficult, and they may not be able to serve in the best and most important assignments. Nor could they do the job for which they have been trained. Other agents see this and balk at high-risk assignments, further compromising agency effectiveness. These are people who travel regularly and who speak multiple languages fluently.[103] Some have apparently already lost property because of foreign prosecutions.[104] Others who may wish to retire abroad will find that impossible. For example, in 1979 Dominic Perrone, an American intelligence officer, was declared persona non grata for alleged interference in Italy's internal affairs and had to leave the country.[105] Perrone, who spoke fluent Italian, had decided to retire in Italy, and had bought a home. He was given twenty-four hours to leave, and suffered great personal and financial loss. Ironically, he had not done anything illegal but had authored a report highly critical of certain Italian agencies, the leaking of which irritated Italy's government. Perrone lived out the remainder of his life in Florida. Present-day intelligence agents implicated in unlawful renditions from other nations face similar disabilities. For these agents, confinement to the United States is decidedly a burden. While they may never face imprisonment, their lives are confined in ways that hurt both them and the effectiveness of the intelligence institutions they serve.

The case of Egyptian cleric Osama Mustafa Nasr, more commonly known as Abu Omar, illustrates the way in which the war on terror has demoralized our intelligence services and reduced their effectiveness. Beyond demoralization arising from the moral and legal fallout from rendition, this case also demonstrated a bumbling, hapless, "Maxwell Smart" side to the agency that contributed to public disclosure and heightened the agency's humiliation.

According to allegations that surfaced during an Italian prosecution, twenty-six Americans, and six Italians snatched Abu Omar from the streets of Milan in broad daylight and in front of witnesses as he walked to noon prayers. Operating in the open, using traceable cell phones, and staying openly at expensive hotels paid for with easily traceable credit cards, this kidnapping seems not so much heroic as tragically inept.[106] Journalist and author Stephen Grey notes, "Even if an Italian official had given the green light, there was consternation at the tradecraft employed by the CIA team that had allowed their movements to have been so closely tracked. One former senior officer of the directorate of operations told me: 'Even if the Italians were involved, this whole operation was botched. Using such a large team, involving the local stations, staying in such luxury, and making such a large scale use of cell phones and traceable credit cards was only asking for trouble."[107] The trail that they left suggests complicity at the highest levels of the Italian government.[108]

Nonetheless, Abu Omar, who was suspected of connections to terrorist organizations, including the infamous Abu Musab al-Zarqawi, was rendered to Egypt (which has a ferocious reputation for torturing political prisoners[109]) where he was confined and "tortured with electric shocks, hung upside down, and sexually abused."[110]

The details are not as important as the consequences. Abu Omar was ultimately released and filed civil suit against his kidnappers and cooperated with the Italian prosecution. This prosecution received a difficult blow that weakened the case when Italy's highest court ruled that important parts of the evidence collected by prosecutors could not be used because of the country's state secrets law.[111] The prosecution continued with the remaining, lawfully obtained evidence, and Judge Oscar Magi rejected a defense effort to end the proceedings.[112] Italy allows prosecutions in absentia and thus does not require the defendant's presence.[113] Six Italian intelligence agents including the former chief of military intelligence, Niccolò Pollari, were also charged. The judge ultimately convicted twenty-three of the Americans, most of whom were CIA agents and one of whom was a CIA station chief. He then sentenced them to prison terms and awarded damages to Abu Omar and his wife. All appealed the decision. The three remaining Americans were acquitted because they enjoyed diplomatic immunity.[114]

In the course of his opinion, the judge stated that Italian secret services "were most likely aware of 'and perhaps complicit in'" Abu Omar's abduction by the CIA. However, because the Constitutional Court had made the contract between the two agencies a state secret, the judge wrote that it was "not possible" to prove the point.[115] Under the circumstances, it seems remarkable that two Italian agents were also convicted and given prison terms.[116]

The United States will not extradite any of these agents, and none is expected to serve any prison time. At least one, however, CIA station chief Robert Lady, may lose his 2.2-million-dollar retirement home in Italy. Courts there have ordered it sold to pay damages. According to the New York Times, this was the "first time a judge in an allied country had placed CIA agents on trial."[117] The *New York Times* compared the Italian court's handling of state secrets with the U.S. Second Circuit Court of Appeals in Arar and said, "The Italian court got it right. The American court got it miserably wrong."[118]

This case continues to impede the effectiveness of our intelligence services. Besides demoralizing a large numbers of agents, with the decreases in efficiency and agency humiliation noted earlier, this episode created four shorter-term problems for U.S. intelligence agencies:

1. The premature actions of the U.S. agents thwarted a competing Italian investigation that might have borne fruit. CIA agents in the field thought at the time of the operation that Italian counterterrorism efforts were "doing just fine against al-Qaeda in Milan."[119] Italian domestic police were actively investigating Abu Omar and others; the kidnapping interfered with this ongoing investigation. According to the Italian prosecutor Armando Spataro, "We could have discovered other illegal links. . . . This kidnapping was also very dangerous because it pushed [the] Islamic moderate part of the community to become extremists."[120] There is reason to believe that, but for his illegal kidnapping and rendering to torture, Italian justice would have put Abu Omar behind bars because he may well have committed criminal acts in Italy. Spataro has said, "The kidnapping of Abu Omar was not only a serious crime against human rights, it was a [defeat] in the fight against terrorism," and "if he was not kidnapped, he would still be in jail today."[121]

2. "The CIA's increasingly toxic reputation in Europe is causing some serious headaches, and may be making vital co-operation in the war against terrorism even harder to maintain."[122] The authoritative Marty Reports to the Council of Europe make it difficult to repair this problem.[123] The information is now too widely disseminated, and the report's prestige makes it politically difficult to ignore. Abu Omar's case is not alone. It is (like the Arar case) only one of the more completely investigated—and therefore believable—of the many extraordinary rendition cases that have become known. It will be difficult for many intelligence agencies to fully cooperate with our intelligence agencies in light of this history.

3. More generally, it temporarily strained relations with Europe. This problem is being addressed by the Obama administration and is likely to be the least of the problems stemming from this or any other rendition.

4. This case has radicalized the moderate Muslim. Spataro's point about how kidnappings and torture can serve to radicalize moderate Muslims has been replicated in other contexts. An important investigative report by Tom Lassiter reveals, "In a classified review of 35 men released from Guantanamo, Pakistani police intelligence concluded in 2005 that the men—most of whom had been subjected to 'severe mental and physical torture'—had 'extreme feelings of resentment and hatred against U.S.A.'" And, "'A lot of our friends are working against the Americans now, because if you torture someone without any reason, what do you expect?' Issa Khan, a former detainee from Pakistan, said in an interview in Islamabad. 'Many people who were in Guantanamo are now working with the Taliban.'"[124]

If kidnapping and torture creates more enemies, then Abu Omar's case became illustrative of that process.

# 5

---

# State Secrets Privilege
# Trumps Justice

## *Mohamed v. Jeppesen Dataplan*

That U.S. intelligence agents kidnapped and rendered people to bloody, medieval torture in countries such as Egypt and Morocco will not surprise anyone who regularly reads a newspaper. The U.S. government no longer contests the basic facts about its extraordinary rendition program. Nonetheless, the government continually invokes the state secrets privilege whenever its battered victims seek compensation in its courts.[1] U.S. courts acquiesce in this tactic, using an overbroad construction of the privilege to scuttle all such cases.[2] In contrast, our closest allies, the United Kingdom and Canada, while far from perfect, do not allow state secrets to destroy civil damage claims, yet they protect national security.

Apparently, some democracies can stand the discomfiture of governmental wrongdoing while protecting vital secrets, sources, and methods. This suggests that the United States asserts the state secrets privilege not to protect legitimate secrets but rather to avoid embarrassment and scrutiny. This chapter examines the states secrets privilege as outlined in the *Jeppesen Dataplan* case in light of publically known facts about extraordinary rendition. It then examines our allies' response to this problem, concluding that the United States could protect national security without relying on overbroad assertions of the state secrets privilege.

In September 2010 the Ninth Circuit Court of Appeals ruled en banc that Binyam Mohamed and other plaintiffs could not proceed

beyond the initial pleadings with their civil lawsuit seeking redress
for their having been rendered to torture as a part of the U.S. extraordinary rendition program. Doing so, the majority opined, would run a
risk of revealing state secrets.[3] State secrets were not merely ruled out
of bounds for purposes of the litigation, nor was the matter remanded
to the trial court to see if the case could fairly be tried with the
remaining publicly available evidence; in an unusual move, the entire
lawsuit derailed because of the possibility that some secrets might by
chance be revealed. This result merits close examination, beginning
with the evidence that at least some and perhaps all plaintiffs were
tortured by U.S. agents and knowingly rendered to other countries for
even worse treatment.

## The Fact of U.S. Torture

As we saw in chapter 4, Binyam Mohamed has repeatedly and unquestionably proved that he was tortured both by and on behalf of U.S.
intelligence agencies with the complicity and knowledge of British
intelligence services. After years of denial and dissembling,[4] the U.S.
government no longer seriously disputes his account.[5] It concedes the
beatings and mock executions by U.S. agents in Pakistan; the rendition
to Morocco; the two years of torture including repeated and bloody
slicing with a scalpel and genital mutilation; the hot, burning liquids
poured onto his wounds; the beatings to the point that Mohamed collapsed onto the floor vomiting and urinating on himself; the threats of
rape, electrocution, and castration. During torture sessions, Mohamed
was given information and told to verify it.[6] Not surprisingly, he eventually "confessed" to and confirmed whatever his tormentors wanted.

Binyam Mohamed's supposed confessions became a crucial ele-
ment in a habeas proceeding by another detainee, Farhi Saeed Bin
Mohammed, before the Federal District Court for the District of Columbia.[7] Binyam Mohamed had "confessed" to all manner of conspiracies—
while under torture so brutal as to be beyond most people's ability to
comprehend. He confessed to plots that could never have happened
while conspiring with people he had never met and did not know. As
we saw in chapter 4, the government eventually and belatedly dropped

its criminal prosecution of Binyam Mohamed long after its position had become wholly untenable. Nonetheless, the government defended the instant habeas proceeding by seeking to use Binyam Mohamed's supposedly cleaned-up-after-the-torture statements as a basis to continue holding Farhi Saeed Bin Mohamed. In short, Binyam Mohamed's false evidence originally given under torture and then "cleansed" by after-the-fact new interrogators using only standard techniques for questioning was offered to justify continued detention of a different prisoner.

These proceedings compelled Judge Gladys Kessler to conclude that Binyam Mohamed's "lengthy and brutal experience" rendered his "confessions" unreliable and inadmissible. Even statements made after his transfer to Guantánamo Bay, well after the torture had stopped, remained tainted and inadmissible. Judge Kessler concluded, unsurprisingly given the government's concessions: "In this case, even though the identity of the individual interrogators changed (from nameless Pakistanis, to Moroccans, to Americans, and to Special Agent [TEXT REDACTED BY THE COURT], *there is no question that throughout his ordeal Binyam Mohamed was being held at the behest of the United States.*"[8]

As a result, the United States remains responsible for all that the Moroccans, Pakistanis, and others inflicted. The judge also found:

Binyam Mohamed's trauma lasted for two long years. During that time, he was physically and psychologically tortured. His genitals were mutilated. He was deprived of sleep and food. He was summarily transported from one foreign prison to another. Captors held him in stress positions for days at a time. He was forced to listen to piercingly loud music and the screams of other prisoners while locked in a pitch-black cell. All the while, he was forced to inculpate himself and others in various plots to imperil Americans. The Government does not dispute this evidence.[9]

Courts in the United Kingdom also accept that Binyam Mohamed was actively tortured by and on behalf of the United States. As the Court of Appeal, Civil Division, in the United Kingdom put it,

There is no secret about the treatment to which Mr. Mohamed was subjected while in the control of the U.S. authorities. We are no longer dealing with the allegations of torture and ill treatment; they have been established in the judgment of the court, publicly revealed by the judicial processes with the USA itself. . . . It is therefore now in the public domain, as a fact found by a U.S. court in proceedings win which the U.S. Government was a party, that he was mistreated, indeed tortured, in the ways in which he has described, when under U.S. control and interrogation, and that representatives of the U.S. intelligence services knew of the mistreatment.[10]

His is a clear and well-documented case, but it is not the only one. For example, in the civilian criminal trial of Ahmed Khalfan Ghailani, who was alleged to have participated in the 1998 U.S. embassy bombings in Kenya and Tanzania, the Federal District judge ruled that one of the government's proposed witnesses could not testify because he had implicated Ghailani while under duress.[11] Ghailani's trial proceeded without the duress-tainted evidence, and a federal jury found him guilty of a single count of conspiracy to destroy buildings and property of the United States. He was found not guilty of the remaining 284 counts of murder and conspiracy. In January 2011 the trial judge upheld the verdict, overruled defense motions for either acquittal or a new trial, and sentenced him to life in prison on the remaining count for which he stood convicted.[12]

What makes Binyam Mohamed's case significant, beyond the simple fact of torture percolating into and affecting the decisions of America's trial courts, is that his statements were relevant in multiple related cases on both sides of the Atlantic. In the Federal District Court for the District of Columbia habeas corpus action, his statements were found to be the product of brutal and intended torture at U.S. hands. At least in that case, his torture at U.S. hands (and with British complicity) was proved. That same torture became relevant across the Atlantic in the British case, which accepted that the torture was proved. The U.K. court in turn released independent evidence demonstrating U.S. and U.K. complicity in that torture. In that sense, his torture was doubly proved. In any event, the facts of U.S. torture, British complicity, and the bad faith actions of both governments are as completely proven in Binyam

Mohamed's case as anything can be in this otherwise contingent world. Like the cases of Maher Arar, Abu Omar, and Khalid El-Masri, Binyam Mohamed's case has become one of the most thoroughly documented of all the renditions. Many other cases of extraordinary rendition to torture undoubtedly took place, but few others have been so well documented in multiple court proceedings in two independent nations.

Given the level of proof and amount of publicly available documentary evidence available to Binyam Mohamed, one might have thought that a civil action seeking damages in a U.S. court would have been straightforward. One would have been wrong. When he and others sought redress for that torture in yet another U.S. courtroom, his case was silenced not on the merits but under the state secrets doctrine.

Other cases, such as that of Ghailani, mentioned earlier, are relevant in that they bolster claims of systemic U.S. rendition to torture. Binyam Mohamed's case, however, provides direct evidence that the state secrets privilege thwarts redress for the intentional, brutal torture of an innocent man. His case demonstrates the injustice of closing the courthouse without assessing any publically available (and therefore not secret) evidence.

Analysis of the state secrets privilege in the extraordinary rendition context must begin with the obvious: victims of this program were provably subjected to the most brutal, medieval torture possible. Their misery at U.S. insistence is unimaginable, beyond what most of us can conceive. Given U.S. rendition to torture, which is criminal under both international and domestic law, it is not surprising that the government sought to use the state secrets privilege to bar all such civil lawsuits.[13] What is surprising is the extent to which U.S. courts yield to these claims of privilege notwithstanding the obvious injustice to people whose torture at America's hands can no longer be challenged.

The majority in *Mohamed v. Jeppesen Dataplan* repeatedly refers to the plaintiff's allegations of torture as "alleged" as if the use of the word "alleged" could somehow stuff the facts back in time making them secret again, or at least making the question of torture seem open. As the U.K. court put it, these are no longer "allegations"—they are as solid fact as one may ever encounter. As the dissent points out, "The majority minimizes the importance of the [rule requiring the trial court to construe the complaint in the light most favorable to the plaintiffs] by gratuitously attaching 'allegedly' to nearly each sentence . . . and by quickly dismissing the voluminous publically available evidence."[14]

That Binyam Mohamed was an innocent bystander, caught up in the war on terror, tortured for information he did not and could not have, remains irrelevant—even if he were guilty of the most heinous crimes, his treatment would have been wholly unconscionable, without redemptive feature.[15] That he was innocent yet nonetheless brutally tortured for years on end without hope of succor adds color, context, and human interest to the story but does not change the legal conclusion.

### *Mohamed v. Jeppesen Dataplan*: ### The Case in a Nutshell

Six people (including Binyam Mohamed) sued defendant Jeppesen Dataplan under the Alien Tort Statute advancing seven theories of liability.[16] They asserted the defendant's complicity with the U.S. government in its now publicly acknowledged extraordinary rendition program to torture. Jeppesen Dataplan, the government's private contractor for rendition flights, made all of the logistical arrangements and used its jets and pilots to carry people to places of torture. Thousands of pages of publicly available documents supported the complaint that the defendant, Jeppesen Dataplan, knew or should have known that it was flying people to be tortured and that its employees recklessly conspired with governmental agents whose goal was to render human beings to places where they faced torture.

On the face, it would seem a well-supported claim asserting an obvious and terrible injustice to people—some of whom were manifestly innocent of any wrongdoing—by a private governmental contractor, which could hardly claim not to have known what they were doing. If they knew nothing else, they knew that they were taking hooded, shackled, and diapered prisoners to countries such as Egypt, Jordan, and Morocco, whose reputations for human rights abuses are well known. One of Jeppesen's senior employees described these flights as "torture flights" or "spook flights" that the company was going to do because "rendition flights paid very well."[17]

While the case was at a preliminary stage and the facts had not been proved before the lower trial court, the majority in the Ninth Circuit Court of Appeals knew that overwhelming available evidence could establish that at least some of the plaintiffs were rendered by the CIA to other nations and then tortured. Based solely on publicly available documents, the employees at Jeppesen Dataplan would have had to be remarkably ignorant not to know their role in facilitating torture. The Ninth Circuit implicitly conceded the point, saying, "We assume without deciding that plaintiff's prima facie case and Jeppesen's defenses may not inevitably depend on privileged evidence."[18]

If that were where the case rested, the appellate court would presumably have simply remanded the case to the trial court to determine whether the plaintiffs could make a prima facie case based on publicly available documents and whether the defendant could fairly defend without the privileged evidence. By not deciding the case on this basis, the court implicitly allowed that, if that were all there were to it, the issue should have gone back to the Federal District Court for a determination on whether the case could fairly proceed, notwithstanding the state secrets privilege. With the thousands of pages of publicly available documents demonstrating the truth of plaintiff's claims, it could hardly have been otherwise. The court's "assume without deciding" language appears to be a fig-leaf pretext in what otherwise looks to be an implicit concession to the mass of evidence demonstrating both the fact of extraordinary renditions to torture and Jeppesen Dataplan's almost certain knowledge of its part in rendering people to be tortured.

Notwithstanding this, the Ninth Circuit ruled that "dismissal is nonetheless required . . . because there is no feasible way to litigate Jeppesen's alleged liability *without creating an unjustifiable risk of divulging state secrets*."[19] The dissent fairly recast this holding as requiring dismissal "out of fear of 'compelled or inadvertent disclosure'" which "assumes that the government might make mistakes in what it produces, or that district courts might compel the disclosure of documents legitimately covered by the state secrets privilege."[20] The state secrets privilege then trumps plaintiff's redress for torture because someone may blunder in the fog of trial and divulge something that ought not be revealed.

Two things suggest that the majority was embarrassed by (or at least defensive about) its ruling. First, it took the unusual step of assessing costs on appeal to be paid by the government—the winning party.[21] Ordinarily costs other than attorney's fees "are allowed to the prevailing party."[22] The Ninth Circuit's order suggests discomfort at ordering the victims pay the torturer's costs.

Second, it tried to evade responsibility for the obvious injustice of the result by suggesting that the government or Congress could remedy the wrong by compensating the victims, investigating alleged governmental wrongdoing, or enacting private bills.[23] The dissent points out that this is not only suggests the injustice of the result but also deprives "the judiciary of its role" and deprives "Plaintiffs of a fair assessment of their claims by a neutral arbiter."[24] The notion that the present Congress or executive branch will rectify this remains as absurd as it did for Japanese internees who waited more than fifty years for partial redress.[25] The court suggests that if an injustice is done, the courts are not to blame; others participate in and share the responsibility.

One may ask whether courts ought to shift responsibility for justice away from the branch dedicated to that cause. While judges are supposed to remain apolitical, they are no doubt aware that as a practical matter their decision means that this injustice will not be rectified—that U.S. government and its agents and contractors will not be held accountable, and that the victims remain victims without redress. The mention of (practically speaking) nonexistent political avenues for redress appears to be an implicit acknowledgment that the courts are permitting an injustice without redress of any kind in the pursuit of protecting national security. While nations do sacrifice people and trample on individual rights in exchange for a perception of greater security, this becomes more difficult in an open democracy when honestly and transparently done. One cannot avoid the conclusion that in this case the majority on the Ninth Circuit Court of Appeals sought to obscure as much as possible the true import of its decision.

The public also loses. As Justice Brandeis famously wrote, "Publicity is justly commended as a remedy for social and industrial diseases. Sunlight is said to be the best of disinfectants; electric light the most efficient policeman."[26] While no one doubts that the government may properly protect true state secrets, there is also little doubt that the government overclassifies much that it need not.[27] A trial would have at least exposed to the public whatever evidence legitimately could be laid out in the open. As it is, one is left to speculate about how much of that which is hidden is merely embarrassing and not justly a state secret.

## Activist Judging: Legislating from the Bench

The state secrets privilege stems from two Supreme Court cases, *Totten v. United States* and *United States v. Reynolds*.[28] *Totten* wholly barred all proceedings but only where the very subject matter of the action was itself secret, such as concerning a contract to engage in spying or the storage of nuclear weapons, neither of which was involved in the case at bar.[29] *Reynolds*, by contrast, created an evidentiary privilege to withhold secret evidence, but the *Reynolds* decision is usually read as only limiting the evidence that can be admitted at trial and was not thought (prior to *Jeppesen Dataplan*) to be an outright bar to proceeding. It was thought that application of *Reynolds* would have, in the normal course of proceedings, allowed the case to go back to the trial court to determine whether the case could be fairly tried without the secret evidence.

Generally, this sort of fine-grained evidentiary sifting is left in the first instance to the trial courts, with appellate courts sitting in review after the trial court has made detailed findings of fact. Trial courts are supposed to develop great competency in finding and winnowing the underlying facts of a case. Appellate courts lack the experience and the fact-finding expertise of trial courts. This is one reason why appellate courts usually defer to trial courts on factual findings, and usually refer matters back to a trial court when further factual matters need developing. Plainly, the Ninth Circuit Court of Appeals rejected that approach in this case.

The five-judge dissent pointed out that, before this case, the nonconstitutional, nonstatutory, judge-made state secrets privilege had never before applied the state secrets privilege to wholly cut-off a case at the pleadings stage outside the narrow *Totten* context.[30] As one legal scholar put it, "the court stretched the privilege to its outer edges" and the ruling therefore "represents a breathtaking application of the privilege."[31] It is true that the Fourth Circuit Court of Appeals in the *El-Masri* case had, in a confusing opinion that conflated *Totten* with *Reynolds*, thrown out the plaintiff's case.[32] The Ninth Circuit correctly refused to follow *El-Masri*, but in so doing, it also stretched Supreme Court precedent.

As we will see in the following, the United States' closest democratic allies require legislation before expanding their versions of the state secrets privilege. The Ninth Circuit bypassed Congress, thereby insulating extraordinary rendition from review. This punctures the notion that conservative judges do not make law, and that they only act with restraint in applying the law. Here a conservative majority on the Ninth Circuit Court of Appeals created judge-made law that expanded the power of government to hide its secrets from review, and left the practice of rendition to torture unaccountable. The court, then, was doubly activist in that it subverted the usual procedure privileging trial courts as the primary fact-finder in the federal system, and it simultaneously stretched the judge-made law of privilege in order to cloak governmental and contractor wrongdoing.

### The Embarrassment Factor

The majority in *Mohamed v. Jeppesen Dataplan* denies that its holding serves to allow the government to "avoid embarrassment or to escape scrutiny of its recent controversial transfer and interrogation policies, rather than to protect legitimate national security concerns."[33] Since this claim is made after the judges had "reviewed the government's public and classified declarations" and thus is predicated on documents that the public cannot see, this claim cannot be conclusively evaluated. The facts, however, leave ample room to doubt the majority's contention. The five judges in dissent assess the record differently, saying, "It is true that, judicial construct though it is, the state secrets doctrine has become embedded in our controlling decisional law. Government claims of state secrets therefore must be entertained by the judiciary. But the doctrine is so dangerous as a means of hiding governmental misbehavior under the guise of national security, and so violative of common rights to due process, that courts should confine its application to the narrowest circumstances that still protect the government's essential secrets."[34]

The *Reynolds* case involved an experimental air force jet that crashed, killing its crew. The crew's families sued and the government successfully interposed the state secrets privilege, ultimately thwarting the case. However, *Reynolds* was never supposed to hide things just to save the government from embarrassment or scrutiny. *Reynolds* had a troubled birth. As the dissent in *Mohamed v. Jeppesen* pointed out,

> Even in Reynolds, avoidance of embarrassment—not preserva-
> tion of state secrets—appears to have motivated the Executive's
> invocation of the privilege. There the Court credited the govern-
> ment's assertion that "this accident occurred to a military plane
> which had gone aloft to test secret electronic equipment," and
> that "there was a reasonable danger that the accident investiga-
> tion report would contain references to the secret electronic
> equipment which was the primary concern of the mission." . . . In
> 1996, however, the "secret" accident report involved in that case
> was declassified. A review of the report revealed, not "details
> of any secret project the plane was involved in," but "instead,
> . . . a horror story of incompetence, bungling, and tragic error."
> . . . Courts should be concerned to prevent a concentration of
> unchecked power that would permit such abuses.[35]

As the *New York Times* pointed out, the *Reynolds* "privilege turned out to be conceived in sin: the now-declassified report contains no secrets. Instead, it recounts how the engine failure that led to the crash might have been avoided. A lawyer involved said the report 'expressly finds negligence' by the Air Force."[36] This misuse of the privilege from the very beginning suggests caution in assessing its use in the present war on terror. The fact that the government asserted the state secrets privilege in its defense in the civil actions by Mahar Arar and Khalid El-Masri—both of whose allegations of rendition to torture have been conclusively established—adds to the suspicion that embarrassment, not secrets, are predominately at issue.

To cut a case off at the pleading stage without allowing the case to proceed on publicly available documents solely on the risk that someone might foul up and inadvertently expose a secret seems extreme. The public is entitled to wonder whether we will discover, in a few decades, that the court helped the government to hide "a horror story of incompetence, bungling, and tragic error." We do know that at least some, and perhaps all, of the plaintiffs were subjected not just to torture but also to years of the most medieval tortures imaginable.

Do other similar democratic nations find this level of expansive privilege necessary for their national security? If not, it sheds doubt on the U.S. claims for the privilege.

## State Secrets Privilege in the United Kingdom and Canada: How Other Democracies Balance Secrets and Justice

### The United Kingdom

Binyam Mohamed's ordeal raises three remarkable points of comparison between the United Kingdom and the United States: first, the United Kingdom was complicit with the United States in his torture; second, the United Kingdom and the United States shared intelligence on and about Mr. Mohamed, and thus shared many of the same state secrets surrounding his case; and third, he litigated, as part of a larger group of plaintiffs, in civil actions sounding in tort in both countries. This gives us a precise comparison as to how each country handled shared state secrets and gives us a basis for assessing the balance between justice and the need for governmental secrets.

In May 2010, just four months before the Ninth Circuit derailed Binyam Mohamed's U.S. torture suit, the England and Wales Court of Appeal ruled in *Al Rawi v. Security Service* that British intelligence agencies MI5 and MI6 could not use secret evidence in defense of abuse allegations in a civil lawsuit brought by Binyam Mohamed and others.[37] This judgment overturned a lower court ruling that would have allowed a "closed material procedure."[38]

The United Kingdom's courts allow closed material proceedings in certain circumstances, such as in control orders and financial restriction proceedings, and in certain narrowly defined cases involving terrorism and in certain parole hearings.[39] Courts in the United Kingdom are permitted to withhold information from claimant's lawyers where "disclosure would be contrary to the interests of national security, the international relations of the United Kingdom, the detection of and prevention of crime or in any other circumstances where disclosure is likely to harm the public interest."[40] In such cases, a special advocate is appointed to guard the claimant's interests. The special advocate cannot, however, disclose the secret information to the claimant, which indubitably hobbles the claim. Unlike the U.S. position in the *Jeppesen Dataplan* instance, the claim would not, even under this procedure, be entirely foreclosed.

Nonetheless, this procedure, had it gone forward, would have allowed the government to use secret evidence in court that would not have been shown to opposing counsel, thus making a successful prosecution of the claim far less likely.[41] However, the issue before the court of appeals was whether, outside of very narrowly limited circumstances, a closed material procedure should be used in an ordinary civil case. The Court of Appeals in the United Kingdom ruled that "the principle that a litigant should be able to see and hear all the evidence which is seen and heard by a court determining his case is so fundamental, so embedded in the common law, that, in the absence of parliamentary authority, no judge should override it, at any rate in relation to an ordinary civil claim, unless (perhaps) all parties to the claim agree otherwise . . . this principle represents and irreducible minimum requirement of an ordinary civil trial."[42]

Unlike the Ninth Circuit Court of Appeals, the England and Wales Court of Appeals declined to invent law to protect the government from embarrassment. If such is to be the case, the parliament will have to do it. To emphasize the point, the court cited Lord Shaw: "There is no greater danger of usurpation than that which proceeds little by little, under cover of rules of procedure, and at the instance of the judges themselves, and that the policy of widening the area of secrecy is always a serious one, but this is for parliament, and those to whom the subject has been consigned by Parliament to consider." And, citing Lord Brown of Eaton-under-Heywood, the court said, "it is the integrity of the judicial process which is at stake here. This must be safeguarded and vindicated whatever the cost."[43] Contrast this decision with that of the Ninth Circuit, which indubitably went beyond anything the Supreme

Court had required in *Reynolds* and thus proceeded "little by little under
the rules of procedure" to widen the secrecy privilege.

The *Al Rawi* case is not the only instance where courts in the United
Kingdom ordered the release of state secrets in order to obtain justice;
but it is the case most similar to that of the *Jeppesen Dataplan* case and
is thus most relevant for comparative purposes. In a related and earlier case arising out of the war against terror, the issue was whether
to release secret reports that tended to demonstrate the innocence
of then–Guantánamo detainee Binyam Mohamed (the same man as
in both the U.S. and U.K. appellate court decisions analyzed earlier,
who had confessed to terrorist conspiracies under brutal torture).[44] At
the time, the United States refused to admit either his innocence or
the fact of his torture, and British intelligence had information that
had been shared with them by the CIA. The United States, which had
generated the intelligence, and which under the "control principle"
was allegedly allowed to control its dissemination, objected to British
courts releasing the information—even though the evidence strongly
tended to substantiate Binyam Mohamed's defense against capital
charges before a military commission at Guantánamo Bay. This may
seem convoluted, but it came down to this: as we saw in chapter 4, the
United States wished to keep secret evidence that tended to exculpate
someone in custody (Binyam Mohamed) who faced the death penalty.
Put another way, the United States was prepared to execute an alleged
terrorist detainee notwithstanding secret evidence in their hands that
he was innocent.

Not surprisingly, Binyam Mohamed's lawyers sued in the U.K.
courts, seeking access to the information in the hands of the British
government but gained from the U.S. government. The trial court
overrode the foreign secretary's objections and ordered release of the
evidence, which in turn triggered Binyam Mohamed's release from
Guantánamo Bay to the United Kingdom. Thus, an innocent man was
spared an unfair trial that might have led to his execution, had the U.S.
government had its way. However, the court redacted seven paragraphs
of its opinion, which tended to show not only that Binyam Mohamed
had been tortured but also that the torture had happened at the behest
of the United States with the knowledge and complicity of the British

intelligence services. The issue of redacting these seven embarrassing paragraphs went to the Court of Appeal, which ordered their release.[45]

The British court system has repeatedly released supposed state secrets that turned out to be not so much real secrets but embarrassing information that was kept secret more to evade scrutiny than to protect national security. Pressure continued to build on the government to disclose what their intelligence agencies knew about the torture of Britons abroad, including the case of Binyam Mohamed.[46] Because of that pressure, including the lawsuits, the British government—without admitting legal liability—agreed to pay former (and one current) Guantánamo detainees millions of dollars to settle suits that claimed British complicity in their renditions and torture. In a statement to Parliament, Justice Secretary Ken Clark said, "The alternative to any payments made would have been protracted and extremely expensive litigation in an uncertain legal environment in which the government could not be certain that it would be able to defend . . . security and intelligence agencies without compromising national security."[47]

Settlement with those claiming to have been tortured allows Britain to maintain some of its mutual secrets shared with the United States. This cuts against the public's right to know. Three considerations mitigate this observation, however. First, at least on some level justice, was done—the victims received compensation from the less culpable but nonetheless complicit government. This is no small victory for those who were wronged. Second, the United Kingdom, through its court system, has already released a great deal of important information and has set precedents that will make rendition to torture harder to perpetrate in the future. Finally, the United Kingdom will continue to inquire about its intelligence practices with a view to preventing recurrence. While not perfect, these are important steps. Conversely, the British government is proposing legislation that, if enacted, could undercut the courts power to order disclosure for the sake of individual justice.[48] Thus, as of this writing, the relative openness of the British system compared with that of the United States remains uncertain.

It is difficult to directly compare the U.S. and U.K. legal systems. What seems clear is that the courts of the United Kingdom are, at least thus far, more open to allowing a legal proceeding go forward notwithstanding the fact that some state secrets may intertwine in the proceedings. Both countries protect essential secrets. The United Kingdom is no less a safe county than the United States. The British courts, however, at least attempt to do justice. The U.S. courts, by distinction, close off proceedings entirely even if it means perpetuating a manifest injustice.

## Canada

While the state secrets privilege in the United States is entirely judge-made law, in Canada the evidentiary privilege stems from the Security of Information Act and is therefore has a legislative pedigree. Canada's Evidence Act also plays a role in shaping the contours of the privilege. This legislative foundation notwithstanding, Canadian courts have had a profound impact on both the scope and the application of the privilege.

Like the United Kingdom, Canada also generated cases where their government became complicit with the United States in rendering people to torture and involving civil litigation in both countries with each government asserting the state secrets privilege. Canada provides a useful comparison on how democracies can balance the state secrets and national security against the imperatives of justice for victims of governmental wrongdoing. Neither the United Kingdom nor Canada necessarily got the balance right. Some Canadian scholars are quite critical of the Canadian approach to state secrets and point out that in addition to the limitations of the inquiry process and the civil tort route, civilian oversight mechanisms of the police and intelligence services have proved inadequate.[49]

Both the United Kingdom and Canada may be found to fail international standards for taking "effective measures to provide civil compensation to victims of torture."[50] However, victims of torture do not inevitably fail in their quest for redress in either of those countries. Their record is immeasurably healthier in that regard than that of the United States. One irony noted by scholars and politicians alike is that the least culpable governments whose complicity with torture remained consistently indirect—Canada and the United Kingdom—have provided some redress while the more culpable nation, the nation that made the decisions to render people to torture, has consistently denied relief to those it rendered to torture.[51]

Canadian citizens Maher Arar, Ahmed El-Maati, Muayyed Nureddin, and Abdullah Almalki were all detained and tortured by Syrian officials using questions that originated with Canadian intelligence and police services. While all have attempted to clear their names and "expose the truth," only one, Maher Arar (whose case is more fully told in chapter 4), has fully succeeded.[52] In his case, a commission of inquiry fully exonerated him, the government has apologized, and he was awarded 10.5 million Canadian dollars.

However, even the other three have, through the inquiry process (the Iacobucci Commission), managed to expose more about their cases than any victim of extraordinary rendition has succeeded in doing in civil lawsuits in the United States. Moreover, "based on the Arar Commission's precedent and recommendation, the Canadian Government has relaxed its national security confidentiality claims to a 'significant degree.'"[53]

Section 38 of the Canada Evidence Act deals with state secrets by requiring the judge to balance the public interests involved and requires disclosure if the public interest warrants it.[54] Advocates and scholars have criticized this procedure because the judge deciding the privilege is not the trial judge but is rather a federal court judge. Nonetheless, the Supreme Court of Canada has upheld the provision in a criminal case.[55] Presumably, the Supreme Court would also uphold the constitutionality of the act in a civil matter because that presents a seemingly stronger case for constitutionality in that a defendant's freedom would not be in issue in a civil case. In the one civil case to date involving a torture victim suing for damages because of Canada's alleged complicity, the Ontario Court of Appeals upheld the constitutionality of section 38 of the Canada Evidence Act.[56] Because this case only involved pretrial discovery and did not result in ending the entire lawsuit, it provides inferential support for the proposition that Canadian courts would not likely stop a lawsuit at that stage. It is difficult to imagine a case like *Jeppesen Dataplan* being decided by a Canadian court.

The Canada Evidence Act also contains a provision that allows the attorney general to block even court-ordered disclosure.[57] The constitutionality of that provision has not been presented to the Supreme Court.[58] Lawyers and scholars in Canada have attacked the procedure as inadequate, but at least unlike U.S. practice, this procedure does not completely bar disclosure once the state secrets privilege is established.[59] At least as to a criminal trial where a defendant's liberty is in issue, the Court has said, "Where the conflict is irreconcilable, an unfair trial cannot be tolerated."[60] One can only presume that principle would also apply in a civil case, albeit perhaps to a lesser extent given that an individual's liberty would not be in issue.

It appears that Section 38 of the Canada Evidence Act creates an evidentiary privilege and would not completely end a lawsuit—if the case (whether criminal or civil) could proceed without the privileged evidence. If this is a correct interpretation of the new law, in light of the few precedents that currently exist, then Canada remains far more receptive to a delicate balancing of interests that does not create the sort of injustice seen in U.S. jurisprudence with the *Arar*, *El-Masri*, and *Jeppesen* cases. The Canadian inquiry process, which operates independently of the civil court tort system, can yield limited relief and, more importantly from the public's perspective, access to far more information about governmental wrongdoing than is available through the U.S. court system.

The fact that Canadian and U.K. courts (and commissions of inquiry) sometimes rectify victims of torture notwithstanding state secrets suggests that the United States could, without diminishing its security, relax its grip. That the United Kingdom and Canada could do better does not excuse the wholesale closure of the courthouse to U.S. victims of rendition to torture. In a democracy, there will always be some tension in how the government balances national security against transparency. And governments of all sorts seem to lean toward secrecy. However, democracies may be more transparent than authoritarian governments, and some democracies seem to be more open than others. In this regard, the United States has much to learn from its nearest allies.

# 6

---

# The Illegality of the Iraq War
# and How Rendition Sparked It

War is an evil thing; its consequences are not confined to the bel-
ligerent states but affect the whole world. To initiate a war of aggression . . . is the supreme international crime.

The Nuremberg Trials[1]

Before the coalition of the willing invaded Afghanistan (and later
Iraq), Secretary of Defense Donald Rumsfeld told President George W.
Bush that "international law allowed the use of force only to prevent
future attacks and not for retribution."[2] President Bush responded, "I
don't care what the international lawyers say, we are going to kick some
ass."[3] At a meeting of his national security advisors on September 11,
2001, he said, "Any barriers in your way, they're gone."[4] It is now well
understood that while 9/11 forced the United States to first deal with
Afghanistan, Iraq was always the preferred target.[5] These statements
suggest that the administration offered pretexts rather than legal justifications for these wars. Even more strongly in the case of the war in
Iraq, it suggests that irrespective of legal or moral constraints, regardless of whether Iraq possessed weapons of mass destruction (WMD) or
had trained al-Qaeda terrorists in their use, the issue was decided.

A few statements taken out of a larger context, while suggestive,
are not conclusive. If the invasion met the formal legal requirements
of Security Council authorization under the UN Charter, then the war
would have been lawful regardless of subjective (and difficult to prove)
intent. If the war met the requirements of self-defense, it would also
have been lawful—irrespective of the president's words—so long as the

movement to war was not wholly pretextual and thus prosecuted in bad faith. Measuring a person's intent remains difficult; gauging a government's intent takes even more evidence.

We leave aside for the moment the question of whether the doctrine that was ultimately advanced—that of anticipatory or preemptive self-defense in the absence of a plausibly imminent threat—could ever satisfy the requirements of international law. However, if the premise that the war was necessary to prevent the use of WMDs was not only false but was also asserted in bad faith, then the conclusion becomes inescapable that war began illegally. If initiated in bad faith, then jurisprudential or philosophical differences about when and where state practices have legitimated preventive wars become irrelevant. No view of international law allows a bad faith preemptive war; under any plausible view of the law, the belief in a real danger necessitating a preemptive war must be honestly held.

Even though the United Nations provided an after-the-fact cover by passing Resolution 1483 (which allowed the coalition forces to administer Iraq following the successful invasion), the initiation of an aggressive and illegal war remains relevant, particularly because 1483 did not purport to legitimize the war retroactively. It is at this curious juncture that extraordinary rendition and rendition to torture becomes relevant. As we will see, evidence from one controversial rendition not only contributed to cause this war but also provides powerful evidence that the U.S. administration either knew or should have known that its basis for war was wrong.

Contrast the "kick some ass" language with former President Bush's words in 2010, when he said of the failure to find the WMDs (which were the heart of the arguments justifying the war) in his post-presidency memoir, *Decision Points*, "No one was more shocked and angry than I was when we didn't find the weapons."[6] How do we interpret these contrasting statements? The first statement suggests going to war under a pretext and suggests that the reasons given for war (primarily self-defense and humanitarian intervention) are not to be believed. The later, after-the-fact statement suggests good faith shock at the error. Which version is likely true? We cannot know what was in Bush's mind or that of any in his administration. We can, however, while guarding jealously against the distorting effects of hindsight, review the facts as were known to the administration at the time.

Scholars have argued that an anticipatory or preemptive war cannot be squared with the UN Charter and that all such wars are illegal. Professor Onder Bakircioglu of Queen's University, Belfast, argues that preemptive war not only exceeds the right of self-defense set out in Article 51 of the UN Charter but also "reaches well beyond the bounds of the controversial notion of anticipatory self-defense . . . which . . . must be 'instant' and 'overwhelming,' 'leaving no choice of means' and 'no moment for deliberations.'" Bakircioglu points out that the United States never faced even a plausibly imminent threat, and nations may not as a matter of state practice eliminate the imminence requirement, and, in any event, the preventive war doctrine has no "significant international approval."[7]

Notwithstanding Bakircioglu's argument, a few scholars argue that state practice makes such wars plausibly legal so long as the necessity is great. They further argue that WMDs falling into the hands of terrorists creates such a necessity. Finally, they argue, the ultimate absence of WMDs is not dispositive so long as those who engage in preemptive war have a good faith belief that the world faces the real threat of WMDs falling into terrorists' hands. They conclude that such good faith legitimates the war in Iraq.[8] Most international legal scholars reject this characterization of international law, but the fact that some reputable scholars and lawyers vigorously argue the point makes it a minimally plausible interpretation of international law. However, even that minority view of the law fails if the belief in Iraq's WMDs was not reasonably held, if not held in good faith.

This chapter will review the formal reasons why the war in Iraq is considered by most international lawyers to have been illegal. It will then take seriously the claim that the war was a good faith, and therefore justifiable, preemption of Saddam Hussein's WMDs. It demonstrates that given the circumstances of Ibn al-Shaykh al-Libi's rendition to Egypt, the administration's claim of good faith is implausible, unreasonable, and the product of willful blindness.

## Before the War

Two events undercut the U.S. position even before the first soldier went into action against Iraq. Neither is sufficient to conclusively prove that the administration acted in bad faith. However, they add important context and, combined with later information, demonstrate the flimsiness of the prowar reasoning.

### UN Inspections

One of the requirements for a cease-fire to end the first Gulf War in 1991 and to free Kuwait from Iraqi invasion and occupation was that Saddam Hussein's government would have to forfeit all WMDs. The regime refused to comply, and years of economic sanctions followed. As a condition for the lifting of sanctions, Iraq was compelled to admit inspectors from the UN Monitoring Verification and Inspection Commission (UNMOVIC) and the International Atomic Energy Agency. By 2003, immediately before the invasion, UNMOVIC was headed by a highly respected Swedish diplomat and lawyer, Hans Blix. One month before the commencement of hostilities (February 14, 2003), Blix reported to the United Nations on his agency's progress. While not exonerating Iraq, he refused to hold the country in material breach of its obligations, further pointing out that his agency had conducted more than four hundred inspections, all without evidence that the Iraqi's "knew in advance that the inspectors were coming." He reported, "UNMOVIC has not found any such weapons."[9] It was clear from his report that he thought that he was getting belatedly sufficient support from the Iraqi's that inspections should continue.

Although not everyone accepted Blix's report or its conclusions, there were voices at the time who argued that there was no good case for war.[10] Blix's report was a major obstacle to the administration's plans to invade. Rather than accept his report, it immediately began to attack the messenger as naïve and dangerously wrong, a "fool and a dupe." Blix's report, they claimed, had "no credibility."[11] These same administration officials have never apologized for their vicious ad hominem attacks on Blix. While his report does not prove the U.S. administration acted in bad faith, it constitutes potent evidence pointing in that

direction. As Blix later pointed out, had Bush given him and his inspectors and experts more time, they "would have been able to interview
the many people who destroyed weapons of mass destruction in 1991."
However, the "U.S. government had 'the same mind frame as the witch
hunters of the past'—looking for evidence to support a foregone conclusion."[12] While admitting that one can never conclusively prove a negative, Blix plainly felt that his job could have properly been done without
the bloodshed of war and without the breeding of yet more terrorism
brought about by that war.

### UN Resolutions

On November 8, 2002, the UN Security Council unanimously adopted
Resolution 1441, which among other things declared Iraq in material
breach of its obligation to disarm itself completely of all WMDs. Sig-
nificantly, earlier drafts of 1441 circulated by the United States and the
United Kingdom would have expressly authorized the use of military
force and would have permitted member states to decide for themselves
whether Iraq had complied. This would have given the United States and
Great Britain the unilateral power to invade lawfully Iraq if they decided
that Iraq had not complied with the UN resolution. Too many Security
Council member states objected and that draft failed. The history of
Resolution 1441 makes clear that the United States and its coalition
partners needed a second resolution before they could lawfully invade.
Despite strenuous efforts, the United States and Great Britain failed to
secure explicit authorization from the Security Council, and it is at that
point that they chose to rely on the weak argument that Resolution 1441
combined with other resolutions to provide all the authorization necessary to invade Iraq lawfully. The history of this resolution, however,
does not support the U.S. and U.K. position. Most governments, save
those of the United States the United Kingdom and their small coalition
partners, plainly thought that any invasion without additional explicit
Security Council authorization would violate international law. The
overwhelming majority of international law specialists also agree that
the war was on this basis illegal.[13] While this history is not conclusive of
the law, it points in the direction of requiring something more than the
extant UN resolutions to justify the war on Iraq.

## The Laws of War: Iraq and Afghanistan
## in Light of the UN Charter

Military use of force has been limited under international law by the United Nations Charter. The United States, like nearly every other state in the world, has both signed and ratified the UN Charter, which entered into force on October 24, 1945. It is thereby obligated under international law to adhere to its principles. Indeed, as one of the founders and original signatories to the charter, the United States has strong moral as well as legal obligations under the charter.

Read literally, the UN Charter appears to prohibit all wars except those conducted in self-defense or under a Security Council authorization relating to the "maintenance or restoration of international peace and security." Any war not authorized by a Security Council resolution or fitting restrictive notions of self-defense would then be considered an aggressive war and hence would be illegal.

From time to time, however, state practice has varied from a literal reading of the charter and has thus opened arguments for the legality of various humanitarian interventions and an expanded notion of self-defense.[14] Without endorsing these more permissive rationales for legitimating war, one must nonetheless consider them seriously when asserted by an exceptionalist nation such as the United States. Such analysis allows consideration of the plausibility of claims that the wars thus waged were lawful; if those claims fail regarding the U.S. invasion of Iraq (or Afghanistan) under these permissive and expansive interpretations of the law, then they were unlawful regardless of any state practice or custom.

It is true that no international court is likely to declare either of these wars illegal. Even if one did, the United States would not obey the judgment. The United States does not consider itself bound by any court system other than its own, having disentangled itself from the jurisdiction of the World Court for such matters after it lost its case before that body during the Reagan administration's mining of the harbor at Managua, Nicaragua, in 1986.[15] However, the fact that no international court may adjudicate the legality of the Iraq War does not render such analysis meaningless. Nations pay a steep price for being perceived to have violated international law.

## The Charter and the Laws of War

Chapter 1, Article 2(4) of the UN Charter, if read in isolation, may appear to be an absolute prohibition of the use of force under any circumstances. It states: "All Members shall refrain in their international relations from the threat or use of force against the territorial integrity or political independence of any state, or in any other manner inconsistent with the purposes of the United Nations."

Since it is difficult (although not impossible) to conceive of a war without at least one aggressor, all wars are from this perspective illegal—at least as to whichever combatant is the aggressor.[16] The founders of the United Nations, created on the heels of the greatest and most destructive war in history, were not naïve and did not think that they could simply outlaw war. They also understood that determining which nation or party is the aggressor may not always appear obvious.

They did, however, wish to radically limit war, and they sought to delegitimize and discourage the use of aggressive wars such as the naked aggression exhibited by the Axis powers in World War II. Article 2(4) purports to eliminate all aggressive wars, but Chapter VII of the charter realistically creates two very narrow exceptions—self-defense and wars initiated by the United Nations through a positive resolution of its Security Council. Had war been limited to these two extremely narrow circumstances, there would have been very few wars in the years following World War II. Wars, however, have not been so limited, and this circumstance permits arguments that state practice (a component of emerging international customary law)[17] has widened the circumstances for a lawful war.

Self-defense remains a reasonable and important exception. Anyone is allowed to defend oneself from an unlawful assault, robbery, or attack without having to await the constable's arrival. Similarly, a nation under attack may defend itself without having to await approval from the United Nations. Article 51 also provides that "nothing . . . shall impair the inherent right of individual or collective self-defense if an armed attack occurs." Many scholars and jurists view this narrow rule limiting self-defense to a response to an actual ongoing (as opposed to merely imminent) armed attack as absolute, not subject to exception.

The doctrine of anticipatory self-defense appears to be foreclosed both by Article 2(4) and by the limitation in Article 51 to self-defense only "if an armed attack occurs." The latter formally rules out preemptive wars that anticipate rather than follow an armed attack. This aspect of the doctrine has not proved to be workable, and state practice has created space for a limited notion of preventive or anticipatory self-defense. Importantly, a nation might anticipate an attack to be imminent and find it necessary to use proportionate means to repel that attack. The notions of imminence, necessity and proportionality are very important in international law and appear in other contexts. It is not enough that a hostile force might at sometime in the indefinite future launch some sort of undefined attack.

The Iraqi regime, however, did not plausibly pose an imminent threat to the United States or any other nation. A decade of sanctions following its massive defeat in the first Gulf War left it no immediate threat to anyone beyond its own borders. The administration's argument for war in that case revolved around the calamitous consequences of allowing Saddam Hussein to obtain WMDs, including the possibility of nuclear weapons. A few international lawyers (mostly, it must be said, in the government's employ) substituted the direness of the consequences of allowing a rogue regime access to WMDs for the imminence requirement. In their view, the necessity of removing WMDs from a rogue state such as Iraq eliminated or at least softened the imminence requirement. Alternatively, the imminence requirement was thought to be met because the consequences of failing to act immediately were so dire. "If necessity can be demonstrated before the attack, then a nation should not be required to wait to be attacked before it can defend itself, especially if the first blow is potentially devastating"[18] The ability to deliver and detonate a nuclear weapon of any sort, including the so-called radioactive or dirty bomb, plainly qualifies under that standard.

We will assume—contrary to the view of the vast majority of international lawyers—that preemptive or anticipatory self-defense is allowed as a matter of state practice even where the threat is not arguably imminent, so long as the consequences of delay are seen in good faith as dire. We do this to assess the probability that the U.S. administration could have acted in a good faith belief that war was justified even under this greatly expanded and mostly rejected doctrine. Before we turn to that possibility, however, we will address two other legitimating possibilities—whether the war was a justifiable humanitarian intervention, and whether the United Nations Security Council, contrary to the history cited earlier, in fact authorized a military intervention in Iraq.

## Humanitarian Intervention

One question that arises in the aftermath of the ashes of World War II is whether a state (or coalition such as NATO) may use military force simply to stop widespread human rights abuses. Indeed, one may argue with considerable plausibility that humanitarian intervention is precisely what legitimated NATO's intervention in the affairs of the former Yugoslavia, including the bombing campaign that attempted to stop ethnic cleansing in the Kosovo region. Put another way, does a genuine and well-intended humanitarian intervention to save human lives become a legitimate state practice notwithstanding the formal requirements of the UN Charter, which did not allow for such actions? (The United Nations has since the Iraq invasion embraced the "Responsibility to Protect" project, but even this initiative does not appear to authorize armed intervention without a formal Security Council resolution.)[19]

Even though the bombing campaign in the former Yugoslavia in the 1990s lacked formal, explicit UN Security Council authorization, nonetheless, the Independent International Commission on Kosovo called the NATO bombing campaign in the former Yugoslavia "illegal, but legitimate." One can see the germ of a problem here. If a war is legitimate even though not authorized by the UN Security Council and not plausibly prosecuted in self-defense, then the notion of what constitutes a lawful war has stretched and become more permissive. Indeed, it is difficult to parse what a legitimate but nonetheless illegal act of war might be. One view would be to see the Kosovo bombing campaign to end ethnic cleansing to have been at the margins—formally illegal under existing law but creating a narrow state practice, or perhaps customary law exception for a humanitarian military action.

Some international legal scholars as well as some moral philosophers say that there is a humanitarian exception that legitimates armed force—subject to very narrow and precise criteria.[20] The United Nations' formal embrace of the Responsibility to Protect Project bolsters this argument.[21] Even then, one must meet stringent criteria before acting:

1. The purpose (at least in part) of any humanitarian intervention must be to stop widespread threats to life. Additional humanitarian purposes pose no theoretical problem. But sometimes a nation also has self-interest at stake, and that does cause problems. For example, what if one invades in part in the hope of gaining access to a region's resources—say oil? It is very difficult to disentangle self-interest from humanitarian motivations, and this is what makes this criterion so difficult to evaluate. It is why many international jurists and moral philosophers would not make any exception for humanitarian intervention unless accompanied by a Security Council resolution under chapter 7 of the UN Charter. The countervailing problem, however, is that any one of the five permanent veto-wielding members of the Security Council can stymie even the most justified of such humanitarian interventions. The world is left with either allowing humanitarian interventions whose purpose may be muddied by self-interest or awaiting a sometimes-paralyzed Security Council. The no-fly zone created by NATO in March 2011 over Libya and the attendant bombing of Gaddafi's forces pursuant to UN Security Council Resolution 1970 appears to be an exception to the usual logjam in that body.

2. Proportionate means are required—no more force than necessary can be used, and great care must be taken not to make the situation worse—a calculation, not a certainty in any case. The problem with this criterion revolves around its vagueness. Who is to say what degree of force would be proportionate in a given circumstance? Plainly, military planners' foresight may differ from the hindsight of humanitarian organizations assessing after-the-fact civilian casualties. In chapter 3, we saw that Human Rights Watch

criticized the numbers of civilian casualties that occurred during the invasion of Panama and the apprehension of Manuel Noriega. No doubt military planners thought their use of force proportionate, and no doubt Human Rights Watch felt justified in questioning that very conclusion. The very elasticity of this criterion renders it difficult to apply.

3. Attempts must be made for a peaceful resolution. As we saw in the case of Hans Blix, many thoughtful observers have contended that the war in Iraq was premature in that UN inspections should have been allowed to continue. In any humanitarian crisis, war is considered a last option. However, the point at which all other options have run out will likely always remain disputable. It is revealing that former President Bush continues to argue that his administration "ultimately gave Saddam Hussein the chance to leave peacefully. And I do believe that he chose war."[22]

4. The intervention ordinarily ought to be collective; ideally, more than one nation should participate. One reason for this is to mitigate the possibility that the war is driven primarily by self-interest rather than the desire to end a humanitarian crisis. The United Nations lacks an armed force of its own and can only act through the efforts of coalitions of nations, and this is one good reason why the effort in the Iraq War was from the beginning characterized as a "coalition of the willing." Coalition forces can resist excessive uses of force, and their presence can threaten to expose a partner's wrongdoing. As a result, the use of coalition forces may provide limited protection against the disproportionate use of force, thus mitigating the worst effects of self-interest and militating against disproportionate uses of force.

5. Finally, and most importantly, the danger must be imminent and the action necessary to avert the mass killings. Because war is widely acknowledged to be so terrible, to be such a blunt instrument of policy, only the worst and most plainly imminent humanitarian disaster resulting from mass killings can justify it. This criterion is likewise imprecise. As the world saw in the case of the Rwandan genocide, humanitarian disasters can rapidly accelerate, and the means and methods can be quite crude. It is never easy to assess

such situations, and the international community, even when not riven with political crosscurrents, moves ponderously, if at all.

The United States and its coalition allies initially attempted to portray the invasion of Iraq as a humanitarian intervention.[23] However, notwithstanding the mass killings of Kurds in the early 1990s, there was no imminent threat to large numbers of lives, no genocide imminent or even threatened as of the March 2003 war in Iraq. With no recent genocide and no imminence of mass lethal violence, all one is left with is the suffering of the Iraqi people and the cruelty of Saddam Hussein's jails and prisons where torture and killing continued, albeit on a smaller scale than in the 1990s. Former president George Bush continues to argue that relieving the Iraqi people of this cruel dictator justified the war in Iraq.[24]

However, unless one were to massively relax the criteria for humanitarian interventions to include removal of any nasty dictator of whom we disapprove, it is difficult to see how the war in Iraq can be justified on this basis. However one might view the military action in the former Yugoslavia, those circumstances were greatly different from those obtained in Iraq in 2003 and cannot be used to justify a so-called humanitarian intervention there.

## The U.S. Invasion of Afghanistan as
## Precedent for the War in Iraq

The war in Afghanistan may be distinguished from the war in Iraq in two respects. Although the United States and the United Kingdom claim similar authorization for the war in Iraq, we will see that this is erroneous. Afghanistan, then, presents a much stronger case for a lawful war authorized by Security Council resolution pursuant to its power under chapter 7 of the UN Charter.

First, the United Nations Security Council, through a series of formally adopted resolutions, authorized the "deployment to Afghanistan of a United Nations–authorized security force."[25] In addition, from the perspective of the United States, Afghanistan presents a stronger case for self-defense.

Professor Michael Mandel of the Osgoode Hall Law School, York University in Toronto, forcefully argues that the war in Afghanistan was pretextual and illegal. First, he points out that the Security Council resolutions regarding Afghanistan do not explicitly authorize war; indeed, they do not even use the formulaic "all necessary means" language that ordinarily is used in authorizing the use of force. Secondly, he points out that the earlier resolutions, relied on by the United States and United Kingdom (referring to the right of self-defense) do not mention Afghanistan by name and are unspecific and therefore cannot authorize war. Finally, he refers to President Bush's "kick some ass" language as pointing to pretext rather than legitimate self-defense.

Professor Mandel makes a strong case and may well be correct in his reading of the law.[26] However, a plausible argument revolving around the doctrine of self-defense can be made, and if one gives the administration the benefit of the doubt in order to assess the strongest case for war, then the war in Afghanistan must be distinguished from the war in Iraq.

The war in Afghanistan occurred shortly after the massive 9/11 attacks on the United States, which resulted in thousands of lives lost and billions of dollars in property damage by al-Qaeda, a terrorist group that not only operated with impunity from its bases in Afghanistan but also had such close ties to the government that it fairly could be said to have been part of that government. It appeared at the time that al-Qaeda was both aided and abetted by the Afghan government, and it made no secret of its intent to strike the United States again. From the perspective of the United States, it appeared that al-Qaeda and the Afghan government was thoroughly enmeshed with each other such that the actions of the one could be imputed to the other. It also appeared that the Afghan government would not extradite or otherwise give up the al-Qaeda leaders.[27]

Conversely, the United States made only a minimal effort "to demonstrate that it was acting in the UN framework,"[28] spent only three weeks of diplomatic effort to convince the Taliban to turn over al-Qaeda operatives for trial in the United States, and shortly after the war began refused a Taliban offer to turn bin Laden and associates over to an international court for trial.[29]

Nonetheless, "the reasonableness [of the war in Afghanistan] was widely accepted by the entire spectrum of countries active in world politics."[30] This last bit of realpolitik provides the honest answer—even though the war's critics may be correct on a formal level, the world has moved on—most of the world's nations consider the war as if it were lawful and act accordingly. Under these circumstances, many scholars of international law argue that while the invasion of Afghanistan may have had some humanitarian purpose, it was more in the nature of self-defense. The United States had security interests that they claim justified the war regardless of any humanitarian considerations, and the UN resolution emphasizing the right of self-defense bolsters that claim.

## Iraq: UN Resolutions Did Not Authorize War

Iraq presents a factually and legally complex case. In the run-up to war in Iraq, the United States relied on earlier UN Security Council Resolutions that authorized the first Gulf War and declared that Iraq was in violation of the postwar cease-fire agreement with the United Nations. Most, but not all, legal scholars (some estimates run as high as nine out of ten, for whatever that is worth) thought this illegitimate and that the United States and its "coalition of the willing" needed an explicit authorization for this war. The reasoning involves interpretations of the various UN resolutions on Iraq and the Vienna Convention on Treaties. The basic problem is that the original Security Council resolution only authorized liberation of Kuwait, not regime change. The later resolutions do not support an interpretation that allows military imposition of regime change, and no treaty or provision of international law allows an individual nation (or group of nations) to decide for itself the consequences that attend Iraq's material breach of the cease-fire. The relevant UN resolutions relied upon by the United States and its coalition partners were

> Resolution 678—which authorized removing Iraq from Kuwait
>
> Resolution 687—which authorized the cease-fire with conditions including disarmament and proscription of WMDs
>
> Resolution 715—which provided for monitoring for WMDs

Resolution 1141—which provided a new timetable and found Iraq in material breach of its obligations.

Resolution 1154—which promised "severest consequences" for any breach, however minor.

Resolution 1441—which held Iraq in material breach of its disarmament obligations under previous resolutions. Specifically, the resolution did not contain any language automatically leading to war and was understood to require additional action by the Security Council.

Resolution 1483—which provided post hoc authority to the coalition forces to occupy Iraq, allowed the coalition to administer Iraq, gave the United Nations an assisting role in Iraq's administration, and lifted sanctions.

The United States relies on the finding of material breaches and the promise of "severest consequences" (military action, in diplomatic-speak) in Resolution 1154 to bootstrap 1441's "material breaches" language into authorization to invade Iraq. But none of this amounts to an explicit authorization by the Security Council as required. Only the Security Council retained this power, not any single nation or group of nations. For the United States and United Kingdom to determine for themselves when military action was authorized is a clear perversion of what the Security Council thought it was doing when it passed Resolution 1441 stripped of language automatically authorizing war. The United States and United Kingdom did not rely solely on this contorted legal justification until after it had failed to secure the requisite Security Council resolution authorizing war. The argument that the Resolution 1441 authorized war notwithstanding what its drafters intended became an argument by necessity once it became obvious that a second resolution authorizing war was impossible. The argument that Resolution 1441 legitimated the war in Iraq is both historically inaccurate and legally frivolous.

Alternatively, the United States and United Kingdom claim that the Iraqi regime committed material breaches ending the cease-fire authorized by Resolution 687. These material breaches, they argued, permitted the resumption of hostilities under Resolution 687. But this makes no sense. Resolution 678 only authorized the freeing of Kuwait—which was not in doubt in 2003. It did not authorize the further invasion of Iraq, and it is for this reason that the original Gulf War stopped when it did. If Resolution 678 did not allow for the complete defeat and occupation of Iraq during the First Gulf War then, a fortiori, the resolution authorizing a cease-fire to that war did not allow the second invasion in 2003 to do just that. Put another way, if the original war authorization never authorized the invasion of Iraq beyond what was necessary to free Kuwait, then a breach in the terms of the cease-fire not affecting Kuwait's freedom could not plausibly be interpreted to authorize the further invasion of Iraq.

The United Kingdom Iraq Inquiry released declassified documents in June 2010 showing that former attorney general Peter Goldsmith warned former prime minister Tony Blair that the Iraq invasion was illegal without UN support. He stated, "In view of your meeting with President Bush on Friday, I thought you might wish to know where I stand on the question of whether a further decision of the [UN] security council is legally required in order to authorize the use of force against Iraq. I remain of the view that the correct legal interpretation of resolution 1441 is that it does not authorize the use of force without a further determination by the Security Council. My view remains that a further [UN] decision is required."[31]

While the U.K. attorney general's opinion may not be conclusive on the point, it is in line with the vast majority of international lawyers and scholars. Some have suggested that the invasion was that of a "coalition of the willing to disregard international law."[32] The fact that the United States and Great Britain turned quickly from a formal analysis of the UN resolutions to the argument that the war was a necessary preemptive strike to prevent acquisition of WMDs and to stop the training terrorists in the use of such weapons suggests that even the government's own lawyers recognized the flimsiness of their formal arguments based upon the UN resolutions.

## Weapons of Mass Destruction

Before the war, the administration made sweeping claims about Iraq's possession of WMDs and the ability and intent to use them. However, there were also many cautious analysts who thought these claims were overstated, or, as the British press has put it—"sexed up." Most of the rest of the world was skeptical about WMDs. Even Paul Wolfowitz, the deputy secretary of defense, characterized the evidence used to justify regime change as "murky." No WMDs were ever found, and there is no evidence—absolutely none—that points toward Iraqi training of al-Qaeda agents in their use. The only remaining argument is whether the United States could have been in good faith in making those claims in light of what they knew or should have known at the time.

## Iraqi Links to Terrorism and Specifically al-Qaeda

There seems to have been little, if any, evidence linking prewar Iraq to al-Qaeda. There do seem to have been jihadists entering Iraq after the invasion to fight off the United States, but that seems hardly relevant to prewar justifications. Even President Bush has admitted that there is no evidence to link Saddam Hussein to the events of September 11, 2001.

While opinion polls taken shortly after the invasion showed that upward of 70 percent of the American public believed that Saddam Hussein was personally involved in the attacks of September 11, these allegations are false. What links there were seem to be low level and of little threat to the United States. A midlevel Hamas leader was found in Iraq; Hussein did pay rewards to the families of persons who blew themselves and others up in the Palestine/Israeli conflict. In short, Iraq's links to terrorism were not great, and not an immediate threat to the United States.

## Retroactive Justification—Nation Building

None of the prewar arguments for the war in Iraq appear to be very strong. Richard Falk argues that the war "still could be judged as legitimate due to a series of effects: the emancipation of the Iraqi people from an oppressive regime, reinforced by the overwhelming evidence that the Baghdad rulers were guilty of systematic, widespread, and massive crimes against humanity, and an occupation that prepares the Iraqi people for political democracy and economic success."[33]

After-the-fact instrumental rationalization seems a particularly flimsy justification—particularly given the near unanimity of opinion that the war was formally outside of any plausible authorization under the UN Charter. Such retrospective arguments do not make the initial decision lawful; at most, they mitigate the effect of an illegal action. Much like the thief who, after an attack of conscience returns one's purloined purse, the initial act remains unlawful.

## Ibn al-Shaykh al-Libi: How a Rendition to Torture Helped Justify War

We have seen that the formal arguments for the Iraq War's legality are all meritless. We now turn to the notion that the war in Iraq was justified because of the administration's (good faith) belief that Iraq had and would use WMDs, and that this fact justified war.

Depending on how one looks at it, Ibn al-Shaykh al-Libi's suicide in a Libyan prison in early May 2009 was either extraordinary good luck or another dead-end in the effort to uncover the facts surrounding America's extraordinary rendition program.[34] Almost immediately after his death, Human Rights Watch suggested that the United States had hidden the facts about his torture.[35] Even before his death, some suggested that the Bush administration was trying to hide al-Libi, that he was sent to Libya precisely because he was such an embarrassment and needed to be kept away from the press and anyone else who might report on what he knew. Al-Libi was reported to be an important potential defense witness in the trials of alleged terrorists and would almost certainly been an embarrassment for the Bush administration.

When President George W. Bush ordered the 2006 transfer to Guantanamo Bay, Cuba, of high-value detainees previously held in CIA custody, Libi was pointedly missing. Human rights groups had long suspected that Libi was instead transferred to Libya, but the CIA had never confirmed where he was sent. "I would speculate that he was missing because he was such an embarrassment to the Bush administration," said Tom Malinowski, the head of the Washington office of Human Rights Watch. "He was Exhibit

A in the narrative that tortured confessions contributed to the massive intelligence failure that preceded the Iraq war."[36]

Many in the former Bush administration were undoubtedly relieved at al-Libi's death; detainees who have sought his testimony were undoubtedly less happy. Within a day after his death (reportedly by hanging himself with bed sheets) suggestions surfaced that al-Libi knew too much. Insinuations percolated that his death may not have been suicide, and others speculated outright that he was murdered.[37]

These suspicions are rooted in al-Libi's capture, rendition, the tale he told under Egyptian torture, and the use U.S. officials made of that tale in the run-up to war in Iraq. Pakistani agents scored a major intelligence coup in late 2001 when they captured al-Libi, a high-ranking al-Qaeda figure, who had, among other things, run a terrorist training camp in Afghanistan.[38] Newspapers speculated from the day the news broke that his capture carried potentially enormous intelligence value.

In early January 2002 the Pakistanis had handed al-Libi over to the United States, which transferred him to Kandahar, Afghanistan.[39] The FBI was particularly interested in al-Libi because Richard Reid (the shoe bomber) and Zacarias Moussaoui (thought at one time to have been the twenty-first hijacker in the 9/11 conspiracy) had both trained at the training camp run by al-Libi. The FBI stood to gain evidence in two of its most important and difficult cases and, understandably, wanted to elicit information that would later be usable in federal district court. FBI agent Jack Cloonan "worried that 'neither the Moussaoui case nor the Reid case was a slam dunk.'" But if they could turn al-Libi into a state's witness, he thought it could make all the difference. "Cloonan became intent on securing al-Libi's testimony as a future witness. . . . he advised his FBI colleagues in Afghanistan to question al-Libi respectfully 'and handle this like it was being done right here, in my office in New York.'"[40] This meant following U.S. constitutional and evidentiary rules designed to give defendants a fair trial.

FBI and CIA agents then took turns using conventional interrogation techniques, and the FBI interrogators thought that they were making good progress.[41] The CIA, however, disagreed and rendered al-Libi to Egypt.[42] Here the story took a dark turn, leading to the widespread skepticism about his later suicide.

Al-Libi began to talk, and the information he gave pleased the Bush administration so much that both the president and the secretary of state, Colin Powell, repeated it to the world. Among other things, al-Libi claimed that Saddam Hussein's regime in Iraq was giving training in the use of chemical and biological WMDs to al-Qaeda terrorists.[43] President Bush trumpeted this "intelligence" in a speech "in his push to get Congressional approval of the resolution authorizing . . . war in Iraq."[44] Most famously, however, Secretary of State Colin Powell used al-Libi's Egyptian "confession" in his address to the United Nations to make the argument to justify the coming invasion of Iraq. A number of news services reported at the time that "most of Powell's case on Iraq's links to terrorism is based on interrogation of captured terrorists such as al-Libi and accounts from foreign intelligence services. It did not contain the telephone intercepts and extensive spy satellite images he deployed to show how Iraq is deceiving UN weapons inspectors."[45] It turns out that al-Libi's torture-induced confession was nearly the whole of the government's evidence that the Saddam Hussein regime in Iraq was training al-Qaeda terrorists in the use of WMDs.[46]

One of the major predicates for the war in Iraq—that the Iraqis were training al-Qaeda agents in the use of chemical and biological weapons—was primarily based on the statement of one man without significant corroboration. There was ample reason at the time to doubt the veracity of al-Libi's claims. A classified Defense Intelligence Agency report at the time expressed skepticism about al-Libi's credibility.[47] Dan Coleman, a retired FBI agent, has said, "It was ridiculous for interrogators to think Libi would have known anything about Iraq. . . . I could have told them that. He ran a training camp. He wouldn't have had anything to do with Iraq. Administration officials were always pushing us to come up with links, but there weren't any. The reason they got bad information is that they beat it out of him. You never get good information from someone that way."[48]

Al-Libi later recanted, saying that he had just wanted to stop the pain. The statement linking Saddam Hussein to training al-Qaeda agents in the use of WMDs turned out to have been false and made under torture.[49] Mamoun Youssef points out:

> The president used this tortured evidence to defend the war, alongside the confession of Ibn al-Shaykh al-Libi, who was cited by Colin Powell at the United Nations as a first-person source of the Saddam–Al-Qaeda connection. But al-Libi was also tortured. And we know that such an operational connection did not exist. And we also now know that what Zubaydah and al-Libi provided were false confessions, procured through torture techniques designed by the communist Chinese to produce false confessions. In other words, the first act of torture authorized by Bush gave the United States part of the false evidence that it used to go to war against Saddam.[50]

Al-Libi's case and suicide raises a host of questions. First, and foremost, did the Bush administration push the use of harsh interrogation (and even outright torture) in order to obtain otherwise unavailable evidence linking al-Qaeda and the regime of Saddam Hussein? Did they use torture to get information that they knew or should have known was unreliable and likely false?[51]

Did the desire for a reason to invade Iraq overwhelm the available (and contrary) evidence? Ron Suskind reports that before the war, British intelligence provided the United States with access to the head of Iraqi intelligence who advised that if the Americans invaded, they would not find any WMDs—information that was ignored. He also reports that the administration had other lesser sources from inside the Hussein government, which corroborated the claim that Iraq did not possess WMDs. Suskind goes on to quote a prominent British intelligence officer as saying that if "the British had known everything that both men were saying . . . 'We never would have gone to war.'"[52]

Suskind's revelations suggest something stronger than simple groupthink laden with a strong dose of confirmatory bias. It tells us that the administration suppressed evidence that would likely have kept the British out of the war, and without the British, it seems unlikely that the administration would have been able to invade Iraq.

Al-Libi's sad case combined with the suppression of intelligence causes one to ask whether the administration intentionally sought to manufacture evidence that it knew or should have known to be false; that "enhanced interrogation" techniques were used in order to "invent evidence linking Saddam Hussein to al-Qaeda."[53] At a minimum, we now know that the administration recklessly used uncorroborated evidence obtained with torture that it ought to have treated more skeptically. Jonathan S. Landay reports that the "Bush administration applied relentless pressure on interrogators to use harsh methods on detainees in part to find evidence of cooperation between al Qaida . . . and the late Iraqi dictator Saddam Hussein's regime." He goes on to point out the administration's desire to make such a link, notwithstanding evidence to the contrary, in order to bolster the case for invading Iraq and overthrowing the Hussein regime.[54] Similarly, Joe Conason points to evidence that the former vice president ordered the additional use of harsh interrogation techniques after al-Libi had become compliant in order to establish a link between Iraq and al-Qaeda. He argues that "whether Bush, Cheney and their associates were seeking real or fabricated intelligence, they knowingly employed methods that were certain to produce the latter."[55]

Would the United States have gone to war had it not had "evidence" of a link between Saddam Hussein's Iraq and WMD training for al-Qaeda? The argument for war admittedly turned on more than simply the allegation that Iraq was training al-Qaeda agents in the use of WMDs. There was also the related argument, now thoroughly debunked, that Iraq possessed WMDs—weapons that Iraq might use against the United States, or that it might provide to terrorists.[56] But the United States hid evidence that there were no such WMDs and but for that hiding of evidence, the British would likely not have accompanied America to war.[57] The only good reason for withholding this information from the British seems to be that it underscored the weakness of the U.S. position. When combined with the flimsiness of the al-Libi torture-derived evidence, and with the Blix report, the conclusion that the United States should and likely did know better becomes inescapable. Both prongs of the argument were defective in that they relied on cherry-picked data such that the unraveling of one might well have unraveled the other.

In retrospect, the invasion of Iraq hung on what appears to have been deception, or at the least a positive refusal to consider, and an effort to obscure, all inconveniently contrary evidence, on both counts. Full disclosure on either count might well have derailed the war effort. Seen in this light, al-Libi's death and the evidence that went to the grave with him seems fortuitous indeed. It massively undercuts U.S. claims of good faith.

Was al-Libi's death a suicide? If not, how did he die? If murdered, then who ordered his death and why? What would his evidence have been had he lived and been willing to testify? Finally, al-Libi was sent by the United States to Libya. Why was he not held and tried for his crimes against the United States? While we cannot answer these questions, the secrecy that shrouds this case further calls the U.S. position into question.

Of all of the post-9/11 renditions, Ibn al-Shaykh al-Libi's may safely be said to have been the most disastrous. As embarrassing as other more highly publicized renditions were (such as that of Binyam Mohamed, Maher Arar, Khalid El-Masri, and Abu Omar), at least no other rendition can fairly be said to have been a contributing factor in starting a war. Al-Libi's case also provides one of the strongest arguments against the effectiveness of using torture to gain information that might save lives.[58] In this case the use of torture led to false information that contributed to starting a war in which thousands of lives have been lost.[59] It provides empirical evidence that information acquired using torture can misfire badly.

Thomas M. Franck writes, "If voters want the United States to play the imperial superpower, it is for historians to warn of the discouraging precedents and for economists to count the costs. It is for the press to portray fairly and fearlessly how that policy affects the people and societies at which it is directed."[60]

## Conclusion

When UN Secretary-General Kofi Annan declared that the war in Iraq was illegal, and when most other nations failed to join us there, they have the support of the vast majority of the world's international lawyers. More importantly, we now know what we did not know at the time. The Bush administration either knew or should have known that the war against Iraq was predicated on misinformation. Former president Bush still may argue that he and others in his administration really thought that Iraq maintained WMDs and was training al-Qaeda in their use. This, however, can only be maintained if one adopts the "pure heart, empty head test" more often applied to commercial paper rather than international law. It is no longer plausible to maintain that the administration reasonably relied on a good faith belief in Iraqi WMDs or the training of terrorists in their use. It is enough that the justifications given for the war in Iraq were unreasonable and therefore illegal and immoral. We come to that understanding in part through the tortured body of al-Libi, whose rendition to torture contributed to causes of war and helps explain why the administration should have known better.

# 7

## European and Canadian Complicity in Rendition and Torture

A U.S.-centered focus on rendition to torture, with the occasional spotlight on allied complicity—such as Canada's role in Maher Arar's rendition to and torture in Syria, or Italy's part in Abu Omar's abduction and transfer to Egyptian torture chambers—fails to capture the extent of allied collusion. Aided and abetted in countless ways, large and small, allied participation in renditions and torture cannot be adequately captured by isolated anecdotes. The United States could not have succeeded in rendering so many to such brutal confinements without the direct help, and a sizable dollop of deliberate indifference, of its democratic friends and allies. Some close U.S. allies also found their own not-so-unique ways, with eyes wide shut, of transferring humans to torture gulags. Whatever excuses may be available for governments that merely ignored CIA use of their airspace and airports to facilitate renditions, no such excuse can be made for countries that actively conveyed prisoners to torture chambers. This book would not be complete without acknowledgment of the role other democracies played in creating and maintaining the world's torture chambers.

As early as 2006 the European Parliament recognized the near certainty that European nations had facilitated the CIA's extraordinary rendition program. That body resolved that the Parliament

> considers it implausible, . . . that certain European governments
> were not aware of the activities linked to extraordinary rendition

taking place on their territory; in particular, considers it utterly
implausible that many hundreds of flights through the airspace
of several Member States, and a similar number of movements
in and out of European airports could have taken place without
the knowledge of either the security services or the intelligence
services and without senior officials from those services at least
giving thought to the link between those flights and the practice
of extraordinary rendition; notes that this assumption is supported by the fact that senior figures in the U.S. administration
have always claimed to have acted without encroaching on the
national sovereignty of European countries!

This last part, where the European Parliament assumed the truth of
U.S. denials of encroaching on European sovereignty, is only plausible
if European officials knew and condoned CIA use of airspace, landing,
and refueling privileges on European soil. By 2006 too much evidence
had surfaced to claim that no rendition through Europe ever happened.
Recall that by 2005 Secretary of State Condoleezza Rice had admitted
using European airspace and facilities for the extraordinary rendition
program (albeit denying purposive torture). So, the U.S. rendition program, at least in broad outline, was well understood by 2006 to have
involved European airspace and airport refueling facilities. However,
any surreptitious CIA use of any nation's airspace or facilities to effect
renditions would have been a gross breach of national sovereignty.
Renditions clearly went over and through European territory, and the
European Parliament admits in the resolution that no nation's sovereignty was violated. If this concession as to the sanctity of European
sovereignty is accurate, it follows that U.S. officials received high-level
license to render people to torture with an allied wink and a nod. This
chapter will demonstrate that many European governments craved
plausible deniability even as they approved, aided, and abetted, and
that they traded sovereignty for America's goodwill in furthering its
rendition program.

    The muted European response to former Secretary of State Con-
doleezza Rice's claims also suggests complicity. Had Rice's statements
been untrue in any important way, one would have expected outraged

denials from leaders across Europe. Notwithstanding Rice's assertion that renditions existed solely to facilitate interrogations and render people to justice, too much evidence had by then surfaced to deny that people rendered to places like Syria and Egypt were being brutally mistreated. As we saw in chapters 3 and 4, it was wholly implausible that U.S. and European officials remained unaware that the likely conclusion to rendition entailed torture.

Even as senior governmental officials across Europe denied knowledge of or complicity with rendition and torture, special rapporteur Dick Marty specifically found that "the blame does not lie solely with the Americans but also, above all, with European political leaders who have knowingly acquiesced in this state of affairs" and added that, "some European governments have obstructed the search for the truth and are continuing to do so by invoking the concept of 'state secrets.' Secrecy is invoked so as not to provide explanations to parliamentary bodies or to prevent judicial authorities from establishing the facts and prosecuting those guilty of offences. This criticism applies to Germany and Italy, in particular."[2] That European governments vigorously obstructed investigations buttresses the thesis that they were complicit in the rendition program. One generally hides and obstructs when one has a motive to hide and obstruct, and it is hard to see what these governments were hiding if not their knowledge of and complicity with rendition.

The assertion of state secrets privilege in the United Kingdom, Germany, and Italy provides additional support. While governments assert the state secrets privilege for a variety of reasons, in this context one is hard-pressed to see a more plausible explanation than complicity in rendition and torture. If highly placed governmental officials had been truly unaware of the CIA's activities on their national territories—if the United States had truly and surreptitiously breached their national sovereignty—one would think that those officials would release any information at their disposal that tended to exonerate them individually while also exonerating their respective national governments. One does not usually hide helpful information.

By early 2007 the European Parliament approved a report criticizing fifteen different European nations plus Turkey for helping the CIA in its extraordinary rendition program, and for failing to cooperate with investigations whose object was to expose that program.[3] As evidence continued to leak out from nation after nation, it became plain that many European nations, including those with otherwise good human rights records, knowingly gave the CIA the right to use airspace and the rights to land and refuel to facilitate renditions to torture. The evidence continues to mount that, despite official denials, several of the former Soviet bloc nations of Europe, including Poland, Romania, and Lithuania, provided space for secret CIA "black site" prisons facilitating both CIA "harsh" interrogations and provided way stations for renditions to nations that torture.[4]

The European Parliament, through its Temporary Committee on the Alleged Use of European Countries by the CIA for the Transport and Illegal Detention of Prisoners, has been actively investigating the cases of persons extraordinarily rendered by the CIA. Its mandate included cases where member countries' airspace was used or where "there are indications" that the countries assisted "with the transport, the communication of information to facilitate arbitrary arrest, participation in interrogations, etc." In short, the committee was concerned with European member states (and candidate countries or accession States) that had either provided airspace or, worse, participated in CIA renditions. The committee's rapporteur investigated eighteen Europe-connected rendition cases, which constitute "only a portion of the actual number of cases."[5] Nonetheless, the findings offer an indictment of the various European nations that aided and abetted the rendition program.

Evidence continues to mount that ties European nations to both renditions and secret detentions, even as many of these same nations have sought to block investigations into wrongdoing (such as Germany blocking the El-Masri investigation).[6] While this chapter can only skim the surface, the next sections will cover a few of the more important or just plain interesting cases, each of which illustrates the larger problem.

## Sweden

Human rights–conscious Sweden—a nation renowned for its human rights adherence and sensibilities—willingly enmeshed itself in the CIA's rendition program.[7] Shortly after the attacks of September 11,

2001, Swedish police "lodged objections to applications for asylum from two Egyptians, Ahmed Agiza and Mohammed El Zari." Because of a CIA briefing note, the Swedish government rejected the men's asylum applications. That same day, the expulsion order become final, and the men were arrested and carried to Bromma airport in Stockholm by about 8:30 P.M. By 9:00 P.M. Swedish officials handed both men over to CIA agents who stripped them naked, drugged and shackled them, and put them on a CIA-chartered plane bound ultimately for Cairo, with a refueling stop in Scotland (thus adding Scottish and U.K. complicity to this rendition to torture).[8]

Once in Egypt, both men were tortured for months before being brought to trial. The Egyptian court sentenced Agiza to twenty-five years in prison, where he remains; El Zari was released—he lives in Egypt, where he has been kept under constant surveillance.[9]

Before the rendition, the Swedish government obtained vague Egyptian governmental assurances in which the Egyptian government proclaimed its "full understanding of all items of this memoire concerning the way of treatment" upon repatriation to Egypt. However, Swedish diplomats failed to visit either prisoner for five weeks after the transfer and then only in the presence of Egyptian prison officials.[10] Given the Egyptian's ferocious reputation for ill-treating and torturing prisoners, it seems implausible that Sweden (or anyone else) would in good faith accept or believe such an ambiguous understanding as if they were concrete assurances from a benign democracy. "Egypt's promise not to torture was a mere fig leaf for the Swedish authorities."[11] In any event, the UN Committee against Torture and the Human Rights Committee ruled that Sweden's rendition via the CIA to Egypt violated the prohibition on torture "and that Egypt's diplomatic assurance did not provide a sufficient safeguard against that manifest risk of torture and other ill-treatment."[12] Subsequently, the Swedish chancellor of justice awarded compensation to the two men, which likely provides little solace to Agiza since he languishes in an Egyptian prison, or to El Zari, who no doubt would have preferred that he be allowed to return to Sweden as a permanent resident.[13]

This sad story leaves as many questions as it answers. Why did the Swedish government so readily expel these men based on information provided by the CIA? Why was the CIA so interested in the men that it would not only intervene in their asylum applications but also provide Sweden with the planes and manpower to render them immediately to Egypt? What was the Scottish and U.K. role? Was it limited to refueling the plane? Were their authorities aware of the cargo? And, most importantly, why did the Swedish government rely on what were at best fig-leaf assurances from the Egyptian government—assurances that were almost certain to fail even cursory inspection, assurances that the government must have known were misleading, if not false? All we can really know in this matter is that the CIA found a willing accomplice in its rendition to torture. Before this rendition, one might have thought Sweden a most unlikely nation to participate in actions that were almost certain to result in torture. Just as plainly, this particular set of renditions could not have taken place without Swedish help; moreover, Scottish help contributed to the ease with which it was effected. Even though Sweden was a most unlikely partner for a rendition to torture, it was not alone.

## Poland

Even as a former Polish prime minister denied knowledge of a CIA secret prison on Polish soil, evidence of complicity mounted from two independent sources.[14] Before the prime minister's denials, former CIA agents confirmed the use of black site secret CIA prisons on Polish territory, where interrogations included torture. In one case, the CIA's own records show that a "debriefer entered the detainee's cell and revved the drill while the detainee stood naked and hooded."[15] Mock executions are prohibited and the agent was reprimanded. The agent left the CIA but then returned to work for the agency as a contractor. Meanwhile the station chief, who witnessed the interrogation, has been promoted to head of the Central European Division.[16] (As we saw in El-Masri's case in chapter 4, the CIA often overlooks its agent's mistakes and rule and policy violations. This, combined with aggressive use of the state secrets privilege, adds to a lack of accountability.)[17]

What makes the former prime minister's denial implausible revolves in part around context. First, Polish officials "lied on at least a few occasions," denying even the existence of secret American prisons.[18] Only when it became plain that such prisons not only existed but also were on Polish soil with official approval did the story change to a claim of ignorance—a denial that these officials knew anything. Notwithstanding these denials, the Council of Europe reported "a Polish intelligence official who claims that 'Poland's approval came from the very top.'"[19] Plainly, Polish officials have been tying themselves in knots with each new revelation of complicity with rendition and torture.

The CIA's black site prison was located in a rural part of Poland that happened to be close to a small airport associated with extraordinary rendition flights.[20] Such bold use of territory for a prison combined with flights regularly going in and out would be hard to hide. As one reporter put it, "The Americans could have tortured prisoners there without our knowledge only if the Polish government consented to the establishment of a base on Polish territory that was completely controlled by the Americans."[21] It seems improbable that any western democracy would allow another nation—even one as powerful as the United States—a blank check to run a secret prison, with no oversight or even knowledge of its activities. If true, such would constitute a remarkable relinquishment of sovereignty. Former prime minister Leszek Miller's response evaded almost to the point of admission:

[REPORTER] Do you acknowledge a possibility that the Americans tortured without your knowledge?

[MILLER] I will not say anything more.

[REPORTER] Could you not have known, as prime minister, what went on at a secret CIA prison on Polish territory?

[MILLER] I cannot say anything more.

[GAZETA WYBORCZA] And if it were true? Would that worry you?

[MILLER] I do not want to comment on that.[22]

The European Parliament's Temporary Committee on the Alleged Use of European Countries by the CIA for the Transport and Illegal Detention of Prisoners was able to track eleven CIA rendition flights to multiple Polish airports and facilities, some of which were clearly extraordinary rendition flights.[23] Such use of multiple airports to facilitate extraordinary renditions, given the tracking abilities of modern air traffic controls, makes hiding difficult. Not only did the CIA operate secret prisons but, apparently, it shipped people in and out at will.

We now know through the Polish equivalent of a Freedom of Information Act inquiry that Poland's Air Navigation Services Agency "actively collaborated with the CIA to create 'dummy' flight plans to cover-up the true destinations of some of the flights."[24] This is perhaps the most damning evidence yet to surface. Bureaucrats in any country rarely take massive, illegal risks without higher-level approval. Their jobs and professional reputations depend upon closely following official policies without deviation and, unless authorized at the highest and most protective levels, without breaching domestic law. How likely is it that low-level civil functionaries would deliberately conspire on their own with a foreign intelligence agency to hide the true flight plans for illicit aircraft runs? In most countries, such would be considered treasonous and potentially espionage. Spying, treason, and doctoring flight plans remain criminal everywhere. High-level approval at a political level seems almost certain in such a situation.

The February 2010 UN Joint Study on Secret Detention found evidence supporting "the notion that one of the secret detainees held in Poland . . . is currently detained and awaiting trial . . . in Guantanamo Bay."[25] Absent high-level approval, it would seem that Poland's sovereignty would have been violated by this act. We also know from former President George Bush's memoirs that "the former President admitted that he authorize the 'waterboarding' . . . of Abu Zubaydah,"[26] and that Zubaydah has been granted victim status by a Polish prosecutor. This is the same Abu Zubaydah who was waterboarded 83 times, all before it became apparent that he had never been a high-level al-Qaeda operative. This seems strong additional evidence of Polish complicity. And Abu Zubaydah was not alone—Khalid Sheikh Mohammed, the al-Qaeda mastermind for the 9/11 tragedy, was waterboarded 183 times and was interrogated in Poland.[27] To be innocent, the Polish government would have to have been ignorant of the fact that some of the highest-level and most-wanted al-Qaeda terrorists were being held and tortured in secret prisons on Polish soil. Finally, there is the odd coincidence that only one week after the *Washington Post* revealed the existence of secret prisons in Eastern Europe, the CIA destroyed its terrorist interrogation tapes.[28]

Secret CIA-run European prisons, or black sites, which began almost immediately after 9/11, were not closed until a full year into President Obama's presidency by executive order in 2008.[29] Polish and Romanian secret CIA-run prisons became particularly notorious places for harsh interrogations and other human rights violations.[30] Thus, we are asked to believe that successive Polish governments from 2001 until sometime in 2009—a period of nearly eight years—knew nothing much of what was going on in their own territory even as their own agencies assisted.

None of these things taken singly proves that high-level governmental officials knew that Poland was facilitating renditions and torture. However, how likely is it that all of these things could have occurred over such a time span without official approval?

## The United Kingdom

In chapter 4, we saw in detail how the British government became entangled with the CIA in successive episodes of torture and rendition in the case of Binyam Mohamed. That case is interesting because of the parallel treatment in both the U.S. and U.K. court systems, and the ways that each nation dealt with sensitive national secrets. However, the case was not isolated, and the United Kingdom was perhaps as complicit with U.S. rendition and torture as any other nation. Both of its intelligence agencies (MI5 covers counterintelligence and MI6 deals with foreign intelligence) became deeply entangled in renditions and in interrogations of persons who had been tortured.

In November 2010 the U.K. government entered into out-of-court settlements of the cases of with sixteen former Guantánamo Bay detainees who had alleged that their security service had been complicit in U.S.-led renditions and torture.[31] Reports claim that one of the sixteen plaintiffs, Moazzam Begg, will receive millions of pounds from the British government and that "the details of the settlement have been made subject to a legally-binding confidentiality agreement. No admissions of culpability have been made in settling these cases nor have any of the claimants withdrawn their allegations."[32] The gag order is particularly interesting in that it limits what the plaintiff can reveal publicly;

while not proof positive of British complicity with their torture and illegal detention, it at least points in that direction.

Credible evidence existed at the time of the settlements to tie the United Kingdom to

- Being present at, and participating in interrogations of detainees;
- Providing information that led to the arrest and detention of persons by the United States or other countries where the United Kingdom knew or should have known that they risked torture and illegal detention;
- Sending questions for these detainees (at Guantánamo and elsewhere) where the United Kingdom knew or should have known that they risked torture and illegal detention;
- Receiving information thereby extracted; and
- Participating in extraordinary renditions that used U.K. territory.[33]

In return for avoiding a full trial on the merits, in which all of the evidence would likely have been exposed, the detainees got "a very large payout" and the inference of some wrongdoing or complicity by the U.K. government; this settlement allowed the government to proceed with an official inquiry into the government's involvement, which might "strengthen . . . determination for such involvement never to happen again."[34] The British government, conversely,

> gets the protection it craved against disclosure in open court of many tens of thousands of classified documents. Not only does this relieve MI5 and MI6 of months of work on the documents and legal arguments about what and how much should be handed over. It also, absolutely crucially from the intelligence and UK government points of view, means that London can now tell Washington and other allies that names and details in their shared secrets will not in future end up in British courts. . . . But they are umbilically linked to the intention, . . . to publish a green paper next year, with legislation to follow, which will massively tighten the terms on which intelligence information can be disclosed in courts. . . . Mr. Clarke made clear that he intends these restrictions to apply not just in civil cases, like the

Guantanamo case, but in criminal cases and in inquests like the current 7/7 case too.[35]

Not surprisingly, the United Kingdom's intelligence services continue to proclaim their innocence. These same intelligence officials can point to the need to avoid protracted and expensive court proceedings as the reason for the out-of-court settlements.[36] However, in summary, we know that information eventually leaked out in drips, linking U.K. intelligence services to Binyam Mohamed's questioning under torture (and those of the others as well); that a legally binding gag order has been placed on the plaintiffs; and that a large amount of money is apparently involved in paying off sixteen persons to remain quiet about their rendition to torture with British complicity. It seems probable that the frontline officers involved in carrying out Britain's role acted under orders from higher-level management officials within the security services.[37] Indeed, it seems reasonable to conclude that, next to the United States, the United Kingdom became the most culpable nation of all in using and becoming complicit with torture. In fairness, it also seems to have done the best job of any nation in disclosing its role in rendition and torture and in acting to avoid such complicity in the future.

## Other Complicit Nations

Complicity with rendition and torture filtered down throughout much of Europe, reaching countries large and small, new democracies and old. Recall that Khalid El-Masri was picked up in Macedonia before being rendered to Afghanistan, and that Germany frustrated attempts to learn about that country's complicity when its government asserted state secrets privilege to stymie a parliamentary inquiry. Macedonia, however, also played a crucial role. Despite denials, the European Court of Human Rights in 2010 decided to "communicate" (that is, inquire about and review) El-Masri's rendition from Macedonia.[38] As a result, Europe's highest human rights court put a series of questions to the parties that, among other things, calls upon Macedonia to account for its part in his rendition to Afghanistan.[39] This is the first time that the Human Rights

Court has agreed to move to the merits of a rendition case and the first time it has called on a member state to explain its part in the rendition program.[40] Only about 10 percent of cases brought before this court reach the communication stage.[41] In this case, Khalid El-Masri alleges that "Macedonian security forces seized Khaled El-Masri at the request of the United States in December 2003 and held him—incommunicado—for 23 days. El-Masri was then handed over to the CIA and flown to a detention center in Kabul, Afghanistan, where he was confined in appalling conditions, interrogated, and abused. After several months, El-Masri was finally released and dumped on a roadside in Albania."[42]

If these allegations prove true, both the major power, Germany, and the little new state, Macedonia, played critical roles in El-Masri's rendition to torture. Amnesty International calls the European Court of Human Rights Court's decision to formally inquire into the matter a "landmark case."[43] Merely by opening this case, the court has set an important precedent, and if the case demonstrates Macedonia's active help in detaining El-Masri and turning him over to the CIA, it will become truly landmark. If the court can move on a small country such as Macedonia, it then sets a precedent as to larger countries such as Sweden, Germany, and even the United Kingdom The case also has the potential of unraveling Germany's role. With this case, European complicity with El-Masri's rendition and torture continues to come undone—and investigations continue on El-Masri's behalf in Germany and Spain as well.[44] According to Dick Marty, who originally investigated renditions for the Council of Europe, "there is no doubt whatsoever regarding the el-Masri case."[45] Poland, Lithuania, and the United Kingdom are also continuing to investigate rendition cases, thus continuing the pressure to unravel European complicity in torture.

Romania and Lithuania have also been identified as countries harboring CIA secret prisons. Each nation has attempted to dissociate itself from these prisons, but the evidence continues to mount.[46]

As we saw in chapters 1 and 4, much of what the CIA wanted to do would have been illegal if performed in the United States. Setting up the Guantánamo Bay prison in Cuba provided one part of the answer for the agency. Renditions to places such as Egypt, Syria, and Morocco provided another. However, both of these responses had deficiencies. Even though Guantánamo Bay was intended as a law-free zone, the agency could not be certain it would remain so (and as we have seen, it did not). It was too large with too many people from outside the agency to keep it completely secret. Rendition to Middle Eastern countries, where there were no restraints on the extent of torture, was also insufficient. In those cases, the CIA had to give up possession of the detainee and could not directly handle the interrogations—something it was loath to do with its more valuable catches. Thus, with the exception of al-Libi, the agency needed a place to imprison and interrogate high-value prisoners such as Khalid Sheikh Mohammed outside of the United States (and even outside of the Guantánamo Bay prison complex) but fully within U.S. control. European black sites provided that "middle way" between harsh U.S. interrogations at Guantánamo Bay and medieval Middle Eastern torture chambers; the United States could thereby maintain control of interrogations and could institute harsh practices secretly and with fewer restraints.

The CIA needed fueling and landing rights in multiple European nations to ferry prisoners to its black sites in Europe and to render others to Middle Eastern torture chambers, and it needed way stations to render people to and from Guantánamo Bay. Secret prisons provided hubs from which to make all of the other networks go, and provided independent bases for secret interrogations as well. Secret European black sites served all three functions well. In short, black site prisons, together with European airports, landing, fueling, and airspace, became a crucial part of a much larger network without which the entire program would likely have faltered and would indubitably have been much smaller.

By the time former President George Bush shut down the U.S. secret prisons in Europe in 2006, much of Europe had become fully complicit in a sophisticated torture network. Even as this is written, investigations continue and information continues to surface, which demonstrates the extent of European cooperation in rendition and torture.

## In-Theater Renditions

Some nations, such as Canada and Great Britain, went beyond complicity with American rendition and torture programs and found their own unique way to turn people over to torturers. In what has come to be known as "in-theater renditions," both Canadian and British troops turned over captured prisoners to Afghani forces known to use torture.[47] Canada's relatively small military contingent in Afghanistan (never more than 2,800 troops out of a total force of 140,000 at its peak),[48] as part of the NATO force in Afghanistan, lacked sufficient resources to detain indefinitely those whom it captured on the battle-field. Their solution was to turn prisoners captured on the battlefield to others, first the Americans and next Afghani forces, ostensibly for safekeeping.[49] However, in each case the Canadians and British (as well as the other NATO allies involved in the war) had reason to know that the people it turned over for safekeeping were in danger of maltreat-ment. People were turned over for interrogations that included both torture and cruel, inhuman, and degrading treatment. This in turn yielded information. Thus, the war provided incentives to avoid look-ing too closely at what happened to prisoners turned over "in-theater."

This differs from extraordinary rendition in that it occurred within the confines of a single nation—Afghanistan; thus, the transfer of pris-oners captured in that war and then turned over to others can be seen as a form of "in-theater" rendition. This is not to suggest that these ren-ditions were all necessarily unlawful. Unlike extraordinary rendition, at least at first there may well be a lawful process in place.

In the beginning, the Afghanistan conflict qualified as a war in which the Geneva Conventions (including the prohibitions on torture and sending people to places where they risked torture) applied, as did the Convention against Torture and the International Covenant on Civil and Political Rights. With the exception of the United States, the other NATO allies, including both Canada and the United Kingdom, accepted that the Geneva Conventions fully applied.

Once the new Afghani government came into power, the struggle became an internal one, which eliminated the full scope of protec-tions under the Geneva Conventions. However, Common Article 3 of the Geneva Conventions applies during internal conflicts, and that part of the Geneva Conventions prohibits torture and further provides that the prohibition against torture and inhumane treatment applies "in all circumstances," and "at any time and in any place whatsoever."

Furthermore, Protocol II to the Convention, to which Canada is bound, requires her armed forces to look to the safety of prisoners upon release; this appears to require a nation capturing prisoners in such an internal conflict to avoid sending them to torture or other ill treatment.[50] Finally, other international treaties including the Convention against Torture also prohibit "refoulement" or the sending of people to torture. Thus, whether the conflict is categorized as an international conflict triggering the full spectrum of Geneva Convention protections, or an internal conflict under Common Article 3, with its lesser protections, there would seem to be an absolute prohibition against torturing people or sending them to places where there is a substantial likelihood of torture.

The phrase "in-theater rendition" provides a useful catchphrase, allowing one to distinguish this way of rendering someone to abuse and torture from extraordinary rendition. The proscription against sending people to places where they risked being tortured remains in both instances.

Initially, during the early stages of the war, Canadian forces along with the British, the Dutch, and the Danes turned all prisoners over to the Americans, who maintained a prison at its Bagram Air Base.[51] However, Canada and the United Kingdom were parties to both the Convention against Torture and the Rome Statute that created the International Criminal Court; hence, Canadian military and political officials were to at least some degree sensitive to suggestions that they might personally be criminally liable for war crimes, including the crime of torture. Among other things, the Geneva Conventions prohibit a nation from sending prisoners during war to any other armed force that did not adhere to the Geneva Conventions. The United States had declared early in the war that it was not bound by those "quaint" relicts of another age. Specifically, the United States refused to provide status determination hearings for captured combatants in Afghanistan in order to determine whether those captured were entitled to prisoner of war status.

By transferring prisoners to a power that was not itself in compliance with the Geneva Conventions, Canada and the United Kingdom as well as other nations found themselves in formal violation of international law from the beginning. This was viewed as a technicality because, without doubt, these nation's officials thought that U.S. forces would obey the spirit of international law even as it eschewed that law's formal trappings; surely, it was reasonably thought, the United States would not engage in torture. As Professor Michael Byers warned in Canada's foremost newspaper, "Canada, by choosing to hand the detainees over, also violated the Third Geneva Convention. The transfers did not, however, violate Canada's obligations under the torture convention, since there was no reason to believe that U.S. forces would abuse the detainees."[52]

The disturbing torture photographs from Abu Ghraib as well as revelations leaking out of Guantánamo Bay and other black prison sites punctured these assumptions. As Professor Byers put it,

> Today, we know better. Photographs, news reports and official investigations into abuses at Abu Ghraib Prison in Iraq, Bagram Air Base in Afghanistan and Guantanamo Naval Base in Cuba indicate that, at best, the U.S. military has failed to educate its soldiers about human rights and the laws of war. At worst, the revelations suggest a policy of law-breaking that extends all the way up the chain of command. Leaked legal opinions that seek to justify torture, the denial of access to legal counsel, and the removal of detainees from occupied Iraq provide additional cause for concern. So does the practice (to which Maher Arar fell victim) of subcontracting interrogations to the notorious intelligence services of Egypt, Jordan and Syria.[53]

Byers further pointed out that assurances by the United States that it would treat detainees properly could not be relied upon because "torturing governments almost always seek to conceal their actions. What matters is the recent track record."[54]

Canada, like Britain and other nations with even smaller military forces in Afghanistan, found itself in a difficult spot. These countries were too small individually to create their own prisons to properly house those that they captured in the conflict. Continuing to send prisoners into U.S. custody risked violations of international criminal law. Prosecution in the International Criminal Court seemed plausible.

By December 2005 Canada began to turn prisoners over to Afghani forces instead.[55] Canadian officials in particular appear to have known and ignored repeated warnings that they were likely turning prisoners over to abuse. Canada failed to put into place monitoring protections that the British and Dutch had placed in their agreements with the Afghanistan government, allowing those nations to monitor those whom they turned over. Thus, Canadian forces ignored the problem of sending people into prisons where torture was likely.

There were three problems with this arrangement. First, the memorandum of agreement lacked any provisions that would allow Canadian officials to monitor or track prisoners once they were in Afghani hands. Second, it was not clear which, if any, Canadian officials bore any responsibility for detainees once they left Canadian control. Finally, this diffusion of responsibility led to a situation where even those in a position to know about the potential for abuse were able to, and did, evade responsibility. Evidence is gradually accumulating that Canadian military and their political overseers intentionally ignored repeated warnings not only from nongovernmental organizations such as Human Rights Watch and Amnesty International but even from their own top diplomats. The British are finding similar, perhaps somewhat lesser problems with their own transfers of prisoners, some of whom faced the most brutal forms of torture.

Paraphrasing Howard Baker's famous Watergate question, the issue has become, what did Canadian officials know and when did they know it? If, as appears increasingly likely, those officials turned a blind eye to torture, then they may well have violated international law, including international criminal law. The British have also begun an investigation into the extent to which their military sent prisoners captured in Afghanistan to face torture.

Crucially, many of those detained by Canadian forces were turned over to Afghanistan's intelligence service, the National Directorate of Security (NDS). According to the Afghan Independent Human Rights Commission, "torture is a commonplace practice in Afghanistan's law enforcement institutions," including the NDS.[56] Moreover, "the continuing use of torture and other abuse against detainees by the NDS is well-established."[57] Human Rights Watch's documentation of individual cases of people tortured in NDS custody is stomach churning and includes stories of beatings, whippings, starvation, freezing, choking, hanging people upside-down for days at a time, and electrical shocks. The British have had similar problems with prisoner transfers to the NDS. Human Rights Watch reports "at least 9 separate instances," most of them as late as 2009, in which detainees "were allegedly abused in NDS custody."[58]

The Canadian government continues to stall inquiry into the situation, declining either to launch a public inquiry or to institute criminal or other investigations. However, Canadian claims that the government did not know about any such abuse, or that such abuse did not actually occur, are becoming increasingly difficult to credit. Apparently, almost from the beginning, the International Committee of the Red Cross warned Canada about Afghan prison torture and complained that Canada was not reporting prisoner transfers in a timely manner.

In November 2009 Richard Colvin (who had been Canada's second-highest diplomat in Afghanistan) testified to Parliament that he had repeatedly warned military and diplomatic officials about the risk of torture for those whom Canada transferred to Afghani prisons; that many were likely innocent of any connection to the conflict; that most were tortured; and that, when he had tried to make his concerns known, he had been told not to commit his information to writing.[59] To opposition members of Parliament, this began to suggest a cover-up.

The government responded by smearing Colvin, calling him a Taliban dupe and asserting that the public should not take the word of people "who throw acid in the face of schoolgirls." However, these attempts to sully the messenger appear to have backfired. More evidence corroborating Colvin's account continues to surface, and as of this date, 125 retired ambassadors have condemned the attempts to discredit Colvin. Prime Minister Harper's prorogation of Parliament in the face of persistent pressure to release relevant documents may have miscarried. By mid-April 2010 at least three separate witnesses, including Colvin, had detailed how the Canadian government had systematically covered up reports about the mistreatment of prisoners turned over to Afghanistan. Finally, the Military Board of Inquiry has looked into the affair and says that Afghan authorities "regularly beat enemy prisoners 'in the street and elsewhere' and most Canadian soldiers were well aware of the fact."[60] Apparently, higher-level military and political officials remained blind to mounting evidence that Canada was failing its obligations under international law in sending people to places where there was a significant likelihood of their being tortured. And in an apparent attempt to stifle inquiry into the subject, the Harper government has "cut short the mandates of the head of the military complaints commission" while parliamentary inquiry appears to have fallen behind a shroud of secrecy.[61] It remains unclear, as of this writing, how much of this affair will be made public.

An Ipsos Reid poll found that 61 percent of Canadians believe that Afghan torture occurred after transfers from Canadian forces, 59 percent believe that the tactic was routine, and a majority believe that it was wrong and that there was "widespread knowledge of it within the Canadian government."[62] Calls for a public inquiry continue to gain momentum, but it is not clear how this will play out.

Canada is not alone in its in-theater renditions of detainees to suffer torture in Afghan prisons. According to papers filed in a U.K. High Court, British forces turned over prisoners to face being beaten with weapons, hung from the ceiling, deprived of sleep, put in stress positions, and electrocuted at the hands of the National Directorate of Security.

## Conclusion

The United States remains the most culpable of nations for its use of rendition and torture. It was not alone and could not have done what it did without help from other nations. It is important not to draw the wrong conclusions, however. The point is not to exonerate the United States with a fallacious waiver that "everybody else does it too." Nor is it sufficient to diffuse blame to the point where culpability is so diffuse that nothing attaches to anyone. Rather, we must learn to avoid such mistakes for all.

These practices have not been without cost. Cruel, torturous interrogations of prisoners in U.S. custody can no longer be hidden. Renditions outsourcing torture and subjecting its victims to medieval interrogation techniques of bone-breaking and bloodletting are increasingly being exposed. Far from being the product of a "few bad apples," these practices are the result of official government policy. Torture done in our name is for our supposed protection and is proclaimed to be for our greater good.

The government's policies have caused multiple legal, political, and international problems for the United States. Lawsuits filed in the United States and around the world have exposed many things that the Bush administration had tried to hide, and these lawsuits have imposed costs that threaten U.S. intelligence practices. Governments around the world have protested U.S. practices and in doing so have also imposed additional burdens on U.S. counterterrorism efforts.

The U.S. torture policy has failed. It has not deterred terrorism, it has impeded intelligence gathering, and it has put the United States at odds with its closest allies. It has obstructed foreign policy initiatives and interfered with legitimate prosecutions in multiple countries. And it has demoralized intelligence agents while radicalizing opponents. Yet transnational resistance to U.S. renditions is slowly curbing the worst excesses and may ultimately force the United States into greater compliance with international law. The various pressures on the United States seem, when viewed singly, quite small. The cumulative effect, however, has been to continually make it harder for the United States to operate freely.

Although the new administration in Washington may have less appetite for using no-marks torture domestically, growing international and domestic pressures are making such practices more difficult. The United States could not return to so-called harsh interrogations if it wanted to. No later administration will find it possible to return to the policies of the Bush administration.

The United States has paid a dear price, and change is being forced upon it. International human rights law, and the international community more generally, provides a modest but material "push and pull" effect, moving the United States reluctantly and intermittently toward compliance. The United States has already begun to reduce its euphemistically labeled "harsh" or "alternative" interrogation practices. While the Obama administration claims the right to continue renditions, few suppose that the practice will continue as before, or that large numbers of people will be abducted, tortured, and "disappeared." However, revelations on May 11, 2010, by the BBC that the United States continues to operate a secret prison on the Bagram Air Base in Afghanistan where prisoners are allegedly abused suggests that, notwithstanding the backlash, some level of abusive practices remain.

None of this was inevitable. The U.S. use of torture after 9/11 was not a foregone conclusion, and the pressure forcing the United States to back away from it was likewise not predictable. This is not a steady march to progress, but the pressures are real and important. Although the Obama administration maintains the right to continue with extraordinary renditions, international and domestic pressures make continuance of the Bush program unlikely. While not enough by itself to hobble the United States, working with other domestic forces can and does have a real effect on U.S. behavior.

Under any conceivable utilitarian calculus, the practice of torture proves wanting. Not all moral calculations are instrumental. Renditions to torture cast the United States as an outlaw, as a nation openly presenting a defective moral compass. That is important irrespective of consequences.

# NOTES

## CHAPTER 1   INTRODUCTION

1. Arthur Chaskalson is chief justice of South Africa's Constitutional Court, president of the International Commission of Jurists, and chair of the Eminent Jurists Panel on Terrorism, Counterterrorism, and Human Rights. Quoted in Mike O'Connor, "Champion of Democracy," *Courier Mail* (Australia), July 29, 2009, 21.

2. David Cole, *The Torture Memos* (New York, London: New Press, 2009).

3. Mark Benjamin, "Waterboarding for Dummies," *Salon.com*, March 9, 2010, http://www.salon.com/news/feature/2010/03/09/waterboarding_for_dummies.

4. Christopher Hitchens, "Abolish the CIA," *Slate*, December 10, 2007, http://www.slate.com/id/2179593.

5. Ibid.

6. Jon Henley, "Want to Know if Waterboarding Is Torture? Ask Christopher Hitchens," *Guardian,* July 2, 2008, http://www.guardian.co.uk/world/2008/jul/02/humanrights.usa.

7. Kevin Allen, "Mancow Gets Waterboarded," *Chicago Sun Times*, May 22, 2009, http://blogs.suntimes.com/sportsprose/2009/05/mancow_gets_waterboarded.html.

8. Ibid.

9. Steven G. Bradbury, Principal Deputy, Assistant Attorney General, "Memorandum for John A. Rizzo, Senior Deputy General Counsel, Central Intelligence Agency," May 30, 2005, reprinted in Cole, *Torture Papers*, 224, 271.

10. Christopher Hitchens, "Believe Me, It's Torture," *Vanity Fair*, August 2008, 70, http://www.vanityfair.com/politics/features/2008/08/hitchens200808.

11. A Lexis-Nexis search of U.S. newspapers yields more than three thousand references to the term "waterboarding."

12. Joseph Margulies, *Guantánamo and the Abuse of Presidential Power* (New York: Simon & Schuster, 2006), 6.

13. *In re Guantanamo Detainee Cases*, 355 F. Supp. 2d 443, 474 (2005).

14. Ian Robbins, "We Have Ways . . . How Do Interrogators Bend People to Their Will?" *New Scientist*, November 20, 2004, 44.

15. Ibid.

16. "George W. Bush Delivers Remarks at Ceremony to Honor Cuban Independence Day," *FDCH Political Transcripts*, May 18, 2001.

17. Craig Scott, private correspondence on file with the author.

18. Jake Oresick, "Spain Aided U.S. Rendition Flights: Report," *Jurist*, December 1, 2008, http://jurist.law.pitt.edu/paperchase/2008/12/spain-aided-us-rendition-flights-report.php.

19. Rachel Donadio, "Judge Links Italy Agency to Abduction of a Cleric," *New York Times*, February 2, 2010, 10.

20. Ibid.

21. Carrie Schimizzi, "Rights Groups Confirm CIA Extraordinary Rendition Planes Landed in Poland," *Jurist*, February 22, 2010, http://jurist.law.pitt.edu/paperchase/2010/02/rights-groups-confirm-cia-extraordinary.php.

22. Ibid.; and Michael Bilton, "Post-9/11 Renditions: An Extraordinary Violation of International Law," *Center for Public Integrity*, May 22, 2007, http://projects.publicintegrity.org/MilitaryAid//report.aspx?aid=855.

23. Dick Marty, European Union, Council of Europe Parliamentary Assembly, Committee on Legal Affairs and Human Rights, "Alleged Secret Detentions and Unlawful Inter-State Transfers of Detainees Involving CoE Member States," Doc. 10957, June 12, 2006, http://assembly.coe.int/Main.asp?link=/Documents/WorkingDocs/Doc06/EDOC10957.htm (hereafter, Marty Report I).

24. Alfred W. McCoy, *A Question of Torture: CIA Interrogation, From the Cold War to the War on Terror* (New York: Henry Holt, 2006), 16, citing Edward Peters, *Torture* (Philadelphia: University of Pennsylvania Press, 1996), 1, 14–18, 25–33, 35; Malise Ruthven, *Torture: the Grand Conspiracy* (London: Weidenfeld and Nicolson, 1978), 25, 30–31; Michael Gargarin, "The Torture of Slaves in Athenian Law," *Classical Philology* 91, no. 1 (1996): 1–18; P. A. Brunt, "Evidence Given under Torture in the Principate," *Zeschrift der Savigny-Stiftung für Rechtsgeschichte* 97 (1980): 256–265; Peter Garnsey, *Social Status and Legal Privilege in the Roman Empire* (Oxford: Clarendon Press, 1970), 213–216; and Denise Grodzynski, "Tortures mortelles et catégories sociales: *Les Summa suplica* dans le Droit Romain aux III et IV Siècles," in *Du châtiment dans la cite: Supplice corporels et peine de mort dans le mond antique* (Rome: L'École Française de Rome, 1984), 361–403.

25. Darius Rejali, *Torture and Democracy* (Princeton, N.J.: Princeton University Press, 2007), 446–478 and 493–499.

26. Henry Shue, "Torture," *Philosophy & Public Affairs* 7 (1978): 124–143.

27. Ibid.

28. Mohammed Adam, "Al-Qaeda Associate Actually Had No Ties to Terrorist Group," *Ottawa Citizen*, April 1, 2010, A1.

29. Andy Worthington, "Abu Zubaydah: Tortured for Nothing," *Newstex*, April 5, 2010.

30. Peter Finn and Joby Warrick, "Detainee's Harsh Treatment Foiled No Plots; Waterboarding, Rough Interrogation of Abu Zubaida Produced False Leads, Officials Say," *Washington Post*, March 29, 2009, A1.

31. "RAW DATA: Transcript of Cheney on 'Fox News Sunday'" *Fox News*, August 30, 2009, http://www.foxnews.com/politics/2009/08/30/raw-data-transcript-cheney-fox-news-sunday/.

32. "Human Rights Watch News Release," *Targeted News Service*, May 11, 2009.

33. Xsociate, "Countering a Tortured Argument Revisited," *All Spin Zone*, November 7, 2007.

## CHAPTER 2    CULTIVATING A TORTURE CULTURE

1. George W. Bush, "President Bush Holds Post G-8 Summit News Conference," *Washington Post*, June 10, 2004, http://www.washingtonpost.com/wp-dyn/articles/A32143-2004Jun10.html.

2. Alan W. Clarke, "Rendition to Torture," *Rutgers Law Review* 62 (2009): 29.

3. Stanley Milgram, *Obedience to Authority: An Experimental View* (New York: Harper & Row, 2004); and Phillip Zimbardo, *The Lucifer Effect: Understanding How Good People Turn Evil* (New York: Random House, 2007).

4. Sung Hui Kim, "The Banality of Fraud: Resituating the Inside Counsel as Gate-Keeper," *Fordham Law Review* 74 (2005): 995.

5. David J. Luban, "The Ethics of Wrongful Obedience," in *Ethics in Practice: Lawyers' Roles, Responsibilities, and Regulation*, ed. Deborah L. Rhode (Oxford: Oxford University Press, 2000), 97.

6. Alfred W. McCoy, *A Question of Torture: CIA Interrogation, From the Cold War to the War on Terror* (New York: Henry Holt, 2006), 48.

7. Jean-Paul Sartre, "Introduction" to *The Question*, by Henri Alleg, trans. John Calder (Lincoln: University of Nebraska Press, Bison Books edition, 2006), xxvii, xxviii.

8. Martha K. Huggins, "Moral Universes of Brazilian Torturers," *Albany Law Review* 67 (2003): 527–528. These factors were taken directly from her article.

9. Darius Rejali, "Torture, American Style—The Surprising Force Behind Torture: Democracies," *Boston Globe*, December 16, 2007, D1; and Darius Rejali, *Torture and Democracy* (Princeton, N.J.: Princeton University Press, 2007), 446–478 and 493–499.

10. Rejali, *Torture and Democracy*, 46.

11. Bill Lambrecht, "A War-Torn Document," *St. Louis Post-Dispatch*, September 16, 2007, B1.

12. Anthony Shalid, "Saudis Promise Stronger Role in Right on Terror," *Boston Globe*, December 2, 2002, A1.

13. John Yoo, "Transferring Terrorists," *Notre Dame Law Review* 79 (2004): 1192–1223.

14. Jane Mayer, "Outsourcing Torture," *New Yorker*, February 14, 2005, 106 (quoting telephone interview with John Yoo).

15. George I. Annas, "Human Rights Outlaws: Nuremberg, Geneva, and the Global War on Terror," *Boston University Law Review* 87 (2007): 431.

16. Matthew B. Stannard, "Stanford Experiment Foretold Iraq Scandal," *San Francisco Chronicle*, May 8, 2004, A15.

17. David Luban, "Liberalism, Torture, and the Ticking Bomb," *Virginia Law Review* 91 (2005): 1426.

18. Rejali, *Torture and Democracy*, 554–556.

19. Mark Bowden, "The Dark Art of Interrogation," *Atlantic Monthly*, October 2003, 55–56.

20. Gary Cohn, Ginger Thompson, and Mark Matthews, "Torture Was Taught by CIA; Declassified Manual Details the Methods Used in Honduras; Agency Denials Refuted," *Baltimore Sun*, January 27, 1997; see also James Hodge and Linda Cooper, "Roots of Abu Ghraib in CIA Techniques: 50 Years of Refining, Teaching Torture Found in Interrogation Manuals; The U.S. and Torture; Cover Story," *National Catholic Reporter*, November 5, 2004, 11.

21. "Prisoner Abuse: Patterns from the Past," National Security Archive Electronic Briefing Book No. 122, *National Security Archive*, http://www.gwu.edu/~nsarchiv/NSAEBB/NSAEBB122/ (providing KUBARK manual and 1983 Human Resources Exploitation Manual). The term "KUBARK" is "a cryptogram, KU a random diptych and BARK the agency's code word for itself"; and Tim Weiner, "Word for Word/Interrogation CIA Style: The Spy Agency's Many Mean Ways to Loosen Cold-War Tongues," *New York Times*, February 9, 1997, 7.

22. KUBARK, *Counterintelligence Interrogation* (Washington, D.C.: CIA, 1963), 46, 90, 91, 8.

23. Ibid., 8.

24. *Human Resource Exploitation Training Manual* (Washington, D.C.: CIA, 1983).

25. "Prisoner Abuse."

26. McCoy, *Question of Torture*, 11.

27. According to the U.S. Air Force SERE Specialist Web site, the first SERE training program began in 1947 at Marks AFB, Alaska. Gosere.com, accessed November 9, 2008, http://www.gosere.com. However, according to Michael Otterman, training to "inoculate soldiers against the stress of torture" began in 1953 and was exported to allies in Southeast Asia by the late 1950s. *American Torture: From the Cold War to Abu Ghraib and Beyond* (London: Pluto Press, 2007), 11–12.

28. Jane Mayer, "The Experiment: The Military Trains People to Withstand Interrogation. Are Those Methods Being Misused and Guantanamo?" *New Yorker*, July 11, 2005, 60.

29. Mark Benjamin, "Torture Teachers," *Salon*, June 29, 2006, http://www.salon
    .com/news/feature/2006/06/29/torture/.

30. A. J. Langguth, "Torture's Teachers," *New York Times*, June 11, 1979; A. J. Lang-
    guth, *Hidden Terrors* (New York: Pantheon, 1978), 25; and Alexander Cock-
    burn, "The Wide World of Torture," *Counterpunch*, November 9, 2001, http://
    www.counterpunch.org/torture2.html.

31. Cockburn, "Wide World of Torture"; Langguth, *Hidden Terrors*, 286; and
    Otterman, *American Torture*, 76.

32. See Langguth, "Torture's Teachers."

33. See Langguth, *Hidden Terrors*, 251–253.

34. *In re Guantanamo Detainee Cases*, 355 F.Supp. 2d 443, 474 (2005), *vacated and
    dismissed*; *Boumediene v. Bush*, 2007 U.S. App. Lexis 3682 (D.C. Ct., Feb. 20,
    2007), *cert. granted*, 127 S. Ct. 1478, 167 L. Ed. 578 (June 29, 2007), *decided* 128
    S. Ct. 2229 (June 12, 2008).

35. Joseph Margulies, *Guantánamo and the Abuse of Presidential Power* (New York:
    Simon & Schuster, 2006), 5–6.

36. Binyam Mohamed's case is more fully discussed in chapter 4.

37. Authorization for Use of Military Force, Pub. L. No. 107–40, 115 Stat. 225
    (codified in note following 50 U.S.C. § 1541 [2000, Supp. III]); ibid., §2(b)(1).

38. Philip Shenon, "After the Attacks: The Lone Voice; In One Vote, a Call for
    Restraint," *New York Times*, September 16, 2001, 6, http://www.nytimes
    .com/2001/09/16/us/after-the-attacks-the-lone-voice-in-one-vote-a-call-for-
    restraint.html.

39. Jordan J. Paust, "Post-9/11 Overreaction and Fallacies Regarding War and
    Defense, Guantanamo, the Status of Persons, Treatment, Judicial Review
    of Detention, and Due Process in Military Commissions," *Notre Dame Law
    Review* 79 (2004): 1340–1341.

40. *Hamdan v. Rumsfeld*, 548 U.S. 557, 594 (2006).

41. Jonathan Hafetz, "Torture, Judicial Review and the Regulation of Custodial
    Interrogations," *New York University Annual Survey of American Law* 624
    (2007): 33.

42. Christopher Kutz, "The Lawyers Know Sin: Complicity in Torture," in *The
    Torture Debate in America*, ed. Karen J. Greenberg, 241–246 (New York: Cam-
    bridge University Press, 2006).

43. Luban, "Liberalism, Torture, and the Ticking Bomb," 1427.

44. Jan Crawford Greenburg, Howard L. Rosenberg, and Ariane de Vogue, "Bush
    Aware of Advisors' Interrogation Talks," *ABC News*, April 11, 2008, http://
    abcnews.go.com/TheLaw/LawPolitics/story?id=4635175&page=1b; Press Release,
    "Highest-Level Bush Administration Officials Approved, Discussed U.S. Post-
    9/11 Torture Program," Center for Constitutional Rights, April 10, 2008, http://
    ccrjustice.org/newsroom/press-releases/highest-level-bush-administration-

officials-approved-discussed—post-911-torture-program; "Poll Results: Water-boarding Is Torture," *CNN.com*, November 6, 2007, http://www.cnn.com/2007/POLITICS/11/06/waterboard.poll/; "World Citizens Reject Torture, Global Poll Suggests," *BBC News*, July 26, 2007, http://www.bbc.co.uk/pressoffice/press releases/stories/2006/10_october/19/poll.shtml; and "Torture Is Rejected, Even in Struggle against Terrorism," *BBC News*, http://www.globescan.com/news_ archives/bbctorture06/detail.html (providing detailed country-by-country results from this worldwide poll).

45. *United States v. Van Allen*, 524 F.3d 814, 823 (7th Cir. 2008).

46. Neil A. Lewis, "Official Defends Signing Interrogation Memos," *New York Times*, April 28, 2009, A12.

47. Tim Golden, "After Terror, a Secret Rewriting of Military Law," *New York Times*, October 24, 2004, 1.

48. Gavin Esler, "Will 'Chief Crazy' Cheney Face a War Crimes Trial?" *Daily Mail* (London), December 5, 2005, http://www.highbeam.com/doc/1G1–139445176 .html.

49. On November 6, 2001, Deputy Assistant Attorney General Patrick Philbin provided the memorandum to then Attorney General Alberto Gonzales, lay-ing out the basis for military commissions arguing that the president has the inherent power to order them and citing *Ex Parte Quirin*, 317 U.S. 1 (1942) as precedent.

50. Military Order of November 13, 2001: Detention, Treatment, and Trial of Certain Non-Citizens in the War against Terrorism, 66 Fed. Reg. 57, 833–36 (November 13, 2001).

51. *In re Guantanamo Detainee Cases*, 355 F. Supp. 2d 443, 475 (D.D.C. 2005).

52. Toby Harden, "Hunger Strike at Camp X-Ray Over Ban on Turbans," *Daily Telegraph* (London), March 1, 2002, 15; and Angus MacSwan and Charles Aldinger, "'Worst of the Worst' Captives Arrive in Cuba: Taliban, al-Qaeda Detainees Jailed at U.S. Base Won't Be Protected by Geneva Convention, Says Rumsfeld," *Ottawa Citizen*, January 12, 2002, A10.

53. Ulysses S. Smith, "'More Ours than Theirs': The Uighurs, Indefinite Deten-tion, and the Constitution," *Cornell International Law Journal* 40 (2007): 266–267; Steve Czajkowski, "DOJ Defends Detention of Uighur at Guantanamo," *Jurist*, April 4, 2008, http://jurist.law.pitt.edu/jurist_search.php?q=DOJ+Defends+Detention+of+Uighur+at+Guantanamo; and Seema Saifee, "Guan-tanamo's Uighurs: No Justice in Solitary," *Jurist*, April 6, 2008, http://jurist .law.pitt.edu/forumy/2008/03/guantanamos-uighurs-no-justice-in.php.

54. Military Order of November13, § 4(c)(3).

55. Ibid., § 4(c)(8).

56. Detlev F. Vagts, "Military Commissions: A Concise History," *American Journal of International Law* 101 (2007): 35.

57. David A. Martin, "Judicial Review and the Military Commissions Act: On Striking the Right Balance," *American Journal of International Law* 101 (2007): 355.

58. Military Order of November 13 § 7(b)(2).

59. *Hamdi v. Rumsfeld*, 542 U.S. 507 (2004).

60. Charles Lane, "Terrorism Tribunal Rights Are Expanded: Draft Specifies Appeals, Unanimity on Death Penalty," *Washington Post*, December 28, 2001, A1.

61. Barton Gellman and Jo Becker, "Pushing the Envelope on Presidential Power," *Washington Post*, June 25, 2007, http://blog.washingtonpost.com/cheney/chapters/pushing_the_envelope_on_presi/index.html.

62. Memorandum from Patrick F. Philbin and John C. Yoo, Office of Legal Counsel, Department of Justice, to William J. Haynes, II, General Counsel, Department of Defense, Re: Possible Habeas Jurisdiction over Aliens Held in Guantanamo Bay, Cuba (December 28, 2001), in *The Torture Papers: The Road to Abu Ghraib*, ed. Karen J. Greenberg and Joshua L. Dratel (Cambridge: Cambridge University Press, 2005), 29, 34, 37.

63. 18 U.S.C. § 2340A (2008); Foreign Affairs and Restructuring Act of 1998, Pub. L. No. 105–277, 112 Stat. §§ 2242, 2681–761 (codified at 8 U.S.C. § 1231 [2000]); Giving effect to Article 3 of The Convention against Torture and Other Cruel, Inhuman or Degrading Treatment or Punishment, December 10, 1984, 1465 U.N.T.S. 85.

64. George Lardner Jr., "Legal Scholars Criticize Wording of Bush Order: Accused Can Be Detained Indefinitely," *Washington Post*, December 3, 2001, A10.

65. Alberto R. Gonzales, "Martial Justice, Full and Fair," *New York Times*, November 30, 2001, A27.

66. *Rasul v. Bush*, 542 U.S. 466, 544 (2004); and *Boumediene v. Bush*, 128 S. Ct. at 2262.

67. Karen J. Greenberg, *The Torture Debate in America* (New York: Cambridge University Press, 2006); and Michael Ratner, *The Trial of Donald Rumsfeld* (New York: New Press, 2008), chap. 4.

68. Hugh Ambrose, *The Pacific* (New York: NAL Caliber, 2010), 70

69. Margaret L. Satterthwaite, "Rendered Meaningless: Extraordinary Rendition and the Rule of Law," *George Washington Law Review* 75 (2007): 1333.

70. Scott Horton, "Through a Mirror Darkly: Applying the Geneva Conventions to 'A New Kind of Warfare,'" in *The Torture Debate in America*, ed. Karen J. Greenberg, 136, 145–146, at 140.

71. Alberto R. Gonzales, "Memorandum for the President," January 25, 2002, in *The Torture Papers: The Road to Abu Ghraib*, ed. Karen J. Greenberg and Joshua L. Dratel (Cambridge: Cambridge University Press, 2005), 119.

72. Annas, "Human Rights Outlaws," 463.

73. Memorandum from Jay S. Bybee, Assistant Attorney General, Office of Legal Counsel, Department of Justice, to Alberto R. Gonzales, Counsel to the President, Re: Standards of Conduct for Interrogation under 18 U.S.C. §§ 2340–2340A.

74. David Luban, "Liberalism, Torture, and the Ticking Bomb," in *Torture Debate in America*, ed. Karen J. Greenberg (New York: Cambridge University Press, 2006), 54; and Harold Koh, quoted in Stephen Gillers, "Legal Ethics: A Debate," in *The Torture Debate in America*, ed. Karen J. Greenberg (New York: Cambridge University Press, 2006), 238.

75. Memorandum from Bybee to Gonzales. Emphasis added.

76. Memorandum from Daniel Levin, Acting Assistant Attorney General, Office of Legal Counsel, to James B. Comey, Deputy Attorney General, Re: Legal Standards Applicable under 18 U.S.C. §§ 2340–2340A, December 30, 2004, http://www.justice.gov/olc/18usc23402340a2.htm.

77. Luban, "Liberalism, Torture, and the Ticking Bomb," in *Torture Debate in America*, 36.

78. Josh Meyer and Julian Barnes, "Memos Gave Bush Overriding Powers," *Los Angeles Times*, March 3, 2009, A1.

79. James Bybee, Memorandum for John Rizzo, Acting General Counsel of the Central Intelligence Agency, Interrogation of al Qaeda Operative, August 1, 2002, at 16, http://image.guardian.co.uk/sys-files/Guardian/documents/2009/04/16/bybee_to_rizzo_memo.pdf; and Luban, "Liberalism, Torture, and the Ticking Bomb," in *Torture Debate in America*, 59.

80. David Luban, "Liberalism, Torture, and the Ticking Bomb," in *Torture Debate in America*, 59–62. However, the Bybee Memorandum of August 1, 2002, does acknowledge that "a single event of sufficiently intense pain may fall within this prohibition" if it "is of an intensity akin to the pain accompanying serious physical injury" including "severe beatings with weapons such as clubs, and the burning of prisoners" (10).

81. *Mohamed v. Jeppesen Dataplan*, 614 F.3d 1070 (9th Cir. September 8, 2010); *El-Masri v. Tenet*, 479 F.3d 296, 308 (4th Cir. 2007), cert. denied, 128 S. Ct. 373 (2007); and *Arar v. Ashcroft*, 414 F. Supp. 2d 250 (E.D.N.Y. 2006), *aff'd en banc*, 532 F.3d 157 (2d Cir. 2008), en banc. 585 F.3d 559 (2009).

82. Boumediene v. Bush, 553 U.S. 723 (2008).

83. Jordan J. Paust, "The Absolute Prohibition of Torture and Necessary and Appropriate Sanctions," *Valparaiso University Law Review* 43 (2009): 1565–1567; Brian Tamanaha, "The Collapse of the 'Good Faith' Excuse for Yoo (Bybee, Delahunty)," in *Balkinization*, March 5, 2009, http://balkin.blogspot.com/2009/03/collapse-of-good-faith-excuse-for-yoo.html; Michael Isikoff and Evan Thomas, "Bush's Monica Problem," *Newsweek*, June 4, 2007, 27; Alan W. Clarke, "De-cloaking Torture: *Boumediene* and the Military Commissions Act," *San Diego International Law Review* 11 (2009): 82; Marjorie Cohn, "National Lawyers Guild Calls on Boalt Hall to Dismiss Law Professor John

Yoo, Whose Torture Memos Led to Commission of War Crimes," reproduced in *BuelahMan's Redstate Revolt*, http://buelahman.wordpress.com/2008/04/09/national-lawyers-guild-says-john-yoo-is-a-war-criminal/.

84. David Cole, *The Torture Memos: Rationalizing the Unthinkable* (New York and London: New Press, 2009).

85. Ibid., 4.

86. Steven G. Bradbury, "Memorandum for John Rizzo, Senior Deputy General Counsel, Central Intelligence Agency," May 30, 2005, in Cole, *Torture Memos*, 228.

87. Steven G. Bradbury, "Memorandum for John A. Rizzo, Senior Deputy General Counsel, Central Intelligence Agency," May 10, 2005, reproduced in Cole, *Torture Memos*, 152, 199.

88. Richard E. Mezo, "Why It Was Called 'Water Torture,'" *Washington Post*, February 10, 2008, B7.

89. Lawrence Wright, "The Spymaster: Can Mike McConnell Fix America's Intelligence Community?" *New Yorker*, January 21, 2008, 53.

90. Cole, *Torture Memos*, 32.

91. Ibid., 4.

92. *Chavez v. Martinez*, 538 U.S. 833 (1998); and Cole, *Torture Memos*, 33.

93. Cole, *Torture Memos*, 33.

94. *Chavez v. Martinez*, 32–33.

95. Ibid., 33.

96. "McCain Suggests Torture Ban Has Flexibility in Imminent Cases," *Associated Press State & Local Wire*, December 18, 2005; and Rosa Brooks, "U.S. Attorney General Nominee Fails Easy Torture Question," *San Jose Mercury News* (California), November 2, 2007, Opinion.

97. Cole, *Torture Memos*, 4.

98. The Harris Poll #93, "Majorities of Public Believe that Torture, 'Rendition,' and the Use of Secret Prison Camps Outside U.S. Are Sometimes Justified," Harris Interactive, December 21, 2005, available at http://www.harrisinteractive.com/harris_poll/index.asp?PID=621; ABC News/Washington Post Poll, "Terror Suspect Treatment: Most Americans Oppose Torture Techniques," May 27, 2004, http://abcnews.go.com/sections/us/Polls/torture_poll_040527.html; and "Poll Results: Waterboarding Is Torture," *CNN.com* (November 6, 2007), http://www.cnn.com/2007/POLITICS/11/06/waterboard.poll/.

99. William Glaberson, "6 at Guantanamo Said to Face Trial in 9/11 Case," *New York Times*, February 9, 2008, A1; and "Tactic Called Torture," *New York Times*, February 9, 2008, A8.

100. Quoted in Martin Hodgson, "U.S. Censored for Waterboarding," *Guardian* (London), February 7, 2008.

101. Evan Wallach, "Drop by Drop: Forgetting the History of Water Torture in U.S. Courts," *Columbia Journal of Transnational Law* 45 (2007): 472, 477–494, 499, 502–504.

102. Christopher Kutz, "Torture, Necessity and Existential Politics," *California Law Review* 95 (2007): 235–236.

103. Ian Robbins, "We Have Ways . . . How Do Interrogators Bend People to Their Will?" *New Scientist*, November 20, 2004, 44.

104. Editorial, "Modern Barbarity: The Idea That Torture Can Be 'Clean' Needs Refuting," *New Scientist*, February 23, 2008, 3.

105. Katerina Ossenova, "Spain Judge Drops Extradition Request for UK Residents Released from Guantanamo," *Jurist*, March 6, 2008, http://jurist.law.pitt .edu/paperchase/2008/03/spain-judge-drops-extradition-request.php.

106. Caitlin Price, "White House Memos to CIA Approved Waterboarding: Washington Post," *Jurist*, October 15, 2008, http://jurist.law.pitt.edu/paper chase/2008/10/white-house-memos-to-cia-approved.php; and Joby Warrick, "CIA Tactics Endorsed in Secret Memos: Waterboarding Got White House Nod," *Washington Post*, October 15, 2008, A1.

107. Greenburg, Rosenberg, and Vogue, "Bush Aware of Advisers' Interrogation Talks."

108. Amy Goodman, "On Visit to France, Donald Rumsfeld Hit with Lawsuit for Ordering, Authorizing Torture," *Democracy Now*, October 26, 2007, http:// www.democracynow.org/2007/10/26/on_visit_to_france_donald_rumsfeld.

109. Jonathan H. Marks, "Interrogational Neuroimaging in Counterterrorism: A 'No-Brainer' or a Human Rights Hazard?" *American Journal of Law & Medicine* 33 (2007): 496.

110. Adam Zagorin and Michael Duffy, "Inside the Interrogation of Detainee 063," *Time*, June 12, 2005, 26.

111. Jan Crawford Greenburg, Howard L. Rosenberg, and Ariane de Vogue, "Sources: Top Bush Advisors Approved 'Enhanced Interrogation,'" *ABC News*, April 9, 2008, http://abcnews.go.com/TheLaw/LawPolitics/story?id=4583256 &page=1.

112. Greenburg, Rosenberg, and Vogue, "Bush Aware of Advisers' Interrogation Talks."

113. Ibid.

114. Ibid.

115. Stephen Gillers, "The Torture Memo," *Nation*, April 28, 2008, http://www .thenation.com/article/torture-memo; Scott Shane, "The Question of Liability Stirs Concern at the C.I.A.," *New York Times*, September 16, 2006, A12; and Jeffrey Smith, "Worried CIA Officers Buy Legal Insurance; Plans Fund Defense in Anti-Terror Cases," *Washington Post*, September 11, 2006, A1.

116. 18 U.S.C. § 2441 (2006).

117. Jack Balkin, "War Crimes Prosecutions in the U.S.? Dream On," *Balkinization*, April 9, 2008, http://balkin.blogspot.com/2008/04/war-crimes-prosecutions-in-us-dream-on.html; and Marty Lederman, "A Dissenting View on Prosecuting the Waterboarders," *Balkinization*, February 8, 2008, http://balkin.blogspot.com/2008/02/dissenting-view-on-prosecuting.html.

118. David Luban, "Liberalism, Torture, and the Ticking Bomb," in *Torture Debate in America*, ed. Karen J. Greenberg, 55.

119. Anthony Lewis, "The Terror President," *New York Review of Books* 55, May 1, 2008, 7.

120. *Rumsfeld v. Padilla*, 542 U.S. 426 (2004).

121. "Padilla Given Long Jail Sentence," *BBC News*, January 23, 2008, http://news.bbc.co.uk/2/hi/americas/7203276.stm; and "Padilla Guilty in U.S. Terror Trial," *BBC News*, August 16, 2007, http://news.bbc.co.uk/2/hi/americas/6950333.stm.

122. "Padilla Given Long Jail Sentence."

123. David Rose, "How MI5 Colluded in My Torture: Binyam Mohamed Claims British Agents Fed Moroccan Torturer Their Questions—World Exclusive," *MailOnline*, March 8, 2009, http://www.dailymail.co.uk/news/article-1160238/How-MI5-colluded-torture-Binyam-Mohamed-claims-British-agents-fed-Moroccan-torturers-questions—WORLD-EXCLUSIVE.html.

124. Ibid.

125. The charges brought against Binyam Mohamed under the Military Commissions Act of 2006 are recounted in *R v. Sec'y of State for Foreign and Commonwealth Affairs*, [2008] EWHC 2048 (Admin); All ER (D) 123 (Q.B.D.) (21 Aug. 2008): ¶45.

126. "Saudi American Released to Riyadh," *BBC News*, October 11, 2004, http://news.bbc.co.uk/2/hi/americas/3733942.stm.

127. Marguilles, *Guantánamo and the Abuse of Presidential Power*, 68–69.

128. *Hamdi v. Rumsfeld*, 542 U.S. 507 (2004).

129. Ibid., 533.

130. Ibid., 536.

131. "Saudi-American Released to Riyadh."

132. Otterman, *American Torture*, 71.

133. Peter Finn, "Most Guantánamo Detainees Low-Level Fighters, Task Force Report Says," *Washington Post*, May 29, 2010, http://www.washingtonpost.com/wp-dyn/content/article/2010/05/28/AR2010052803873.html?wpisrc=nl_natlalert.

134. Ibid.

135. Global Security.org, "Guantanamo Bay Detainees," http://www.globalsecurity.org/military/facility/guantanamo-bay_detainees.htm.

136. Devin Montgomery, "UN Torture Investigator Calls on Countries to Accept Guantanamo Detainees," *Juris*, January 5, 2009, http://jurist.law.pitt.edu/paperchase/2009/01/un-torture-investigator-calls-on.php.

137. Alan W. Clarke and Laurelyn Whitt, "Problem without Borders: A Comment on Garrett's Judging Innocence," *Queen's Law Journal* 33 (2008): 619; and Brandon Garrett, "Judging Innocence," *Columbia Law Review* 108 (2008): 55.

138. *Rasul v. Bush*, 542 U.S. at 466 (2004).

139. 28 U.S.C. §§ 2241–2243 (2006).

140. U.S. Const. art. I, § 9, cl. 2. The Bill of Rights came into effect in 1791, two years after the Constitution was ratified in 1789. U.S. Constitution, amendments I–X.

141. *Marbury v. Madison*, 5 U.S. 87, 111 (1803); and *Sanchez-Llamas v. Johnson*, 548 U.S. 331, 354 (2006).

142. "Brief for Amnesty International et al. as Amici Curiae Supporting Petitioners," *Boumediene v. Bush*, 128 S. Ct. 2229 (2007) (Nos. 06–1195, 1196).

143. Caitlin Price, "Guantanamo Tribunal Ignored Evidence Clearing German-Born Detainee: WP," *Jurist*, December 6, 2007, http://jurist.law.pitt.edu/paperchase/2007/12/guantanamo-tribunal-ignored-evidence.php.

144. "Brief for Amnesty International," *Boumediene v. Bush*.

145. "President's Statement on Signing the Department of Defense, Emergency Supplemental Appropriations to Address Hurricanes in the Gulf of Mexico, and Pandemic Influenza Act, 2006," January 2, 2006, http://www.whitehouse.gov/news/releases/2005/12/20051230–8.html.

146. Professor Lederman is a regular commentator on Jack Balkin's Blog. "So Much for the President's Assent to the McCain Amendment," posting by Marty Lederman to *Balkinization*, http://balkin.blogspot.com/2006/01/so-much-for-presidents-assent-to.html.

147. *Hamdan v. Rumsfeld*, 548 U.S. 557 (2006).

148. Stephen A. Saltzburg, "A Different War: Ten Key Questions About the War on Terror," *George Washington Law Review* 75 (2007): 1026.

149. Clarke, "De-cloaking Torture," 59–134.

150. Marc Falkoff, "Politics at Guantanamo: The Former Chief Prosecutor Speaks," *Jurist*, November 2, 2007, http://jurist.law.pitt.edu/forumy/2007/11/politics-at-guantanamo-former-chief.php.

151. "Brief for Amnesty International," *Boumediene v. Bush*."

152. *Boumediene*, 128 S. Ct. at 2275.

153. Ibid., 2283.

154. Ibid., 2275.

155. *In re Guantanamo Detainee Cases*, 355 F. Supp. 2d 443 (D.D.C. 2005).

156. Sarah Miley, "DC Circuit Denies Guantanamo Detainee Habeas Petition," *Jurist*, June 8, 2010, http://jurist.org/paperchase/2010/06/dc-circuit-denies-guantanamo-detainee-habeas-petition.php.

157. Jaclyn Belczyk, "Federal Judge Orders Release of Russian Guantanamo Detainee," *Jurist*, May 14, 2010, http://jurist.org/paperchase/2010/05/federal-judge-orders-release-of-russian-guantanamo-detainee.php; and Peter Finn, "4 Cases Illustrate Guantanamo Quandaries: Administration Must Decide Fate of Often-Flawed Proceedings, Often Dangerous Prisoners," *Washington Post*, February 16, 2009, A1.

158. U.S. Constitution, art. VI, cl. 2.

159. *Marbury v. Madison*, 5 U.S. 137 (1803).

160. *Boumediene*, 128 S. Ct. 2235–36.

161. *Sanchez-Llamas v. Oregon*, 548 U.S. 331, 346–47 (2006).

162. *Boumediene*, 128 S. Ct. 2252.

163. *In re Guantanamo Detainee Cases*, 355 F. Supp. 2d. 465–66.

164. Jeffrey Toobin, "Swing Shift," *New Yorker* September 12, 2005, http://www.newyorker.com/archive/2005/09/12/050912fa_fact.

165. *Atkins v. Virginia*, 536 U.S. 304 (2003); and *Roper v. Simmons*, 543 U.S. 551, 576 (2005).

166. *Al Maqaleh v. Gates*, 604 F. Supp. 2d 205, 208 (D.D.C. 2009).

167. *Maqaleh v. Gates*, 605 F.3d 84 (2010); 2010 U.S. App. LEXIS 10384 (May 21, 2010).

168. Andrea Prasow, "Senior Counter-Terrorism Counsel at Human Rights Watch, the Bagram Detainee Review Boards, Better, but Still Falling Short," *Jurist*, June 1, 2010, http://jurist.org/forum/2010/06/bagram-detainee-review-boards-show-improvement-but-still-fall-short.php.

169. *Maqaleh v. Gates*, at 98.

170. Zach Zagger, "CIA Documents Reveal Possible Cover-Up of Interrogation Video," *Jurist*, April 16, 2010, http://jurist.law.pitt.edu/paperchase/2010/04/cia-documents-reveal-possible-cover-up.php; and Sarah Paulworth, "Federal Judge Tells CIA to Investigate Destruction of Interrogation Tapes," *Jurist*, January 18, 2011, http://jurist.org/paperchase/2011/01/federal-judge-tells-cia-to-investigate-destruction-of-interrogation-tapes.php.

## CHAPTER 3    FROM EICHMANN AND CARLOS "THE JACKAL" TO REAGAN AND CLINTON

1. Amnesty International, "USA: CIA 'Waterboarding': Admission of a Crime, Now There Must Be a Criminal Investigation," February 6, 2008, http://www.amnesty.org/en/library/info/AMR51/011/2008.

2. "The U.S. Government Is Not Jack Bauer," *Brattleboro Reformer*, June 27, 2007, Editorials.

3. Issac A. Linnartz, "The Siren Song of Interrogational Torture: Evaluating the U.S. Implementation of the UN Convention against Torture," *Duke Law Journal* 57 (2008): 1493.

4. Alfred W. McCoy, *A Question of Torture: CIA Interrogation from the Cold War to the War on Terror* (New York: Henry Holt, 2006); and Paul Krugman, "Reclaiming America's Soul," *New York Times*, April 24, 2009, 27.

5. Convention against Torture and Other Cruel, Inhuman or Degrading Treatment or Punishment, Dec. 10, 1984, 39 U.N. GAOR, Supp. No 51, at 197, 1465 U.N.T.S. 243, Art. 3, section 1 [hereinafter CAT] (prohibiting torture and cruel, inhuman and degrading treatment). The United States signed this treaty on April 18, 1988, and ratified it on October 21, 1994. Senate advice and consent was subject to numerous reservations, declarations, and understandings, including the declaration that CAT not be self-executing. 136 Cong. Rec. S 17486 (daily ed. October 27, 1990).

6. 999 U.N.T.S. 171 (Dec. 16, 1966); U.S. signed 5 October 1977, ratified June 8, 1992. United Nations Treaty Collection: Status of Treaties, 137, http://www2.ohchr.org/english/law/ccpr.htm.

7. Human Rights Committee, International Covenant on Civil and Political Rights [ICCPR], General Comment No. 31 [80] Nature of the General Legal Obligation Imposed on States Parties to the Covenant, P 12, U.N. Doc. CCPR/C/21/Rev.1/Add. 13 (March 29, 2004).

8. Jordan Paust, "Post-9/11 Overreaction and Fallacies Regarding War and Defense, Guantánamo, the Status of Person, Treatment, Judicial Review of Detention, and Due Process in Military Commissions," *Notre Dame Law Review* 79 (2004): 1340–1343.

9. Article 3 (Common Article 3) to the1949 Geneva Conventions prohibits torture as well as "outrages upon personal dignity . . . humiliating and degrading treatment."

10. Leila Nadya Sadat, "Ghost Prisoners and Black Sites: Extraordinary Rendition under International Law," *Case Western Reserve Journal of International Law* 37 (2006): 320.

11. Ingrid Detter Frankopan, "Extraordinary Rendition and the Law of War," *North Carolina Journal of International Law, Commerce & Regulation* 33 (2008): 670–671, 689.

12. *Filartiga v. Pena Irala*, 630 F.2d 876, 890 (2d Cir. 1980); *Siderman de Blake v. Republic of Argentina*, 965 F.2d 699, 717 (2d Cir. 1992) (official torture violates *jus cogens*); and *In Re Agent Orange Product Liability Litigation*, 373 F.Supp.2d 7, 110 (E.D.N.Y. 2005).

13. George J. Annas, "The Statue of Security: Human Rights and Post-9/11 Epidemics," *Journal of Health Law* 38, no. 2 (2005): 319n111 and surrounding text.

14. *Filartiga v. Pena Irala*, 863.

15. Sadat, "Ghost Prisoners and Black Sites," 320; Ingrid Detter, "The Law of War and Illegal Combatants," *George Washington Law Review* 75 (2007): 1055–1056; *Prosecutor v. Furundzija*, [1998] No. IT-95-17/1-T; *R (on the application of Mohamed) v. Sec'y of State for Foreign and Commonwealth Affairs*, [2008] EWHC 2048 (Admin); *R. v. Bow Street Metro. Stipendiary Mag., ex parte Pinochet Ugarte* (No. 3) [1999] 1 A.C. 147; *A v. Sec'y of State for the Home Dep't* [2005] UKHL 71, 2006 2 A.C. 221; and *Jones v. Ministry of Interior of the Kingdom of Saudi Arabia* [2006] UKHL 26, 2001 1 A.C. 270.

16. Leila Nadya Sadat, "Extraordinary Rendition, Torture, and Other Nightmares from the War on Terror," *George Washington Law Review* 75 (2007): 1212; and *R. v. Bow Street Metro.*

17. Robert Gammon, "The Torture Professor: Why UC Berkeley Should Fire John Yoo, the Legal Scholar Whose Work Led to Abu Ghraib and Secret Spying on Americans," *East Bay Express* (California) May 14, 2008, citing Columbia University law professor Scott Horton and other unnamed legal scholars.

18. Slavery Convention, September 25, 1926; Supplementary Convention on the Abolition of Slavery, the Slave Trade, and Institutions and Practices Similar to Slavery, April 30, 1956, 18 UST 3201, 266 UNTS 3; ICCPR, December 16, 1966, 999 UNTS 171, Arts. 8, 9, 11, 14; European Convention for the Protection of Human Rights and Fundamental Freedoms, opened for signature November 4, 1950, 213 UNTS 221 Arts. 4, 5, 6, 7; American Convention on Human Rights, November 22, 1969, 1144 UNTS 123, Arts, 6, 7, 8, 9; Genocide Convention of 1948, 78 U.N.T.S. 277 (1948); *Kadic v. Karadzic*, 70 F.3d 232 (2d Cir. 1995); and G.A. Res. 96(I), 1 U.N. GAOR, U.N. Doc. A/64/Add.1, at 188–89 (1946).

19. Alan Clarke, "Creating a Torture Culture," *Suffolk Transnational Law Review* 32 (2008): 1; and Alan Clarke, "De-cloaking Torture: *Boumediene* and the Military Commissions Act," *San Diego International Law Journal* 11 (2009): 59.

20. U.N. CAT/USA/CO/Add. 1 (November 6, 2007).

21. Sadat, "Extraordinary Rendition," 1200n106 and surrounding text.

22. One of the reviewers for this book, Roger S. Clark, made this observation in summarizing this argument.

23. John A. Radsan, "A More Regular Process for Irregular Rendition," *Seton Hall Law Review* 37 (2006): 17 (citations omitted).

24. Margaret L. Satterthwaite, "The Story of *El-Masri v. Tenet*: Human Rights and Humanitarian Law in the 'War on Terror,'" *New York University Public Law and Legal Theory Working Papers*, 538, 542, http://lsr.nellco.org/nyu/plltwp/papers/109/.

25. Matthew Lippman, "Genocide: The Trial of Adolf Eichmann and the Quest for Global Justice," *Buffalo Human Rights Law Review* 8 (2002): 56.

26. *Encyclopaedia Britannica, MICROPAEDIA, Ready Reference* vol. 4 (Chicago: Encyclopaedia Britannica, 2002): 396; Doran Geller, "The Capture of Adolf

Eichman," *Jewish Virtual Library*, http://www.jewishvirtuallibrary.org/jsource/
Holocaust/eichcap.html; and Shlomo J. Shiro, introduction to *The House on
Garibaldi Street* by Isser Harel (1975; repr., Abington: Frank Cass, 1997).

27. "Adolf Eichmann," *Encyclopedia of World Biography*, 2nd ed., 17 vols. (Gale
Research, 1998). Reproduced in *Biography Resource Center* (Farmington Hills,
Mich.: Gale, 2010). http://library.lethbridgecollege.ab.ca:2070/servlet/BioRC
(access to this library resource is restricted to subscribers).

28. "Adolf Eichmann." *People of the Holocaust* (U*X*L, 1998). Reproduced in *Biography Resource Center* (Farmington Hills, Mich.: Gale, 2010), http://library
.lethbridgecollege.ab.ca:2070/servlet/BioRC.

29. Lippman, "Genocide," 53.

30. David Cesarani, "Adolf Eichman: The Mind of a War Criminal," *BBC History*, January 20, 2009, http://www.bbc.co.uk/history/worldwars/genocide/
eichmann_01.shtml#six.

31. United Nations Security Council Resolution 138, Adopted June 23, 1960,
available at http://www.un.org/documents/sc/res/1960/scres60.htm.

32. "Capture of Carlos: French Help for Islamic Junta's War Won Arrest of
Jackal," *Guardian* (London), August 17, 1994, 3; and Terry Davis, "Unlawful
Rendition," *Wall Street Journal*, June 27, 2006, A14.

33. Bill Akass, "I Was Drugged and Kidnapped Claims Carlos; Lawyer for Carlos
the Jackal Says 'There Was No Procedure of Extradition. It Was Kidnapping,'"
*Daily Record*, August 17, 1994, 2.

34. "Carlos the Jackal," *World of Criminal Justice*, 2 vols. (Gale Group, 2002).
Reproduced in *Biography Resource Center* (Farmington Hills, Mich.: Gale,
2010), http://library.lethbridgecollege.ab.ca:2070/servlet/BioRC; *Öcalan v.
Turkey* (ECHR 46221/99): ¶78; *Ilich Sánchez Ramirez v. France*, no. 28780/95,
Commission decision of June 24, 1996, DR 86-B, p. 155; and Sue Quinn,
"Jackal Arrest a Betrayal' Shadowy Deal, Kidnap Alleged by His Lawyer,"
*Advertiser*, August 17, 1994.

35. Paul Webster, "Pasqua Basks in Arrest of the Jackal," *Guardian* (London),
August 16, 1994, 2; and Bruce Wilson, "Jackal, High Priest of Terror," *Advertiser*, August 17, 1994.

36. "Carlos the Jackal," *World of Criminal Justice*.

37. Wilson, "Jackal, High Priest of Terror."

38. Webster, "Pasqua Basks in Arrest of the Jackal," 2.

39. "Carlos the Jackal Faces New Trial," *BBC News*, May 4, 2007, http://news.bbc
.co.uk/2/hi/europe/6623659.stm.

40. *Ilich Sánchez Ramirez v. France*, ¶155; *Öcalan v. Turkey*, ¶78; and Davis, "Unlawful Rendition."

41. *Ilich Sánchez Ramirez v. France*, ¶61.

42. Ibid., ¶162.

43. European Convention for the Protection of Human Rights. Art, 5, ¶ 1.

44. *Ilich Sánchez Ramirez v. France*, ¶160.

45. *Ramirez Sánchez v. France* (ECHR 59450/00, July 4, 2006), ¶71, and ¶62–64.

46. Glenn Kessler, "Rice Defends Tactics Used against Suspects; Europe Aware of Operations, She Implies," *Washington Post*, December 6, 2005, A01; Condoleezza Rice, U.S. Secretary of State, Remarks upon Her Departure for Europe (December 5, 2005), quoted in Louis Fisher, "Extraordinary Rendition: The Price of Secrecy," *American University Law Review* 57 (2008): 1426.

47. Davis, "Unlawful Rendition."

48. Fisher, "Extraordinary Rendition," 1426.

49. Ibid.

50. Alan W. Clarke and Laurelyn Whitt, *The Bitter Fruit of American Justice: International and Domestic Resistance to the Death Penalty* (Boston: Northeastern University Press, 2007), 53. The United States does, however, agree to have its reports (and thus its record) scrutinized by the UN Human Rights Committee and the Committee against Torture, and it gets a hard time before both.

51. Quoted in Matteo M. Winkler, "When 'Extraordinary' Means Illegal: International Law and European Reaction to the United States Rendition Program," *Loyola of Los Angeles International and Comparative Law Review* 30 (2008): 67.

52. Joan Fitzpatrick, "The Unreality of International Law in the United States and the LaGrand Case," *Yale Journal of International Law* 27 (2002): 428.

53. *Öcalan v. Turkey* (Öcalan II) App. No. 46221/99, 37 Eur. Ct. H.R. 10 (2003) (European Court of Human Rights March 12, 2003), available at http://cmiskp.echr.coe.int/tkp197/search.asp?skin=hudoc-en; and *Freda v. Italy*, App. No. 8916/80, 21 Eur. Comm'n H.R. 250 (1981).

54. *Klaus Altmann (Barbie) v. France*, App. No. 10689/83, 37 Eur. Comm'n H.R. 225, 233–234 (European Court of Human Rights, July 4, 1984), available at http://echr.coe.int/echr/en/hudoc.

55. "1983: 'Butcher of Lyon' Returns to Face Trial," *BBC News*, February 6, 1983, http://news.bbc.co.uk/onthisday/hi/dates/stories/february/6/newsid_4149000/4149443.stm.

56. "Klaus Barbie." *Encyclopedia of World Biography*, 2nd ed., 17 vols. (Gale Research, 1998). Reproduced in *Biography Resource Center* (Farmington Hills, Mich.: Gale, 2010). http://library.lethbridgecollege.ab.ca:2070/servlet/BioRC.

57. European Commission for Democracy through Law (Venice Commission), Draft Opinion on the International Obligations of Council of Europe Member States in Respect of Secret Detention Facilities and Inter-State Transport of Detainees, Opinion no. 363/2005, Strasbourg, March 8, 2006, ¶120, http://www.venice.coe.int/docs/2006/CDL-DI(2006)001-e.asp.

58. UN Security Council Resolution 138.

59. Winkler, "When 'Extraordinary' Means Illegal," 55.

60. A. Barton Hinkle, "Suddenly, Fascism Doesn't Look So Bad After All," Editorial, *Richmond Times Dispatch*, February 17, 2009, A11; Marc A. Thiessen, "Tough Questions for Panetta; His Answers Will Shape CIA's War on Terror," *USA Today*, January 28, 2009, A11; Nat Hentoff, "War Crimes," *Village Voice*, February 15, 2005, 26; Dana Priest and Barton Gelman, "U.S. Decries Abuse but Defends Interrogations; 'Stress and Duress' Tactics Used on Terrorism Suspects Held in Secret Overseas Facilities," *Washington Post*, December 26, 2002, A1.

61. Ingrid Detter Frankopan finds rendition's roots tracing to the fugitive slave laws, "Extraordinary Rendition and the Law of War," 658, citing U.S. Const. art. IV, § 2, cl. 3, repealed by U.S. Const. amend. XIII.

62. Many state constitutions received British common law; however, outside of specific provisions, such as habeas corpus, it was not generally received into the federal constitution. Ernest A. Young, "Historical Practice and the Contemporary Debate Over Customary International Law," *Columbia Law Review Sidebar* 109 (2009): 33.

63. Sir William Holdsworth, *A History of English Law*, vol. 5 (London: Ethuen & Co. Ltd., Sweet and Maxwell, reprinted 1966), 50.

64. Arraignment, Judgment, and Execution of John Story, for Treason: State Trials, 14 Eliz. A.D. 1571 in *Howell's State Trials* (1809): 1087–1095, 1090.

65. Thomas A. Walker, *A History of the Law of Nations.* (Cambridge: Cambridge University Press, 1899; Elibron Classics Replica Edition, 2006), 159n1.

66. "Arraignment, Judgment, and Execution of John Story," 1090.

67. Holdsworth, *History of English Law*, 5:50; and Gregory Townsend, "State Responsibility for Acts of De Facto Agents," *Arizona Journal of International and Comparative Law* 14 (1997): 664–665.

68. Holdsworth, *History of English Law*, 5:49–60.

69. Walker, *History of the Law of Nations*, 159n1; see also Holdsworth, *History of English Law*, 5:50.

70. Holdsworth, *History of English Law*, 5:50.

71. Townsend, "State Responsibility," 635; and *Ker v. Illinois*, 119 U.S. 436 (1886).

72. Joseph Miller, "Extending Extraterritorial Abduction beyond Its Limit: *United States v. Alvarez Machain*," *Pace International Law Review* 6 (1994): 221n18 and surrounding text.

73. Townsend, "State Responsibility," 438.

74. *Ker v. Illinois*, 119 U.S. 444, 442 (1886).

75. *Frisbie v. Collins*, 342 US 519, 522–523 (1952).

76. The Hostage Taking Act, 18 U.S.C. 1203 (1984); The Destruction of Aircraft Act, 18 U.S.C. 32 (1984); Act to Combat International Terrorism, 18 U.S.C.

3071 (1984); FBI, Headline Archives, "A Byte out of History: The Case of the Yachted Terrorist," September 15, 2004, http://www.fbi.gov/news/stories/2004/september/yachted_091504.

77. 107 Cong. Rec. S11186 (daily ed. Oct. 30, 2001) (statement of Sen. Specter), http://www.gpo.gov/fdsys/pkg/CREC-2001–10–30/pdf/CREC-2001–10–30-pt1-PgS11185–2.pdf#page=2.

78. Jane Mayer, *The Dark Side* (New York: Doubleday, 2008), excerpt on Fresh Air, National Public Radio, September 18, 2008, http://www.npr.org/templates/story/story.php?storyId=94754692; and Satterthwaite, "Story of *El-Masri v. Tenet*," 538.

79. Elaine Sciolino, "Friend Led Terror Suspect to F.B.I., Lawyer Says," *New York Times*, September 19, 1987, http://www.nytimes.co1987/09/19/world/friend-led-terror-suspect-to-fbi-lawyer-says.html; and *United States v. Yunis*, 924 F.2d 1086, 1089 (D.C. Cir. 1991).

80. Ed Bruske, "Testimony Casts Defendant as Leader of Hijackers," *Washington Post*, February, 28, 1989, A17; Tracy Thompson, "Hijacker Gets 30-Year Term; Case Was First to Involve Air Piracy Overseas," *Washington Post*, October 5, 1989, A39; and *United States v. Yunis*, 924 F.2d 1086 (1991).

81. *United States v. Yunis*, 924 F.2d 1086, 1092 (1991).

82. Ibid., 1089–1092.

83. Convention for the Suppression of Unlawful Seizure of Aircraft, Dec. 16, 1970, art. 4, para. 2, Dec. 16, 1970, 22 UST. 1643, 1645, T.I.A.S. No. 7192. See H. Rep. No. 885, 93d Cong., 2d Sess. 10 (1974), reprinted in 1974 *U.S. Code Congressional & Administrative News* 3975, 3978; and S. Rep. No. 13, 93d Cong., 1st Sess. 1, 3 (1973).

84. 49 U.S.C. 1472; and *United States v. Yunis*, 924 F.2d 1086, 1092 (1991).

85. Sciolino, "Friend Led Terror Suspect"; and Sam Seibert and Richard Sandza, "A Sting on the Mediterranean," *Newsweek*, September 28, 1987, 36.

86. Thompson, "Hijacker Gets 30-Year Prison Term."

87. Seibert and Sandza, "Sting on the Mediterranean," 36.

88. 18 U.S.C. 1203 (1984); and *United States v. Yunis*, 924 F.2d 1086, 1091 (1991).

89. *Murray v. Schooner Charming Betsy*, 6 U.S. (2 Cranch) 64 (1804).

90. FBI, "A Byte out of History"; and Thompson, "Hijacker Gets 30-Year Prison Term."

91. *United States v. Noriega*, 746 F. Supp. 1506, 1529, 1534 (S.D.Fla. 1990), aff'd 117 F.3d 1206 (11th Cir. 1997).

92. Ibid.

93. Geoffrey Robertson, "The Case of General Pinochet," in *The Phenomenon of Torture*, ed. William F. Schultz (Philadelphia: University of Pennsylvania Press, 2007), 318–319; *R. v. Bow Street Metro. Stipendiary Mag., ex parte Pinochet Ugarte* (No. 3) [1999] 1 A.C. 147.

94. *United States v. Noriega*, 117 F.3d 1206, 1212 (11th Cir. 1997).

95. David Nachman, Human Rights Watch, "Human Rights in Post-Invasion Panama: Justice Delayed Is Justice Denied," April 7, 1991, http://www.hrw.org/legacy/reports/1991/panama/.

96. *United States v. Alvarez-Machain*, 504 US 655 (1992).

97. Ibid., 657.

98. *United States v. Caro-Quintero*, 745 F. Supp. 599, 608–10 (1990), aff'd 946 F.2d 1466 (9th Cir, 1991), rev'd sub nom. Alvarez Machain, 504 US 655 (1992).

99. *United States v. Alvarez-Machain*, 504 US 655, 659 (1992).

100. Donald E. Schulz, "Between a Rock and a Hard Place: The United States, Mexico, and the Agony of National Security," *Security Studies Institute, U.S. Army War College*, June 24, 1997, 13, http://www.strategicstudiesinstitute.army.mil/pdffiles/pub37.pdf.

101. Robert Labardini, "Life Imprisonment and Extradition: Historical Development, International Context, and the Current Situation in Mexico and the United States," *Southwest Journal of Law & Trade in the Americas* 11 (2005): 9 (citation omitted).

102. *United States v. Alvarez-Machain*, 504 US 669–670.

103. Ibid., 682.

104. *Sosa v. Alvarez-Machain*, 542 US 692, 698 (2004).

105. Michael J. Glennon, "How International Rules Die," *Georgetown Law Journal* 93 (2005): 961; and Jonathon A. Gluck, "The Customary International Law of State-Sponsored International Abduction and the United States," *Duke Law Journal* 44 (1994): 613.

106. Clarke and Whitt, *Bitter Fruit*, 38.

107. Alan W. Clarke and Laurelyn Whitt, "Problem without Borders: A Comment on Garrett's Judging Innocence," *Queen's Law Journal* 33 (2008): 619.

108. Ibid.

109. Clarke and Whitt, *Bitter Fruit*, 38–39.

110. *R. v. Horseferry Road Magistrates' Court ex parte Bennett* [1994] 1 A.C. 42 ¶ 67F-H.

111. Chris McGreal, "America Accused of Riding Roughshod in Drug Case," *Independent* (London), April 29, 1990, 11; Neil A. Lewis, "U.S. Tries to Quiet Storm Abroad over High Court's Right-to-Kidnap Ruling," *New York Times*, June 17, 1992, A8; Clarke and Whitt, *Bitter Fruit*, 38; and Labardini, "Life Imprisonment and Extradition," 13, 15, 14.

112. European Commission for Democracy through Law, Opinion on the International Legal Obligations of Europe Member States in Respect of Secret Detention Facilities and Inter-State Transport of Prisoners, adopted by the Venice Commission at its 66th Plenary Session (Venice March 17–18, 2006), http://www.venice.coe.int/docs/2006/CDL-A.D.(2006)009-e.asp.

113. Daniel Benjamin, "5 Myths about Rendition (and that New Movie)," *Washington Post*, October 21, 2007, B3.

114. U.S. Department of Justice, *United States Attorney's Manual*, § 15.610, http://www.justice.gov/usao/eousa/foia_reading_room/usam/title9/15mcrm.htm#9–15.610.

115. Hostage Taking Act, 18 U.S.C. 1203 (1984); Destruction of Aircraft Act, 18 U.S.C. 32 (1984); Act to Combat International Terrorism, 18 U.S.C. 3071 (1984); and William J. Clinton, "Memorandum for the Vice President," and others, June 21, 1995, http://www.fas.org/irp/offdocs/pdd39.htm.

116. Jane Mayer, "Outsourcing Torture: The Secret History of America's 'Extraordinary Rendition' Program," *New Yorker*, February 14, 2005, 106.

117. Margaret L. Satterthwaite, "The Story of *El-Masri v. Tenet*: Human Rights and Humanitarian Law in the 'War on Terror,'" *New York University Public Law and Legal Theory Working Papers*, Paper 109 (2008), 536, 538; http://lsr.nellco.org/nyu/plltwp/papers/109/.

118. *United States v. Yousef, et. al.*, 327 F.3d 56, 79, 82 (2003).

119. Satterthwaite, "Story of *El-Masri v. Tenet*," 538.

120. *United States v. Yousef*, 327 F.3d 56, 82 (2003).

121. Ibid., 93.

122. Benjamin, "5 Myths about Rendition."

123. Ibid.

124. Quoted in Mayer, "Outsourcing Torture," 106.

125. Ibid.

126. U.S. Dept. of State, 2006 Country Reports on Human Rights—Egypt, March 6, 2007, http://www.state.gov/g/drl/rls/hrrpt/2006/78851.htm.

127. Human Rights Watch, "Egypt's Torture Epidemic: A Human Rights Watch Briefing Paper," February 2004, http://www.hrw.org/legacy/english/docs/2004/02/25/egypt7658.htm.

128. Amy Zalman, "Egypt Human Rights Violations: History of Torture in Egypt," August 28, 2009, http://terrorism.about.com/od/humanrights/a/EgyptTorture.htm.

129. Mayer, "Outsourcing Torture," 106, quotes Michael Scheuer that the Clinton administration required assurances that the person rendered would not be tortured. However, Michael Scheuer has also been quoted as saying that "before 9/11 we never asked for some guarantee that prisoners would not be tortured or coerced." Jack Wood, "How the United States Kidnaps and Tortures People," *Nye-Gateway to Nevada's Rurals*, March 5, 2009.

130. Peter Popham and Jerome Taylor, "The War on Terror: Inside the Dark World of Rendition," *Independent*, June 8, 2007, www.independent.co.uk/news/world/politics/the-war-on-terror-inside-the-dark-world-ofrendition—452261.html.

See also Human Rights Watch, *Black Hole*, §VI (May 9, 2005), http://www.hrw
.org/en/node/11757/section/6.

131. Mayer, "Outsourcing Torture," 106.

132. Henry Porter, "Into Harm's Way: By 'Rendering' Suspects to Torturers,
America Sinks to the Moral Level of Saddam," *Observer*, December 11, 2005,
www.guardian.co.uk/world/2005/dec/11/usa/print; and Satterthwaite, "Story
of *El-Masri v. Tenet*," 542.

133. Human Rights Watch, "Egypt's Torture Epidemic," 7.

134. Priest and Gellman, "U.S. Decries Abuse."

135. Some estimates run into the thousands: Satterthwaite, "Story of *El-Masri v.
Tenet*," 544n39; Alan Brinkley, Book Review, "Black Sites," *New York Times*,
August 3, 2008; Stephen Grey, *Ghost Plane* (New York: St. Martin's Grifffin,
2007), cover. Jane Mayer puts the number at hundreds of renditions "to
countries where torture is routine." Interview with Jane Mayer by Terry
Gross, on Fresh Air, October 24, 2008, National Public Radio broadcast.

136. Press Release, September 22, 2008, "Handing over Detainees by UK Forces
May Be Unlawful." Legal Opinion Prepared for The All Party Parliamentary
Group on Extraordinary Rendition ("APPG"), by Michael Fordham, Q.C., Tom
Hickman, barristers at Blackstone Chambers specializing in human rights
law, on instruction from solicitors Michael Davison, and Emma Colquhan,
at the law firm Lovells LLP, paragraph 11. http://www.extraordinaryrendition.
org/component/docman/doc_download/152-legal-opinion-publication.html.

## CHAPTER 4   SIGNIFICANT U.S. RENDITIONS TO TORTURE

1. "President Bush: Job Ratings," PollingReport.com, http://www.polling
report.com/BushJob1.htm. George W. Bush's approval rating soared to 88
percent by mid-November 2001, just two months after the attacks of September 11, 2001. Peter Grier, "The New Normal," *Christian Science Monitor*
October 11, 2001, 1.

2. George W. Bush, State of the Union Address, January 30, 2002, http://news
bbc.co.uk/2/hi/americas/1790537.stm.

3. John Barry, Michael Isikoff, and Michael Hirsh, "The Roots of Torture," *Newsweek*, May 24, 2004, 26, 30.

4. David Luban coined the term "torture culture" and argues that administration lawyers sought to "construct a judicially-endorsed practice of permis-
sible torture." Luban, "Liberalism, Torture, and the Ticking Bomb," *Virginia
Law Review* 91 (2005): 1425.

5. Margaret L. Satterthwaite, "The Story of *El-Masri v. Tenet*: Human Rights and
Humanitarian Law in the 'War on Terror,'" in *New York University Public Law
and Legal Theory Working Papers* (2008): 544, http://lsr.nellco.org/nyu/plltwp/
papers/109/.

6. Jane Mayer, *The Dark Side: The Inside Story of How the War on Terror Turned Into a War on American Ideals* (New York: Doubleday, 2008); Stephen Grey, *Ghost Plane: The True Story of the CIA Rendition and Torture Program* (New York, St. Martin's Press, 2007); Trevor Paglen and A. C. Thompson, *Torture Taxi: On the Trail of the CIA's Rendition Flights* (Hoboken, N.J.: Melville House Publishing, 2006); Rachael Meeropol, ed., *America's Disappeared* (New York, Seven Stories Press, 2005); Dana Priest and Barton Gelman, "U.S. Decries Abuse but Defends Interrogations; 'Stress and Duress' Tactics Used on Terrorism Suspects Held in Secret Overseas Facilities," *Washington Post*, December 26, 2002, A1; DeNeen L. Brown and Dana Priest, "Canadian's Case Called Typical of CIA," *Washington Post*, November 5, 2003, A1; Dana Priest, "Italy Knew about Plan to Grab Suspect; CIA Officials Cite Briefing in 2003," *Washington Post*, June 20, 2005, A1; Dana Priest, "Help from France Key in Covert Operations; Paris's 'Alliance Base" Targets Terrorists," *Washington Post*, July 3, 2005, A1; and Jane Mayer, "The CIA's Travel Agent: The Boeing Subsidiary That Helps with Extraordinary Renditions," *New Yorker*, October 30, 2006, 34.

7. Felix S. Cohen, "Transcendental Nonsense and the Functional Approach," *Columbia Law Review* 35 (1935): 814.

8. Tom Engelhardt, "Tomgram: How Bush Took Us to the Dark Side," *Atlantic Free Press*, January 3, 2008, http://www.atlanticfreepress.com/news/1/3175-tomgram-how-bush-took-us-to-the-dark-side.html; Craig Whitlock, "Jordan's Spy Agency: Holding Cell for the CIA: Foreign Terror Suspects Tell of Torture," *Washington Post*, December 1, 2007, A1; and Daniel McGrory, "U.S. Torture Jets 'Were Refueled in Britain,'" *Times* (London), December 16, 2005.

9. Amnesty International, "United States of America the Threat of a Bad Example: Undermining International Standards as 'War on Terror' Detentions Continue," August 18, 2003, 30–31, http://www.amnesty.org/en/library/info/AMR51/114/2003.

10. The first press reports of Mohammed's (also sometimes spelled Mohammad) abduction, transfer to U.S. agents, and rendition apparently appeared in a Karachi paper, *The News International*, October 26, 2001, in "Mystery Man Handed Over to U.S. Troops in Karachi," cited in Grey, *Ghost Plane*, 110. This news was repeated the next day in an article in the *Washington Post*; Rajiv Chandresekaran, "Pakistan Questioning Two Nuclear Scientists," *Washington Post*, October 27, 2001, A20.

11. Declaration on the Protection of All Persons from Enforced Disappearance, GA Resolution 47/133 of December 18, 1992; International Convention for the Protection of All Persons from Enforced Disappearance, entered into force Dec. 23, 2010 (not ratified by United States); Art. 7, Rome Statute of the International Criminal Court, U.N. Doc. A/Conf.183/9*; InterAmerican Convention on Forced Disappearance of Persons, entry into force March 3, 1996 (not ratified by United States). Also see generally, International Covenant

on Civil and Political Rights, G.A. Res. 2200A (XXI), 21 U.N. GAOR Supp. (No 16) at 52, U.N.Doc. A/6316 (1966), 999 U.N.T.S. 171 entered into force Mar. 23, 1976, articles 6(1), 7, 9, 14(1) and 16. The United States ratified the ICCPR in 1992.

12. Rajiv Chandrasekaran and Peter Finn, "U.S. Behind Secret Transfer of Terror Suspects," *Washington Post*, March 11, 2002, A1.

13. Grey, *Ghost Plane*, 111–112.

14. Ken Herman, "Bush Urges Americans to Return to Work as Nation Waits Market Reaction," *Cox News Service*, September 16, 2001.

15. Chandrasekaran and Finn, "U.S. Behind Secret Transfer."

16. *R (on the application of Mohamed) v. Secretary of State for Foreign and Commonwealth Affairs*, [2008] EWHC 2048 (Admin), All ER (D) 123 (Q.B.D.) (21 August 2008); and *Mohamed v. Jeppesen Dataplan, Inc.*, 539 F. Supp. 2d 1128 (N.D. Cal., 2008), reversed, 563 F3.d 992 (9th Cir. 2009) reversed, 563 F.3d 992, 1009 (9th Cir., April 28, 2009) reversed *en banc*, 2010 US App. LEXIS 18746 (9th Cir. 2010).

17. On Obama, see Dahlia Lithwick, "See No Evil," *Slate Magazine*, February 10, 2009, http://www.slate.com/id/2210915; and Brian Beutler, "Obama's State Secrets Mistake," *Guardian Unlimited*, February 13, 2009. On Brown, see Richard Norton Taylor, "Miliband Presses for Gag on CIA Memo: Disclosure Would Harm Security, Judges Told Binyam Mohamed Lawyers Query U.S. Letter of Support," *Guardian*, May 16, 2009, 12.

18. Eli Lake, "U.S. Hushes Britain on Gitmo Detainee; Justice Letter Filed in Court," *Washington Times*, May 12, 2009, A1; John F. Burns, "U.S. Again Warns Britain on Detainee Memo," *New York Times*, May 15, 2009, 10; Duncan Gardham and Alex Spillius, "Release 'Torture' Files and We Won't Share Secrets, Says U.S.; At Your Peril, Warns America," *Daily Telegraph*, May 14, 2009, 12; and Taylor, "Miliband Presses for Gag on CIA Memo."

19. Steve Swan, "Binyam Gives Details of Captivity," *BBC News*, March 13, 2009, http://news.bbc.co.uk/2/hi/uk_news/7941285.stm; and "Binyam Mohamed, "Key Quotes," *BBC News*, March 13, 2009, http://news.bbc.co.uk/2/hi/uk_news/7941745.stm.

20. Alan W. Clarke, "De-cloaking Torture: Boumediene and the Military Commissions Act," *San Diego International Law Journal* 11 (2009): 94–97.

21. "Military Commissions Act of 2006" (109 P.L. 366; 120 Stat. 2600 [October 17, 2006]), enacting Chapter 47A of title 10 United States Code (codified at 10 U.S.C. §§948a-950w and other sections of titles 10, 18, 28, and 42). These charges are summarized in *\*R (on the application of Mohamed) v. Secretary of State for Foreign and Commonwealth Affairs*, [2008] EWHC 2048 (Admin), All ER (D) 123 (21 August 2008) ¶47.

22. *R (on the application of Mohamed) v Secretary of State for Foreign and Commonwealth Affairs*, [2008] EWHC 2048 (Admin), [2008] All ER (D) 123, ¶24, ¶11–22, ¶26, ¶2; "No Repeat over CIA Flights Urged," *BBC News*, June 27, 2006, http://

news.bbc.co.uk/2/hi/europe/5119650.stm; "Profile: Binyam Mohamed," *BBC News*, February 23, 2009, http://news.bbc.co.uk/2/hi/uk_news/7906381.stm; and *Mohamed v. Jeppessen Dataplan Inc*, 563 F.3d 992. 998 (9th Cir. 2009).

23. *R (on the application of Mohamed) v Secretary of State for Foreign and Commonwealth Affairs*, [2008] EWHC 2048 (Admin), [2008] All ER (D) 123 (Aug) ¶31–32; and Jamil Dakwar and Eric Goldstein, "Morocco: Human Rights at a Crossroads," *Human Rights Watch*, October 20, 2004, http://www.hrw.org/en/node/11932/section/2.

24. Andrew O. Selsky, "Gitmo Inmate's Lawyer Urges U.S. on Photos," Associated Press, *USA Today*, December 10, 2007, http://www.usatoday.com/news/topstories/2007–12–10–3587204980_x.htm; and Vanessa Allen, "The Muslim 007 Who 'Proves MI5 Knew of Torture,'" *Daily Mail* (London) May 18, 2009, 28.

25. *R (on the application of Mohamed) v Secretary of State for Foreign and Commonwealth Affairs*, [2008] EWHC 2048 (Admin), [2008] All ER (D) 123.

26. Henry Chu, "Guantanamo Inmate Returns to Britain; Terror Charges against Binyam Mohamed, Held for Seven Years, Were Dropped in 2008. He Has Alleged Torture," *Los Angeles Times*, February 24, 2009, A3.

27. "Profile: Binyam Mohamed," *BBC News*, February 23, 2009, http://news.bbc.co.uk/2/hi/uk_news/7906381.stm; and *R (on the application of Mohamed) v Secretary of State for Foreign and Commonwealth Affairs*, [2008] EWHC 2048 (Admin), [2008] All ER (D) 123 (Aug), ¶2.

28. Selsky, "Gitmo Inmate's Lawyer."

29. Lucas Tanglen, "Guantanamo Ex-Detainee Claims Memos Show UK Involved in Alleged Torture," *Jurist*, March 8, 2009, http://jurist.law.pitt.edu/paperchase/2009/03/guantanamo-ex-detainee-claims-memos.php.

30. Richard Norton-Taylor, "Front: Fight to Stop U.S. Destroying Torture Images: British Resident Says Photographs Are Evidence of Abuse at Guantanamo," *Guardian* (London), July 6, 2009, 1.

31. *Mohamed v. Jeppesen Dataplan, Inc.*, 563 F.3d 992 (9th Cir. 2009), 997, 999 n.1.

32. *Mohamed, v. Jeppesen Dataplan, Inc.*,539 F.Supp. 2d 1136. 28 U.S.C. § 1350; *Mohammed v. Jeppesen Dataplan*, 539 F.2d 1128, 1129–30 (N.D. Cal. 1008), reversed on appeal, 563 F.3d 992 (9th Circuit 2009); reversed by the court *en banc*, 614 F.3d 1070 (9th Cir. September 8, 2010).

33. *R v. Sec'y of State for Foreign and Commonwealth Affairs*, [2008] EWHC 2048.

34. Duncan Gardham, "Britain Asks U.S. to Free Five from Guantanamo," *Daily Telegraph* (London), August 8, 2007.

36. The detainee who was scheduled for release, Shaker Aamer, was not released and remains imprisoned at Guantánamo Bay as of February 12, 2011. Megan McKee, "Rights Group Chides Prolonged Detention of UK Man in Guantanamo," *Jurist*, February 12, 2011, http://jurist.org/paperchase/2011/02/rights-group-chides-prolonged-detention-of-uk-man-in-guantanamo.php.

See also Mike Rosen-Molina, "Guantanamo Detainee Sues UK for Withhold-ing 'Torture' Evidence," *Jurist*, May 6, 2008, http://jurist.law.pitt.edu/paper chase/2008/05/guantanamo-detainee-sues-uk-for.php; and Robert Verkaik, "The Last Briton in Guantanamo Faces Death Penalty: After Being Held Pris-oner by the U.S. for Six Years, Inmate to Be Charged with Terrorism Offences Despite Protesting His Innocence," *Belfast Telegraph*, May 30, 2008.

37. Jon Manel, "U.S. 'Offered Binyam Plea Bargain,'" *BBC News*, March 24, 2009, http://news.bbc.co.uk/2/hi/uk_news/7960357.stm.

38. *R (on the application of Mohamed) v Secretary of State for Foreign and Common-wealth Affairs*, [2008] EWHC 2048 (Admin), [2008] All ER (D) 123 (Aug) ¶105.

39. *Manual for Military Commissions* (2007), http://www.defense.gov/news/ MANUAL%20FOR%20MILITARY%20COMMISSIONS%202007%20signed.pdf. Rule 505a, Military Commission Rules of Evidence, provides for the protec-tion of classified evidence and provides for ex parte and in camera proceed-ings. *R (on the application of Mohamed) v Secretary of State for Foreign and Commonwealth Affairs*, [2008] EWHC 2048 (Admin), [2008] All ER (D) 123 (Aug) at ¶147(x).

40. Manel, "U.S. 'Offered Binyam Plea Bargain.'"

41. *R (on the application of Mohamed) v Secretary of State for Foreign and Common-wealth Affairs*, [2008] EWHC 2048 (Admin), [2008] All ER (D) 123 (Aug) at ¶147(x).

42. Ibid., ¶ 147.

43. Ibid., ¶67.

44. Ibid., ¶147 (vii) and (x)(4)

45. Rule 505, Military Commission Rules of Evidence.

46. *R (on the application of Mohamed) v Sec'y of State for Foreign and Commonwealth Affairs*, [2008] EWHC 2048 (Admin), [2008]All ER (D) 123 (Aug), ¶47 (v).

47. *Canada (Justice) v. Khadr*, [2008] 2 S.C.R. 125 (Can.).

48. *Khadr v. Canada (Attorney General)*, [2008] F.C.J. No. 972, 20008 FC 807.

49. *Slahi v. Canada (Minister of Justice)* [2009] F.C.J. No. 141, 2009 FC 160, ¶8.

50. Paul Koring, "Khadr Hopes Jury Will Hear of Gang-Rape Threats; Interrogator Boasted of Threatening Detainees to Persuade Them to Confess," *Globe and Mail* (Canada), October 30, 2010, A23.

51. Jo Becker and Adam Liptak, "Sotomayor's Blunt Style Raises Issue of Temper-ment," *New York Times*, May 29, 2009, A14.

52. The majority in *Arar v. Ashcroft*, 532 F.3d 157 (2008) treated the matter as an immigration matter. Judge Sack dissented, saying, "This is not an immigra-tion case." Ibid., 126–127.

53. Judge Sack dissenting in *Arar v. Ashcroft*: "The defendants did not themselves torture Arar, they 'outsourced' it." 532 F.3d 157, 204–05 (2d Cir. 2008).

Representative Jerrold Nadler: "The administration, . . . was outsourcing torture." "Rendition to Torture: The Case of Maher Arar," Joint Hearing before
the Subcommittee. on International Organizations, Human Rights and Oversight of the House Committee on Foreign Affairs and the Subcommittee on
the Constitution, Civil Rights and Civil Liberties House Committee on the
Judiciary, 110th Cong. 58 (2007); and Jane Mayer, "Outsourcing Torture: The
Secret History of America's "Extraordinary Rendition" Program," *New Yorker*,
February 14, 2005.

54. Omar El Akkad and Colin Freeze, "Testimony Puts Arar, Khadr at al-Qaeda
Safehouse," *Globe and Mail*, January 20, 2009, A1. and *Arar v. Ashcroft*, 532
F.3d at 194 (Sack, J., dissenting).

55. Judge Saks, *Arar v. Ashcroft*, 532 F.3d at 194 (Sack, J., dissenting).

56. Lorne Waldman, "No One above the Law: Reflections of an Immigration
Lawyer on the Importance of the Rule of Law," *Saskatchewan Law Review* 72
(2009): 150.

57. Ronald-Frans Melchers, "The Maher Arar Case: Implications for Canada—
U.S. Law Enforcement Cooperation," *Journal of the Institute of Justice and International Studies* 6 (2006): 41.

58. Waldman, "No One above the Law," 150 (citing "Commission of Inquiry into
the Actions of Canadian Officials in Relation to Maher Arar, Report of the
Events Relating to Maher Arar: Factual Background," vol. 1 [Ottawa: Public
Works and Government Services, 2006], 53–54).

59. *Arar v. Ashcroft*, 414 F. Supp. 2d 250, 253, 254 (2006).

60. Tonda MacCharles, "9/11 Gaffe Is Old News, U.S. Security Czar Says; Ottawa,
Washington to Assess Border Risks," *Toronto Star*, May 28, 2009, A20; Jed
Borod, "Canada Protests U.S. Refusal to Remove Arar from Terror Watch
List," *International Enforcement Law Reporter* 23, no. 3 (March 2007); and
Kayleigh Shebs, "Arar Decries Alleged Linkage to Khadr Case," *Jurist*, Janu-
ary 30, 2009, http://jurist.law.pitt.edu/paperchase/2009/01/arar-decries-
alleged-linkage-to-khadr.php.

61. "Commission of Inquiry," vol. 1.

62. "Rendition to Torture," 110–118.

63. Ibid., 30–31, 50 (statement of Maher Arar).

64. Melchers, "Maher Arar Case," 41; and "Rendition to Torture," 49 (statement
of Maher Arar).

65. "Rendition to Torture," 49 (statement of Maher Arar).

66. Jules Lobel, "Extraordinary Rendition and the Constitution: The Case of
Maher Arar," *Review of Litigation* 28 (2008): 485.

67. *Arar v. Ashcroft*, 414 F.Supp. 250, 257 (E.D.N.Y. 2006); and Lobel, "Extraordinary Rendition and the Constitution," 485.

68. "Commission of Inquiry," 180; and Lee Carter, "Canada-Syria Case Papers Released," *BBC News*, August 10, 2007, http://news.bbc.co.uk/2/hi/americas/6939866.stm.

69. John R. Crook, "Second Circuit Panel Dismisses Canadian Citizen's Claims Involving Removal to Syria; Court to Rehear en Banc; U.S. Agencies Investigate Handling of the Case," *American Journal of International Law*102 (2008): 882; and "Commission of Inquiry," note 19.

70. Lobel, "Extraordinary Rendition and the Constitution," 488n244.

71. "Commission of Inquiry," 27–28.

72. Waldman, "No One above the Law," 151.

73. Melchers, "Maher Arar Case," 39–40.

74. Carter, "Canada-Syria Case Papers Released."

75. Franz Kafka, *The Trial*, trans. Willa and Edwin Muir (1937; repr., New York: Knopf, 1964), 286.

76. Alan W. Clarke and Laurelyn Whitt, "Problem without Borders: A Comment on Garrett's *Judging Innocence*," *Queen's Law Journal* 33 (2008): 619.

77. Alan W. Clarke and Laurelyn Whitt, *The Bitter Fruit of American Justice: International and Domestic Resistance to the Death Penalty* (Boston: Northeastern University Press, 2007), 120–121.

78. Samuel R. Gross, "The Risks of Death: Why Erroneous Convictions Are Common in Capital Cases," *Buffalo Law Review* 44 (1996): 499–500.

79. Scott Shane, "On Torture, 2 Messages and a High Political Cost," *New York Times*, October 30, 2007, A18.

80. Clarke and Whitt, "Problem without Borders," 632–633; Contrast *Hill v. Hamilton-Wentworth Reg'l Police Servs Bd*, [2007] 3 S. C.R. 129 (Can.) with *Harlow v. Fitzgerald*, 457 US 800, 818 (1982). R.S.C. 1985, c. I-11. See also J. Gomery, "The Pros and Cons of Commissions of Inquiry," *McGill Law Journal* 51 (2006): 783–798; Allan Manson and David Mullan, eds., *Commissions of Inquiry: Praise or Reappraise?* (Toronto: Irwin Law 2003). Contra, Edward L. Greenspan, "Inquiries Are Not Like Courts of Law," *Standard* (St. Catherines, Ontario) November 18, 2005, A6.

81. "Commission of Inquiry"; and Gloria Galloway, "Ottawa Settles with Arar; Harper to Unveil Compensation of at Least $10-million for Canadian Tortured in Syria," *Globe and Mail*, January 26, 2007, A1.

82. *Arar v. Ashcroft*, 585 F. 3d. 559 (2d. Cir. 2009) (state secrets privilege raised by government but issue not reached and decided on other grounds), certiorari denied, *Arar v. Ashcroft*, 130 St. Ct. 3409 (2010).

83. *El-Masri v. United States*, 479 F.3d. 296 (4th Cir. 2006), certiorari denied, *El-Masri v. United States* 128 S. Ct. 373; *Arar v. Ashcroft*, 585 F. 3d. 559 (2d. Cir. 2009); and *Mohamed v. Jeppesen Dataplan, Inc.*, 2010 US App. LEXIS 18746 (9th Cir. 2010).

84. *Certiorari denied*, 130 S.Ct. 3409 (June 14, 2010); *Arar v. Ashcroft*, Petition for Writ of Certiorari, Supreme Court of the United States, 2009 US Briefs 923; 2010 US S. Ct. Briefs LEXIS 1192; and Paul Koring, "Cannon Supports Arar's Request for US Appeal; Foreign Minister's Letter to Supreme Court Says Canadian's Suit Would Not Harm Canada-U.S. Relations," *Globe and Mail*, June 4, 2010, A16.

85. Dick Marty, Committee on Legal Affairs and Human Rights, "Alleged Secret Detentions and Unlawful Inter-State Transfers of Detainees Involving Coe Member States," Council of Europe Parliamentary Assembly, Doc. 10957, June 12, 2006, available at http://assembly.coe.int/Main.asp?link=/Documents/WorkingDocs/Doc06/EDOC10957.htm; and Dick Marty, Committee on Legal Affairs and Human Rights, "Secret Detentions and Illegal Transfers of Detainees Involving Council of Europe Member States: Second Report," Council of Europe Parliamentary Assembly, Doc. 11302 rev., June 11, 2007, http://assembly.coe.int/Documents/WorkingDocs/Doc07/edoc11302.pdf. [Hereinafter Marty Reports I and II].

86. David Johnston, "Rice Ordered Release of German Sent to Afghan Prison in Error," *New York Times*, April 23, 2005, A3.

87. Marty Report II, ¶ 271.

88. Johnston, "Rice Ordered Release of German."

89. Marty Report II, ¶271.

90. Marty Report II, ¶297; and Eric Mink, "CIA-Sponsored Kidnappings and Torture Undermine Anti-Terror Efforts," *St. Louis Post-Dispatch*, February 7, 2007, B9.

91. Bruce Zagaris, "Extradition and Alternatives: Germany Charges 12 CIA Operatives in el-Masri, Rendition Probe," *International Enforcement Law Reporter* (April 2007).

92. John Goetz, Marcel Rosenbach, and Holger Stark, "German CIA Arrest Warrants Strain Ties with U.S.," *BBC Monitoring Europe—Political*, June 27, 2007; and "Bid to Arrest CIA Rendition Team Splits German Cabinet," *Deutsche Press-Agentur* (July 7, 2007).

93. Craig Whitlock, "Germans Drop Bid for Extraditions in CIA Case; 13 Agency Operatives Charged in Kidnapping," *Washington Post*, September 24, 2007, A9.

94. Marty Report II, ¶290–292, 299; and Zagaris, "Extradition and Alternatives.

95. "Bid to Arrest CIA Rendition Team."

96. *El-Masri v. Tenet*, 479 F3d 296 (March 2, 2007).

97. Adam Goldman and Matt Apuzzo, "At CIA, Mistakes by Officers Are Often Overlooked," *Washington Post*, February 9, 2011.

98. Alan Clarke, "Creating a Torture Culture," *Suffolk Transnational Law* Review 1 (2008): 1; and "CIA Torture Tapes Destroyed after Watchdog Concluded Methods Illegal," *Public Record*, December 11, 2008.

99. Richard Owen, "CIA Agents Must Be Charged over "Kidnap and Torture," Says Judge," *Times* (UK), February 17, 2007, 3.

100. Andrew Gilmore, "Spain Judge Weighing Probe of U.S. Lawyers Who Promoted Guantanamo: Reports," *Jurist*, March 28, 2009, http://jurist.law.pitt.edu/paperchase/2009/03/spain-judge-weighing-probe-of-us.php; *El-Masri v. United States*, 479 F.3d. 296 (4th Cir. 2006); *Arar v. Ashcroft*, 585 F.3d. 559 (2d. Cir. 2009); and *Mohamed v. Jeppesen Dataplan, Inc.*, 2010 US App. LEXIS 18746 (9th Cir. 2010). Abu Omar filed a civil lawsuit in Italy against those agents allegedly involved in his rendition. Complaint of Sabrina De Sousa ¶41, *Sabrina de Sousa v. Department of State*, U.S. District Court for D.C., Case 1:09-cv-00896, May 14, 2009; and Clarke, "Creating a Torture Culture," 45.

101. Bruce Zagaris, "European Prosecutors, Legislators Seek Accountability for U.S.," *International Enforcement Law Reporter* 23, no. 41 (April 2007); *Sabrina de Sousa v. Department of State*, U.S. District Court for D.C., Case 1:09-cv-00896, May 14, 2009; Scott Shane, "Woman in Rendition Case Sues for Immunity," *New York Times*, May 13, 2009, http://www.nytimes.com/2009/05/14/us/14diplo.html?_r=1&ref=world; and "Former U.S. Government Employee Sues for Immunity in CIA Rendition Case," *International Enforcement Law Reporter* 25 (2009): 273.

102. Complaint of Sabrina de Sousa, ¶51, ¶ 59, ¶61; "First CIA Rendition Trial Opens," *BBC News*, June 8, 2007, http://news.bbc.co.uk/2/hi/europe/6732897.stm; and Poveldeo Elisabetta, "Judge Halts Italy Trial Testing U.S. Rendition," *International Herald Tribune*, June 19, 2007.

103. The CIA's mission primarily focuses on intelligence abroad; see Central Intelligence Agency, "CIA Vision, Mission and Values," https://www.cia.gov/about-cia/cia-vision-mission-values/index.html. The CIA's focus primarily on information about adversaries places many of its jobs abroad. Central Intelligence Agency, "Careers," https://www.cia.gov/careers/index.html. The CIA's "Professional Trainee Program's" minimum requirements include "a strong interest in international affairs." https://www.cia.gov/careers/jobs/view-all-jobs/professional-trainee-program.html.

104. "First CIA Rendition Trial Opens."

105. "'Impermissible' U.S. Interference in Intelligence Services," *BBC Summary of World Broadcasts*, February 17, 1979.

106. "First CIA Rendition Trial Opens"; Mohamad Bazzi, "The CIA's Italian Job," *Nation*, April 9, 2007, 22; "Italian Spies to Take Stand at CIA Kidnapping Trial," *Agence France Presse*, May 26, 2009; Gordon Corera, "CIA Renditions Strain Europe Goodwill," *BBC News*, March 20, 2006, http://news.bbc.co.uk/2/hi/europe/4822374.stm.

107. Grey, *Ghost Plane*, 212–213.

108. Corera, "CIA Renditions Strain Europe Goodwill."

109. Human Rights Watch, "U.S./Egypt: Bush Mubarak Summit Should Spotlight Torture, Rights Abuses," April 8, 2004, http://www.hrw.org/en/news/2004/04/08/

usegypt-bush-mubarak-summit-should-spotlight-torture-rights-abuses; and Bazzi, "CIA's Italian Job," 22.

110. Peter Jan Honigsbert, *Our Nation Unhinged: The Human Consequences of the War on Terror* (Berkeley: University of California, 2009), 190.

111. Rosa Anna Tremoglie points out that the case was weakened by the Constitutional Court's decision, and that the decision cannot be appealed: "Italian Court Rules in Favor of National Security," Human Events Online, March 19, 2009, http:///www.humanevents.com/article.php?id=31133.

112. "Italian Spies to Take Stand"; and Maria de Cristofaro and Sebastian Rotella, "Italian Judge Lets Trial of CIA Agents Proceed; A Defense Request to End the 'Rendition' Case Is Dismissed, But Some Evidence Is Barred," *Los Angeles Times*, May 21, 2009, A24.

113. "First CIA Rendition Trial Opens."

114. Rachel Donadio, "Judge Links Italy Agency to Abduction of a Cleric," *New York Times*, February 2, 2010, 10; John Hooper, "Italian Court Finds CIA Agents Guilty of Kidnapping Terrorism Suspect; World's First 'Extraordinary Rendition' Trial Ends: Twenty-three Americans Sentenced in Absentia," *Guardian*, November 5, 2009, 24; and Rachel Donadio, "Judge Assails Italian Intelligence Services; Officials Probably Knew About CIA Kidnapping of Cleric, He Contends," *International Herald Tribune*, February 2, 2010, 3.

115. Donadio, "Judge Assails Italian Intelligence Services," 3.

116. "CIA Men Jailed for Kidnap," *Daily Record*, November 5, 2009, 2.

117. Donadio, "Judge Assails Italian Intelligence Services," 3; Michael Isikoff, "A House Is Not a Home," *Newsweek,* November 16, 2009, 12; and Donadio, "Judge Links Italy Agency."

118. Editorial, "A National Disgrace," *New York Times*, November 11, 2009, http://www.nytimes.com/2009/11/11/opinion/11wed1.html.

119. Jeff Stein, "Inside Man," *Washingtonian*, April 2010, 62–65, 109–116.

120. Corera, "CIA Renditions Strain Europe Goodwill,"

121. Isikoff, "A House Is Not a Home," 12.

122.Corera, "CIA Renditions Strain Europe Goodwill."

123. Marty Report I and II.

124. Tom Lasseter, "The Accidental Incubator for Radical Islamists Al Qaeda and Taliban Leaders Managed to Exploit Guantanamo," *Star-Ledger* (Newark), June 17, 2008, 1.

## CHAPTER 5    STATE SECRETS PRIVILEGE TRUMPS JUSTICE

1. We deal only with civil suits seeking compensation or other remedies. For governmental secrecy issues related to releases from detention at Guantánamo Bay, see *In re Guantánamo Bay Detainee Litig.*, 577 F. Supp. 2d 143 (D.D.C.

2008). For pretrial detentions or the return of refugees in Canada, see Canadian Anti-Terrorism Act, C-36, Public Safety Act, C-17, Canadian Immigration and Refugee Protection Act (IRPA), or the U.K. Terrorism Act 2000. For a discussion of preventive detention practices of Canada, the United States, Britain, and Australia, see Craig Forcese, "Catch and Release: A Role for Preventive Detention without Charge in Canadian Anti-terrorism Law," *IRPP Study*, July 7, 2010, available at www.irpp.org.

2. *El-Masri v. United States*, 479 F.3d. 296 (4th Cir. 2006), certiorari denied, *El-Masri v. United States*, 128 S. Ct. 373; *Arar v. Ashcroft*, 585 F. 3d. 559 (2d. Cir. 2009) (state secrets privilege raised by government but issue not reached and decided on other grounds), certiorari denied, *Arar v. Ashcroft*, 130 St. Ct. 3409 (2010); and *Mohamed v. Jeppesen Dataplan, Inc.*, 614 F.3d 1070 (9th Cir. 2010).

3. *Mohamed v. Jeppesen Dataplan*, 614 F.3d 1070 (9th Cir. 2010).

4. Alan W. Clarke, "Rendition to Torture: A Critical Legal History," *Rutgers Law Review* 62 (2009): 38–51.

5. *Mohammed v. Obama*, 689 F. Supp. 2d 38, 68 (2009).

6. Ibid., 59.

7. Ibid.

8. Ibid., 63, 66, 79. Emphasis added.

9. Ibid., 64.

10. *R (on the application of Mohamed) v Secretary of State for Foreign and Commonwealth Affairs*, [2010] EWCA Civ 65; All ER (D) 118 (Feb) ¶ 55, 138.

11. "Blow to U.S. Prosecutors as Terror Case Witness Barred," *BBC News*, October 6, 2010, http://www.bbc.co.uk/news/world-us-canada-11481343.

12. *U.S. v. Ghailani*, 2011 U.S. Dist. LEXIS 5751 (SDNY January 21, 2011); "Ahmed Ghailani Jailed for Life over Bomb Conspiracy," *BBC News*, January 25, 2011, http://www.bbc.co.uk/news/world-us-canada-12279533.

13. *El-Masri v. United States*, 479 F.3d. 296 (4th Cir. 2006); *Arar v. Ashcroft*, 585 F. 3d. 559 (2d. Cir. 2009); and *Mohamed v. Jeppesen Dataplan, Inc.*, 614 F.3d 1070746 (9th Cir. 2010).

14. *Mohamed v Jeppesen Dataplan, Inc.*, 614 F3d dissent at 1095.

15. Clarke, "Rendition to Torture," 38–51; and *R (on the application of Mohamed) v Secretary of State for Foreign and Commonwealth Affairs*, [2010] EWCA Civ 65; All ER (D) 118 (Feb) ¶ 35.

16. 28 U.S.C. § 1350.

17. *Mohamed v. Jeppesen Dataplan*, 614 F.3d 1070 (9th Cir. September 8, 2010), dissent, n. 5

18. Ibid., majority opinion, 47.

19. Ibid., majority opinion, 48 (emphasis added).

20. Ibid., dissent, n. 4.

21. Ibid., majority opinion, 65.

22. *Federal Rules of Civil Procedure* § 54; 28 U.S.C. § 2412; and *American Jurisprudence 2d*, Vol. 5, Appellate Review § 858.

23. *Mohamed v. Jeppesen Dataplan*, 614 F.3d 1070 (9th Cir. September 8, 2010), majority opinion, 59–60.

24. Ibid., dissenting opinion, 92.

25. Ibid., dissenting opinion.

26. Quoted in Steven Aftergood, "Reducing Government Secrecy: Finding What Works," *Yale Law and Policy Review* 27 (2008–2009): 399n1.

27. Ibid., 415.

28. *Totten v. United States*, 92 U.S. 105 (1876); and *United States v. Reynolds*, 345 U.S. 1 (1953).

29. *Totten v. United States*, 92 U.S. 105 (1876); and *Weinberger v. Catholic Action of Hawaii/Peace Education Project*, 454 U.S. 139 (1981).

30. *Mohamed v. Jeppesen Dataplan*, 614 F.3d 1070 (9th Cir. September 8, 2010), majority opinion, 64, 17.

31. Steven D. Schwinn, "Ninth Circuit Dismisses Torture Claims Based on State Secrets Privilege," *Constitutional Law Prof Blog*, September 8, 2010, http://law-professors.typepad.com/conlaw/2010/09/ninth-circuit-dismisses-torture-claims-based-on-state-secret-privilege.html.

32. *El-Masri v. United States*, 479 F.3d. 296 (4th Cir. 2006).

33. *Mohamed v. Jeppesen Dataplan*, 614 F.3d 1070 (9th Cir., 2010), majority opinion, 1090.

34. Ibid., dissenting opinion, 1094 (citations omitted).

35. *Mohamed v. Jeppesen Dataplan*, 614 F.3d 1070 (9th Cir., September 8, 2010), majority opinion, n. 1.

36. "Shady Secrets," *New York Times*, September 30, 2010; see also *Arar v. Ashcroft*, 585 F.3d 559 (2d Circuit, 2009).

37. *Al Rawi and Ors v. Security Service and Ors*, [2010] NPC 51, [2010] EWCA Civ 482 (May 4, 2010).

38. *Al Rawi and Ors v. Security Service and Ors*, [2009] EWHC 2959 (QB).

39. *Al Rawi and Ors v. Security Service and Ors*, [2010] NPC 51, [2010] EWCA Civ 482 (04 May 2010), ¶ 27–29.

40. *Al Rawi and Ors v. Security Service and Ors*, [2009] EWHC 2959 (QB), ¶ 4.

41. Ibid.

42. *Al Rawi and Ors v. Security Service and Ors*, [2010] NPC 51, [2010] EWCA Civ 482 (May 4, 2010), ¶ 30.

43. Ibid., ¶ 37.

44. *R v. Sec'y of State for Foreign and Commonwealth Affairs*, [2008] EWHC 2048 (Admin).

45. *\*R (on the application of Mohamed) v Secretary of State for Foreign and Commonwealth Affairs*, [2010] EWCA Civ 65; All ER (D) 118 (Feb).

46. Frances Gibb, "They Say That They Were Tortured, Now Tell Us the Truth, Urges Watchdog," *Times* (London), February, 20, 2010, 6–7.

47. Quoted in Rebecca Omonira-Oyekanmi and Peter Finn, "Britain Settles with Detainees," *Washington Post*, November 17, 2010, A10.

48. Ibid.; and Richard Norton Taylor, "Guantanamo Bay: Law Must Change to Prevent Guantanamo Payments Happening Again, Says Clarke; All Intelligence Material to be Presented in Secret Government Determined to Avoid Repeat Scenario," *Guardian* (London), November 17, 2010, 5.

49. Jasminka Kalajdzic, "Access to Justice for the Wrongfully Accused in National Security Investigations," *Windsor Year Book Access to Justice* 27 (2009): 171–205.

50. Conclusions and Recommendations of the Committee against Torture: Canada, UN CAT, 34th Sess., UN Doc. CAT/c/CR/34/CAN (July 2005), at 2–3.

51. David Cole, quoted in Kalajdzic, "Access to Justice," 171–205.

52. Ibid.

53. Daniel J. Huyck, "Fade to Black: *El-Masri v. United States* Validated the Use of the State Secrets Privilege to Dismiss 'Extraordinary Rendition' Claims," *Minnesota Journal of International Law* 17 (2008): 435, 465.

54. Erin E. Langley, "The Loss of American Values in the Case of Erroneous Irregular Rendition," *Georgetown Law Journal* 98 (2010): 1463.

55. *R. v. Ahmad*, 2011 SCC 6.

56. *Abou-Elmaati v. Canada* (Attorney General), [2011] ONCA 95.

57. Ibid., at ¶ 6; see also, Kalajdzic, "Access to Justice," 171–205.

58. *R. v. Ahmad*, ¶ 24.

59. *El-Masri v. United States*, 479 F.3d. 296, 396 (4th Cir. 2006).

60. *R. v. Ahmad*, ¶ 2.

### CHAPTER 6    THE ILLEGALITY OF THE IRAQ WAR AND HOW RENDITION SPARKED IT

1. International Military Tribunal, "Trial of the Major War Criminals before the International Military Tribunal," vol. 1 (1947), 186, http://www.holocaust-history.org/works/imt/01/htm/t186.htm.

2. Michael Mandel, "What Right Do We Have to Be in Afghanistan in the First Place? Why the Prisoner Transfer Issue Cannot Be Detached from the Legality and Legitimacy of the War Itself," lecture given February 28, 2010, to the Special Forum on the Canadian Mission in Afghanistan, Osgoode Hall Law

School, 3, http://nathanson.osgoode.yorku.ca///wp-content/uploads/2010/09/Special-Forum-on-Detainees_Session-6_Mandel_edit-Feb-28–2010.pdf (hereafter, Mandel lecture).

3. Richard Clarke, *Against All Enemies* (New York: Free Press, 2004), 23–24.

4. Steve Weissman, "How Torture Worked to Sell the Iraq War," *truthout*, April 25, 2009, http://archive.truthout.org/042509A.

5. Mandel lecture, 4.

6. Quoted in Steve Holland, "Bush Considered Replacing Cheney as VP," *Washington Post*, November 3, 2010, A02.

7. Onder Bakircioglu, "The Right to Self-Defence in National and International Law: The Role of the Imminence Requirement," *Indiana International and Comparative Law Review* 19 (2009): 14, 48; see also Thomas M. Franck, "What Happens Now? The United Nations after Iraq," *American Journal of International Law* 97 (2003): 619–620.

8. David B. Rivkin Jr., Lee A. Casey, and Mark Wendell DeLaquil, "War, International Law, and Sovereignty: Reevaluating the Rules of the Game in a New Century," *Chicago Journal of International Law* 5 (2005): 496.

9. Dr. Hans Blix, Briefing of the Security Council, February 14, 2003, available at http://www.unmovic.org/.

10. Simon Tisdall, "'Moral' Case for War Is Shot," *Manchester Guardian Weekly*, February 26, 2003, 14; and Ian Bruce, "Judgment Day Is Postponed As Inspections Humiliate Powell; UN Findings Point to Holes in American Case for War," *Herald* (Glasgow), February 15, 2003, 4.

11. Mike Carlton, "Government That Won't Offend, Don't You Worry about That," *Sydney Morning Herald* (Australia), July 31, 2010, 14; and Phillip Coorey and Dafna Linzer, "Bush Lays Down Law; Allies Challenge Security Council," *Advertiser*, February 25, 2003, 1.

12. Bonnie Azab Powell, "UN Weapons Inspector Hans Blix Faults Bush Administration for Lack of 'Critical Thinking' in Iraq," UC Berkeley News, March 18, 2004, http://berkeley.edu/news/media/releases/2004/03/18_blix.shtml. Also see "WMDs: Truth and Its Consequences," Web cast, Hans Blix, interview with Christiane Amanpour, *UC Berkeley News*, http://berkeley.edu/news/media/releases/2004/03/18_blix.shtml.

13. William Maley, "Bypassing UN Sets Dangerous Precedent: It Is Feeble to Claim That a Breach of Resolution 1441 Authorizes the Use of Force, Says William Malley," *Canberra Times* (Australia) March 19, 2003, 17.

14. Thomas Buergenthal, Dinah Shelton, and David P. Stewart, *International Law in a Nutshell* (St. Paul: West, 2009), 3–6; and Ronald C. Slye and Beth Van Schaack, *Essentials of International Criminal Law* (New York, Aspen, 2009), 306.

15. "Military and Paramilitary Activities in and against Nicaragua" (*Nicaragua v. United States of America*, available on the International Court of Justice Web

site, http://www.icj-cij.org/docket/index.php?p1=3&p2=3&k=66&case=70& code=nus&p3=4.

16. Slye and Van Schaack, *Essentials: International Criminal Law*, 164.

17. Ibid., 95–99.

18. Mark L. Rockefeller, "The 'Imminent Threat' Requirement for the Use of Preemptive Military Force: Is It Time for a Non-Temporal Standard?" *Denver Journal of International Law and Policy* 33 (2004): 139.

19. International Coalition for the Responsibility to Protect has a relationship with the United Nations, but Security Council resolutions were required prior to UN peacekeeping in Darfur, whereas proposed resolutions as to Burma were vetoed. See, UN and the Responsibility to Protect at http://www .responsibilitytoprotect.org.

20. Richard Falk, "What Future for the UN Charter System of War Prevention?" *American Journal of International Law* 97 (2003): 590; and James P. Sterba, "Terrorism in International Justice," in *Morality in Practice*, ed. James P. Sterba (Thompson, Wadsworth, 2004), 610.

21. International Coalition for Responsibility to Protect, http://www.responsi-bilitytoprotect.org.

22. William McKenzie, "Why He Did What He Did" (interview with George Bush), *Dallas Morning News*, November 14, 2010, 1.

23. Martin Woollacott, "Nothing and No One Will Stop This Drift Towards War: The Debate about Iraq Is Phoney—The Decision Has Been Made," *Guardian* (London), October 4, 2002, 18; "Germany Rejects Role in Iraq Peace Force with Poland, Denmark," *BBC Summary of World Broadcasts*, May 7, 2003; and Johann Hari, Book Review, "The Wrong War for the Right Reasons; Blair's Wars by John Kampfner," *Independent on Sunday* (London), October 26, 2003, 17.

24. Simon Mann, "Bush Breaks Silence with Personal Account of Presidential Hits and Misses," *Age* (Melbourne, Australia) November 10, 2010, 15.

25. United Nations Security Council, Resolution 1386 (2001) Adopted by the Security Council at its 4443rd meeting, on December 20, 2001.

26. Mandel lecture.

27. Michael Kelly, "Despite the Naysayers," *Washington Post*, November 28, 2001, A35.

28. Falk, "What Future for the UN Charter System of War Prevention?" 592.

29. *Morality in Practice*, ed. James P. Sterba, 613.

30. Falk, "What Future?" 592.

31. Sarah Miley, "U.K. Documents Show Legal Advisor Warned PM Iraq Invasion Was Illegal," *Jurist*, July 1, 2010, http://jurist.org/paperchase/2010/07/former-uk-legal-advisor-warned-blair-iraq-invasion-was-illegal.php.

32. Franck, "What Happens Now?" 607.

33. Falk, "What Future?" 590.

34. Ibn al-Shaykh al-Libi is the nom de guerre of Ali Mohammed Abdel Azziz al-Fakeri. Maamoun Youssef, "Report: Al-Quaida Militant Who Once Gave False Confessions of Iraq Link Dies in Libya Prison," *Associated Press*, May 12, 2009, 1; see also Peter Finn, "Detainee Who Gave False Iraq Data Dies in Prison in Libya," *Washington Post*, May 12, 2009, A12.

35. Maamoun Youssef, "Al-Qaida Militant Dies in Libyan Prison," *Associated Press*, May 12, 2009.

36. Dan Froomkin, "Torture Watch," *Washington Post*, May 13, 2009, http://voices.washingtonpost.com/white-house-watch/torture/torture-watch-6.html (reporting that al-Libi was named as a potential witness for the defense in some of the terrorism trials).

37. "Mystery Surrounds Prison Death of Terrorist Whose Testimony Was Key to Iraq Invasion," *Herald Scotland*, May 16, 2009, http://www.heraldscotland.com/mystery-surrounds-prison-death-of-terrorist-whose-testimony-was-key-to-iraq-invasion-1.829036. Youssef, "Al-Qaeda Militant"; Benjamin Davis, "The Man Who Knew Too Much? A Convenient Suicide in a Libyan Prison," *Jurist*, May 13, 2009, http://jurist.law.pitt.edu/forumy/2009/05/man-who-knew-too-much-convenient.php; and Andy Worthington, "Death in Libya, Betrayal in the West," *Guardian Unlimited*, May 15, 2009. ("News of the death, in a Libyan jail, of Ibn al-Shaikh al-Libi . . . has, understandably, raised questions about whether . . . he was murdered.")

38. Elizabeth Neuffer and Colin Nickerson, "Fighting Terror the Military Campaign," *Boston Globe*, January 6, 2002, A22; and Adrienne Lester, "Former High-Value CIA Detainee Dies in Libya Prison," *Jurist*, May 13, 2009, http://jurist.law.pitt.edu/paperchase/2009/05/former-high-value-cia-detainee-dies-in.php.

39. Eric Schmitt with Erik Eckholm, "A Nation Challenged: The Hunted; U.S. Takes Custody of a Qaeda Trainer Seized in Pakistan," *New York Times*, January 6, 2002; and Neuffer and Nickerson, "Fighting Terror the Military Campaign," A22.

40. Jane Mayer, "Outsourcing Torture: The Secret History of America's "Extraordinary Rendition" Program," *New Yorker*, February 14, 2005.

41. Ibid., 104–106.

42. Douglas Jehl, "Qaeda-Iraq Link U.S. Cited Is Tied to Coercion Claim," *New York Times*, December 9, 2005, A1.

43. Ibid.; Mayer, "Outsourcing Torture"; "CIA Questioned Credibility of Intel Behind Claims of Saddam-Al Qaeda Links," *Frontrunner*, June 12, 2008; Lester, "Former High-Value CIA Detainee Dies"; Davis, "Man Who Knew Too Much?"; and Tom Malinowski and Richard A. Clarke, "Restoring Moral Authority: Ending Torture, Secret Detention, and the Prison at Guantanamo Bay," *Annals of the American Academy of Political and Social Science* 618 (July 2008): 148.

44. Malinowski and Clarke, "Restoring Moral Authority," 148; and Davis, "Man Who Knew Too Much?"

45. Youssef, "Al-Quaida Militant."

46. Warren P. Strobel, "Powell Says Iraq Is Harboring a Terrorist Network Headed by Alqaida Associate Iraq Harboring Al-Qaeda Network," *Knight-Ridder Tribune Business News*, February 6, 2003.

47. Jehl, "Qaeda-Iraq Link."

48. Mayer, "Outsourcing Torture."

49. Jack Cloonan, "Retired FBI Special Agent, Coercive Interrogation Techniques: Hearing Before the Senate Committee On Judiciary," 110th Cong. (2008) "Statement of Jack Cloonan Retired FBI Special Agent, Capitol Hill Hearing Testimony," *Congressional Quarterly, Congressional Testimony*, June 10, 2008; Matt Smith, "Powell Aide Says Torture Helped Build Iraq War Case," *CNN. com*, May 14, 2009, http://www.cnn.com/2009/POLITICS/05/14/iraq.torture/ index.html?iret=newssearch; and Evan Thomas, "Flying in the Shadows," *Washington Post*, Book World, discussing the book by Stephen Grey, *Ghost Plane*, November 14, 2006, C3.

50. Youssef, "Report: Al-Qaeda Militant"; see also, Andrew Sullivan, "One Tortured Lie: That's All It Took for War; Bush Needed 'Evidence' and Used Techniques Designed to Produce Lies to Get It," *Sunday Times*, April 26, 2009, 4.

51. Frank Rich, "Obama Can't Turn the Page on Bush," *New York Times*, May 16, 2009, 12, http://www.nytimes.com/2009/05/17/opinion/17rich-5.html?ref= opinion.

52. Ron Suskind, *The Way of the World* (New York: HarperCollins, 2008), 362–64, 383, 385.

53. Joe Conason, "We Tortured to Justify War," *Salon.com*, May 14, 2009, http:// www.salon.com/opinion/conason/2009/05/14/cheney/index.html.

54. Jonathan S. Landay, "Abusive Tactics Used to Seek Iraq-al Qaida a Link," *McClatchy Newspapers*, April 21, 2009, http://www.mcclatchydc.com/227/story/ 66622.html.

55. Ibid.

56. Liz Cho, World News Now Introduction, *ABC News Transcripts*, October 8, 2002.

57. Suskind, *Way of the World*, 362–364, 385.

58. Worthington, "Death in Libya."

59. Aid for Civilian Casualties of War: Hearing before the Subcommittee On State, Foreign Operations, and Related Programs of the Sen. Committee On Appropriations, 111th Cong. (2009) (statement of John Cromy, Board Member, CIVIC [Campaign for Innocent Victims in Conflict]).

60. Franck, "What Happens Now?," 620.

CHAPTER 7    EUROPEAN AND CANADIAN COMPLICITY
IN RENDITION AND TORTURE

1. "European Parliament Resolution on the Alleged Use of European Countries by the CIA for the Transportation and Illegal Detention of Prisoners, Adopted Midway through the Work of the Temporary Committee" (*2006/2027[INI]*) adopted July 6, 2006, ¶ 16, http://www.europarl.europa.eu/sides/getDoc.do?pubRef=-//EP//TEXT+TA+P6-TA-2006–0316+0+DOC+XML+V0//EN&language=EN.

2. Dick Marty, Committee on Legal Affairs and Human Rights, Council of Europe Parliamentary Assembly, "Alleged Secret Detentions and Unlawful Inter-State Transfers of Detainees Involving Coe Member States," Doc. 10957, June 12, 2006 ¶ 4, ¶ 5, http://assembly.coe.int/Main.asp?link=/Documents/Working Docs/Doc06/EDOC10957.htm (hereafter, Marty Report I).

3. Bruce Zagaris, "European Prosecutors, Legislators Seek Accountability for U.S." *International Enforcement Law Reporter* 23, no. 41 (April 2007).

4. Carrie Schimizzi, "Rights Groups Confirm CIA Extraordinary Rendition Planes Landed in Poland," *Jurist*, February 22, 2010, http://jurist.law.pitt.edu/paperchase/2010/02/rights-groups-confirm-cia-extraordinary.php.

5. Giovanni Claudio Fava, Rapporteur, "Working Document 7," European Parliament, Temporary Committee on the Alleged Use of European Countries by the CIA for the Transport and Illegal Detention of Prisoners, (2006), 2, 3, http://www.statewatch.org/cia/documents/working-doc-no-7-nov-06.pdf.

6. Julia Hall, "Current Evidence: Complicity in the CIA Rendition and Secret Detention Programs," *Amnesty International*, January 25, 2011, http://www.amnesty.org/en/library/asset/EUR01/001/2011/en/32c9f8a1–9a67–4355-bd2b-2d271654e30b/euro1001201en.html, 6–7.

7. See the Swedish Government's Human Rights Web site at www.human-rights.gov.se. According to the U.S. State Department's "Country Reports on Human Rights in Sweden," the "government generally respected the human rights of its citizens, and the law and judiciary provided effective means of dealing with individual instances of abuse," http://www.state.gov/g/drl/rls/hrrpt/2006/78841.htm.

8. Michael Bilton, "Post-9/11 Renditions: An Extraordinary Violation of International Law," May 22, 2007, *Center for Public Integrity*, http://www.public integrity.org/militaryaid/report.aspx?aid=855; and Fava, "Working Document 7," 7, 9.

9. Fava, "Working Document 7," 9.

10. Naureen Shah, Summary: "Promises to Keep: Diplomatic Assurances against Torture in U.S. Terrorism Transfers," *Columbia Law School Human Rights Clinic* (December 2010): 2, http://www.law.columbia.edu/human-rights-institute/initiatives/counterterrorism/assurance/promisestokeep; Hall, "Current Evidence," 13; "Aide-Memoire by a Major General of the Arab Republic of Egypt—General Intelligence Serve," dated December 13, 2001, reproduced in

the full report by Naureen Shah, "Promises to Keep," 150; Shah, Summary "Promises to Keep," 2.

11. Holly Cartner, Europe and Central Asia director at Human Rights Watch, quoted in Bilton, "Post-9/11 Renditions."

12. Hall, "Current Evidence," 13, 14.

13. Ibid.

14. Hillary Stemple, "Poland Ex-PM Denies Knowledge of CIA Secret Prison," *Jurist*, September 9, 2010, http://jurist.org/paperchase/2010/09/poland-ex-pm-denies-knowledge-of-cia-secret-prison.php.

15. "Drill Held to Detainee's Head: CIA Agents Confirm Torture at Polish Black Site," *Spiegal Online International*, September 13, 2010, http://www.spiegel.de/international/europe/0,1518,717166,00.html.

16. Adam Goldman and Matt Apuzzo, "At CIA, Mistakes by Officers Are Often Overlooked," *Washington Post*, February 9, 2011.

17. The agency denies that it fails to properly discipline its agents. "CIA spokesman George Little said, 'Any suggestion that the agency does not take seriously its obligation to review employee misconduct—including those of senior officers—is flat wrong.'" Ibid.

18. "Polish Weekly Examines Fate of Terror Suspects Detained at CIA Prison in Poland," *BBC Monitoring Europe—Political*, October 1, 2010, providing the text of a report by Polish newspaper *Polityka*.

19. Ibid.

20. "Drill Held to Detainee's Head."

21. "Former Officials React to Report Naming Poland as CIA Torture Location," *BBC Monitoring Europe—Political*, September 10, 2010, providing the text of a report by Agnieszka Kublik, Wojciech Czuchnowski, and Mariusz Zawadzki, in *Gazeta Wyborcza* Web site on September 9, 2010.

22. Ibid.

23. Giovanni Claudio Fava, Rapporteur, Working Document 8, European Parliament, Temporary Committee on the Alleged Use of European Countries by the CIA for the Transport and Illegal Detention of Prisoners, 53 (November 16, 2006), http://www.statewatch.org/cia/documents/working-doc-no-8-nov-06.pdf.

24. Hall, "Current Evidence," 11.

25. Ibid.

26. Ibid., 12.

27. "Polish Weekly Examines Fate."

28. Ibid.

29. Executive Order 13491, *Federal Register* 74, no. 16 (January 22, 2009), 4893 revoking Executive Order 13440, July 20, 2007.

30. Marty Report I; and Dick Marty, Committee on Legal Affairs and Human Rights, Council of Europe Parliamentary Assembly, "Secret Detentions and Illegal Transfers of Detainees Involving Council of Europe Member States: Second Report," Doc. F-67075, June 7, 2007 (hereafter, Marty Report II).

31. "Detainees Paid off to Avoid Torture Hearings," *Herald* (Glasgow), November 17, 2010, 5; Alistair MacDonald, and Jess Bravin, "UK Plans to Pay 16 Ex-Detainees," *Wall Street Journal*, November 17, 2010, 10.

32. Kat Baldwyn, "Detainee 'Will Get Millions,'" *Birmingham Evening Mail*, November 17, 2010, 8.

33. Hall, "Current Evidence," 14–15.

34. "Paying a High Price: Torture and Terrorism," *Guardian* (London), November 17, 2010, 34.

35. Ibid.

36. Paul Koring, "Will U.K. Payouts Set Precedent for Khadr: Britain Pays Millions to Keep Secret Role Played by Counterintelligence Operatives in Torture of Britons Held Abroad," *Globe and Mail* (Canada), November 19, 2010, A20.

37. Richard Norton-Taylor, "MI5 Officer Escapes Charges over Mohamed Torture Case," *Guardian* (London), November 18, 2010, 17.

38. Date of Decision to Communicate/Date de décision de la communication, 28/09/2010.

39. Questions to the Parties in Khalid El-Masri against the former Yugoslav Republic of Macedonia lodged 20 July 2009 (October 8, 2010), This case can be accessed using the search functions found at the European Court of Human Rights database, http://echr.coe.int/echr/en/hudoc.

40. Hall, "Current Evidence," 10; and Megan McKee, "Europe Rights Court to Review Macedonia Role in CIA Extraordinary Rendition," *Jurist,* October 14, 2010, http://jurist.org/paperchase/2010/10/europe-rights-court-to-review-macedonia-role-in-cia-extraordinary-rendition.php.

41. "Top European Court Demands Answers on CIA Rendition," Press Release, *Open Society Foundations*, October 14, 2010, http://www.soros.org/initiatives/justice/focus/national-security/news/el-masri-european-court-20101014.

42. Ibid.

43. Hall, "Current Evidence," 10.

44. "Top European Court."

45. See the Marty Reports I and II. See also "Macedonia Not to Be Included in Kosovo Organ Trade Probe—Dick Marty," *BBC Monitoring Europe—Political*, (February 3, 2011).

46. Hall, "Current Evidence," 8–9, 12–13.

47. "Special Forum on the Canadian Mission in Afghanistan," Osgoode Hall Law School, York University (February 10, 2010), sponsored by the Nathanson

Centre on Transnational Human Rights, Crime and Security, http://nathanson.osgoode.yorku.ca/programs/conferences-workshops/2009–2010/special-forum-on-canadian-mission-afghanistan/.

48. Alex Neve, "Responsibility of the Canadian State under International Law and in Canadian Law: Charter Review, Public Inquiries, and Civil Liability Lawsuits," presentation at the Special Forum on the Canadian Mission in Afghanistan, Osgoode Hall Law School, York University (February 10, 2010), available at http://nathanson.osgoode.yorku.ca/programs/conferences-workshops/2009–2010/special-forum-on-canadian-mission-afghanistan/; and Michael Mandel, "What Right Do We Have to Be in Afghanistan in the First Place? Why the Prisoner Transfer Issue Cannot be Detached from the Legality and Legitimacy of the War Itself," presentation at ibid.

49. Michael Byers, "Canada's Moral Standing in the World: Does Our Detainee Transfer Record Matter?" presentation at ibid.

50. "Testimony of Andrea Prasow, Senior Counterterrorism Counsel Human Rights Watch" before the Special Committee on the Canadian Mission in Afghanistan, Parliament of Canada (May 5, 2010) 7, available at Nathanson Centre Web site, http://nathanson.osgoode.yorku.ca/programs/conferences-workshops/2009–2010/special-forum-on-canadian-mission-afghanistan/.

51. Byers, "Canada's Moral Standing."

52. Michael Byers, "Afghanistan: We Cannot Risk Complicity in Torture," *Globe and Mail* (Canada), September 27, 2005, A19.

53. Ibid.

54. Ibid.

55. Neve, "Responsibility of the Canadian State," 3.

56. "Testimony of Andrea Prasow," 3.

57. Ibid., 5.

58. Ibid., 4–5.

59. Steven Chase, "All Detainees Were Tortured, All Warnings Were Ignored; Richard Colvin Began Red-Flagging Problems with Afghan Detainee Treatment in May 2006. Now He Tells MPs That Canada Handed Over Innocent People to Certain Torture and Ottawa Disregarded His Alerts," *Globe and Mail* (Canada), November 19, 2009, A1.

60. "Afghan Authorities Regularly Beat Enemy Detainees, Military Inquiry Finds," *Carleton Place*, May 7, 2010, 1.

61. "Another Government Watchdog Bites the Dust," *Toronto Star*, December 15, 2010, A27.

62. "Majority of Canadians Believe Afghan Detainees Tortured after Transfer: Poll," *National Post*, May 10, 2010, A4.

# INDEX

9/11: post-9/11 renditions, 69, 71, 75, 92, 103, 157; terrorist attacks, 1, 2, 35, 94, 135, 147; terrorist connections with, 12, 45, 94, 153, 166; use of torture in the post-9/11 war against terror, 22, 60, 89, 167, 179

*ABC News* (television program), 41, 42
Abu Ghraib, 20, 24, 41, 174
Abu Omar. *See* Omar Abu
Abu Zubaydah. *See* Zubaydah, Abu
accession states/candidate countries, 162
advice of counsel, 26, 27
Afghanistan, 3, 14, 22, 31, 32, 40, 45, 47, 54, 58, 94–96, 101, 106, 107, 110, 111, 135, 140, 146–148, 153, 169, 170, 172–176; intelligence service (National Directorate of Security), 175–177
aggressive wars, 41, 136, 140, 141
Agiza, Ahmed, 163
airspace, 10, 14, 159, 160, 162. *See also* landing rights; refueling
Albania, 89, 90, 110, 170
Alien Tort Statute, 97, 122
al-Libi, Ibn al-shaykh, 9, 11, 13, 14, 138, 152–158, 171
Almalki, Abullah, 104, 133
Al-Qaeda, x, 11, 13, 19, 25, 28, 31, 40, 41, 54, 90, 92, 94, 95, 107, 115, 135, 147, 151, 153, 154, 155, 156, 158, 166
al-Qahtani, Mohammed, 41
*Al Rawi v. Security Service*, 128, 130
*Alvarez-Machain* case, 82, 83, 85–87
al-Zarqawi, Abu Musab, 114
Amal Militia, 78, 79
American Civil Liberties Union, 23
Amnesty International, 92, 170, 175
Annan, Kofi, 157
anticipatory war, 136, 137, 142. *See also* preemptive war
Antihijacking Act of 1974, 79
Appropriations Subcommittee on Foreign Relations (U.S.), 78
Arar, Mahr, 9, 10, 35, 103–110, 115, 121, 127, 133, 157, 159, 174
*Arar v. Ashcroft*, 109, 134
Argentina, 66–68, 86

Ashcroft, John, 41, 42
assurances, *See* diplomatic assurances
asylum, 77, 163, 164
attorney general (U.S.), 32, 36, 38, 41, 43, 133, 150
Authorization to Use Military Force (AUMF), 25

bad faith, 27, 35, 36, 120, 136, 138
Bagram, Bagram Air Force Base (Iraq), 58, 59, 96, 101, 173, 174, 179
Baker, Howard, 175
Bakircioglu, Onder, 137
Balkin, Jack, 42
*Baltimore Sun*, 21
Barbie, Klaus, 73
battlefield/battle zone, 32, 47, 58, 172
Battling Bastards of Bataan, 32
BBC (British Broadcasting Corporation), 179
Begg, Moazzam, 167
Beirut, Lebanon, 78
Benjamin, Daniel, 86
Berri, Nabih, 79
bin Laden, Osama, 69
black sites, 8, 10, 14, 59, 96, 162, 164, 165, 167, 171, 174
Blair, Tony, 150
blank check/blanket permission, 25, 47, 165
Blix, Hans, 138, 139, 145, 156
Bolivia, 73
Bosnia, 45
*Boumediene v. Bush*, xiii, 35, 50, 51, 53–59
Bradbury, Stephen G., 36
Brandeis, Justice Louis, 124
Brazil, 18, 19, 23
breach of (international) peace, 74–76
Brief of Legal Historians, 58
Brookings Institution, 86
Brown, Gordon, 94
Bundestag (Germany), 111, 169
Bush, George H. W., 78, 80, 86
Bush, George W., ix, 7, 13, 16, 17, 19, 25, 27, 28, 30, 40, 42, 43, 51, 53, 57, 60, 135, 136, 139, 145–147, 150, 151, 152, 154–156, 158, 166, 171

Bush administration, xii, 4, 5, 7–9, 20, 26, 29, 32, 34, 35, 38–40, 43, 52, 57, 63, 70, 75, 85, 90, 91, 93, 99, 111, 152–156, 158, 178, 179
Butcher of Lyon, 73
Bybee, James, 32, 34, 42
Byers, Michael, 174

Cairo, Egypt, 89, 163
Canada, ix, x, 3, 7, 9–11, 14, 15, 84, 92, 102, 104–107, 110, 117, 128, 132–134, 159, 171–177; Canadian Security Intelligence Service, 105
candidate countries/accession states, 162
Cannon, Lawrence, 109
Carlos "the Jackal" (Ramirez Sánchez), vii, 7, 60–90 passim
CAT. See Convention Against Torture
cease-fire agreement (with respect to Kuwait and Iraq), 138, 148–150
Central Intelligence Agency (CIA): and abductions or kidnapping, 10, 110, 111; and crimes, war crimes, and defenses thereto, 27, 30, 36–38, 42, 43, 64, 110–112, 115, 170; demoralized, 111–115; and destruction of evidence, 59, 112, 166; and rendition or torture flights, 10, 13, 14, 17, 71, 72, 86–89, 92, 103, 110, 123, 153, 159–167, 170, 171; and secret prisons or black sites, 8, 10, 91, 96, 162, 164–167, 170; and torture/harsh interrogations, 3, 14, 21, 23, 27, 36, 40–42, 59, 96, 97, 100, 111, 130, 132, 152, 153, 162–164, 171
Cesarani, David, 68
Chaskalson, Arthur, 3
Chavez v. Martinez, 38
Chechnya, 45
chemical and biological WMDs. See weapons of mass destruction (WMDs): chemical and biological
Cheney, Dick, 12, 38, 41, 93, 156
Chile, 63, 80, 81
CIA. See Central Intelligence Agency
Clark, Ken, 131
"clean" torture, 19, 21–23, 40
Clinton, William, Clinton administration, 11, 60, 71, 75, 86–90
Cloonan, Jack, 153
closed material procedure, 128, 129
coalition of the willing, 95, 135, 136, 139, 145, 146, 148–150
Cohen, Felix S., 92
Cold War, 21, 22; communist interrogation techniques, 22, 155
Cole. See USS Cole
Cole, David, 35, 37, 54
Coleman, Dan, 154
collective intervention or self-defense, 142, 145
Colvin, Richard, 176
Combatant Status Review Panel (CSRT), 50, 51, 53, 54, 55

Commission of Inquiry (Canada), 104, 107, 109, 132–134
complicity with torture or rendition, 159–179 passim
Conason, Joe, 156
Congress. See U.S. Congress
Constitutional Court (Italy), 114
Convention Against Torture (CAT), 33, 61, 62–64, 66, 69, 81
Convention for the Suppression of Unlawful Seizure of Aircraft (Hague Convention), 79
Costa Rica, 73
Council of Europe, 10, 74, 115, 165
Court of Appeal, Civil Division (U.K.), 119
cruel, inhuman, and degrading treatment (CID), 52, 60, 172
CSRT. See Combatant Status Review Panel
customary international law, 62, 78, 79, 83, 84, 87, 141
Cyprus, 78

"Dark Prison" (Kabul, Afghanistan), 101
Davis, Col. Morris, 53
Davis, Terry, 71
death penalty, 25, 95, 98, 102, 130
Decision Points (G. W. Bush), 136
Defense Intelligence Agency (U.S.), 154
Denmark, 173
Department of Justice, U.S. See U.S. Department of Justice
derogation, 62. See also nonderogable
detainees: British complicity with torture of, 3, 168, 176; Canadian, 133; in Canadian custody, 3, 174–176; legal rules as to access to courts, 8, 30, 31, 33, 44, 48–55, 58, 59, 94, 98, 101, 118, 130, 131, 153, 166, 168; transportation, 10, 30, 152; treatment of U.S., 1, 3, 5, 8, 23–25, 27, 29, 31, 40, 41, 51, 116, 156, 164, 171
Detainee Treatment Act of 2005 (DTA) (U.S.), 51–54, 57
diplomatic assurances, 163
diplomatic immunity, 114
Direction de la Surveillance du Territoire (DST) (France), 69
dirty bomb, 12, 45, 46, 48, 94, 96, 98, 142
DST. See Direction de la Surveillance du Territoire
DTA. See Detainee Treatment Act of 2005
dummy flight plans, 166

Eastern Europe, 14, 22, 166, 171
Egypt: assurances as to torture, 163, 164; rendition to, ix, 10, 11, 14, 59, 87–90, 93, 113, 122, 137, 154, 163, 164, 170; reputation for torture, 65, 88–90, 113, 163, 174; torture in, 2, 8, 9, 10, 11, 13, 65, 89, 90, 117, 153, 159, 161, 163
Eichmann, Adolf, 10, 60–90 passim
Elizabeth I, queen of England, 76
El-Maati, Ahmed, 133

El-Masri, Khalid, 35, 110, 111, 121, 126, 127, 134, 157, 162, 169, 170
El Zari, Mohammed, 163
enemy combatant, 29, 30, 46, 47, 50, 51, 53, 54, 57, 141, 173. *See also* illegal combatant
England, 76, 128, 129. *See also* United Kingdom
England and Wales Court of Appeal, 128, 129
enhanced interrogation, 6, 156
European Commission for Democracy through Law, 74
European Commission of Human Rights, 69, 73
European Convention on Human Rights (also European Convention for the Protection of Human Rights and Fundamental Freedoms), 70, 73
European Court of Human Rights, 73, 169, 170
European Parliament, 159–162
European Union, 92
EUROPOL warrants, 112
Evidence Act (Canada), 133, 134
expulsion order, 163
extradition, 6, 40, 61, 64–66, 68, 70, 73, 74, 76, 77, 80, 82–84, 87, 88, 92, 93, 111, 112, 114, 147

Falk, Richard, 151
false burial, 39
Federal Bureau of Investigation (FBI), 24, 78, 153, 154
Federal Court of Canada, 102
"a few bad apples," 20, 178
fig-leaf assurances, 163, 164
first Gulf War, 138, 142, 148, 150
Fisher, Louis, 72
Foreign Affairs Restructuring Act of 1998 (U.S.), 30
foreign secretary (U.K.), 101, 102, 130
Fourth Circuit Court of Appeals (U.S.), 126
France, 6, 7, 69–71, 73
Franck, Thomas, 157
*Frisbie v. Collins*, 77, 78, 80, 82
fugitive slave laws, 75

gag order, 167, 169
Geneva Conventions, 31, 31, 52, 54, 56, 58, 62, 172–174; Common Article 3, 31, 56, 172, 173; Protocol II, 173
genocide, ix, 61, 63, 67, 81, 145, 146
Germany, 20, 32, 50, 110, 111, 161, 162, 169, 170
Gestapo, 11, 19, 73
Ghailani, Ahmed Khalfan, 120, 121
golden shield, 26
Goldsmith, Peter, 150
Gonzales, Alberto, 31–33
good faith, 27, 35–38, 67, 81, 136–138, 143, 151, 152, 157, 158, 163
grave breaches, Geneva Code, 31

Great Britain. *See* United Kingdom
Great Writ, 53. *See also* habeas corpus
Grey, Stephen, 113
Gross, Samuel R., 108
GTMO. *See* Guantánamo Bay, Cuba
Guantánamo Bay, Cuba (GTMO), 5, 8, 10, 20, 22–24, 30, 40, 41, 44, 47–55, 57–59, 94, 96, 98, 102,116, 119, 130, 131, 152, 166–171, 174
Guantánamo Review Task Force, 48

habeas corpus, 30, 31, 44, 49–56, 58, 59, 118, 119, 120
Hafetz, Jonathan, 26
The Hague, Netherlands, 63, 79
*Hamdan v. Rumsfeld*, 52
Hamdi, Yaser Esam, 29, 46–48
*Hamdi v. Rumsfeld*, 46, 47, 50, 51, 54
Harper, Stephen, 176, 177
harsh interrogation, ix, 1, 3, 5, 6, 10, 12, 14, 16, 17, 24, 28, 33, 36, 37, 42, 46, 59, 64–66, 91, 112, 155, 156, 162, 167, 171, 178
head-of-state immunity, 63, 80, 81
hearsay, 29, 50, 51, 53
High Court (U.K.), 98–102
high-value detainee or prisoner, 27, 40, 152, 171
Himmler, Heinrich, 67
Hitchens, Christopher, 4, 5
Hitler, Adolf, 20, 67
Holocaust, 32, 68, 81
Hostage Taking Act (U.S.), 79
*hostis humani generis*, ix, 62
House of Lords (U.K.), 80, 85, 103
HRW. *See* Human Rights Watch
Huggins, Martha, 18, 20
humanitarian intervention, 136, 140, 143, 144–146, 148
Human Resource Exploitation Manual (1983), 21, 22
Human Rights Committee. *See* United Nations Human Rights Committee
Human Rights Watch (HRW), 13, 81, 89, 144, 145, 152, 175, 176
Hussein, Saddam, 13, 137, 138, 142, 145, 146, 151, 154–156

Iacobucci Commission (Canada), 133
Ibn al-Shaykh al-Libi. *See* al-Libi, Ibn al-shaykh
ICCPR. *See* International Covenant on Civil and Political Rights
illegal combatant, 29, 30, 31, 53, 54, 57, 66, 173. *See also* enemy combatant
imminence (requirement for preemptive war), 136, 137, 142, 143, 146
in absentia judicial proceedings, 88, 89, 111, 114
incommunicado detention, 29, 46, 95, 101, 170
Independent International Commission on Kosovo, 143

International Atomic Energy Agency, 138
International Committee of the Red
    Cross, 176
International Court for the Former
    Yugoslavia, 62
International Covenant on Civil and
    Political Rights (ICCPR), 61, 62, 172
International Criminal Court, 63, 173, 174
international humanitarian law, 32, 57,
    62. *See also* laws of war
interrogation tapes, destruction of by
    CIA, 59, 112, 166
in-theater renditions, 3, 171–173, 177
Iran, 22, 24
Iraq, 9, 11, 13, 22, 32, 135–158 *passim*, 174
Iraq War, 3, 4, 13, 14, 135–158 *passim*
irregular rendition, 60, 64, 65, 66, 71,
    73–76, 80, 87
Islam, 89, 94, 115
Islamabad, Pakistan, 88, 116
Israel, 67–69, 73, 86, 151
Italy, 10, 14, 24, 73, 113–115, 159, 161

Japan, 32, 39, 124
Jeppesen Dataplan, Inc., 97, 122, 123. *See
    also Mohamed v. Jeppesen Dataplan*
JFK airort (New York City), 103, 104
jihadists, 151
Jordan, 17, 78, 88, 92, 93, 104, 106, 122,
    174
Julien, Henry G., 77
*jus cogens*, 62

Kabul, Afghanistan, 101, 170
Kafka, Franz/Kafkaesque, 9, 104, 107, 110
Kandahar, Afghanistan, 153
Karachi, Pakistan, 92, 95
Keitel, Wilhelm, 20
Kennedy, Anthony, 53, 58
Kenya, 94,120
*Ker-Frisbie* doctrine, 78, 80, 82
*Ker v. Illinois*, 77, 78, 83
Kessler, Gladys, 119
Khadr, Omar, 102, 103
*Khadr* case, 102, 103
Khan, Issa, 116
"kick some ass," 135, 136, 147
KUBARK manual, 21, 22
Kurds, 146
Kurnaz, Murat, 50
Kutz, Christopher, 26
Kuwait, 138, 148–150

Lady, Robert, 114
Landay, Jonathan, 156
landing rights, 160, 171. *See also* refueling
Lassiter, Tom, 116
Latin America, 22, 23
law-free zone, 30, 49, 50, 57, 171
laws of war, 20, 25, 62, 67, 135–179 *passim*
Lebanon, 78, 79, 110
Lederman, Marty, 43, 51
Lewis, Anthony, 43

Libya, 144, 152, 157
Lithuania, 10, 14, 170
Lobel, Jules, 105
long-arm jurisdiction, 78
Luban, David, ix, 18, 20, 27, 34

Macedonia, 14, 110, 111, 169, 170
Machain, Humberto Álvarez, 82, 83–86.
    *See also Alvarez-Machain* case
Magi, Oscar, 10, 114
Mandel, Michael, 147
*Maqaleh v. Gates*, 58
*Marbury v. Madison*, 56
Marty, Dick, Marty Reports, 10, 110, 115,
    161, 170
material breach (Iraq's cease-fire
    obligations), 138, 139, 148, 149, 150
MCA. *See* Military Commissions Act of
    2006
McCain, John, 38
McConnell, Mike, 37
McCoy, Alfred, 18
McGill University, 104
*Meet the Press* (television program), 93
Mexico, 82–86
MI5 (U.K. intelligence agency), 128, 167,
    168
MI6 (U.K. intelligence agency), 128, 167,
    168
Middle East, 8, 14, 171
Milgram, Stanley, 17, 18, 67
Miliband, David, 101
military commissions, 29, 30, 52–59
Military Commissions Act of 2006 (MCA)
    (U.S.), 52–59, 100, 102, 134
Military Complaints Commission
    (Canada), 177
Military Order of November 13, 2001
    (U.S.), 28–35
military tribunals, 29, 50
Miller, Leszek, 165
Mitrione, Dan, 23
mock execution, 45, 118, 164
Mohamed, Binyam, 25, 35, 45, 94–103, 110,
    117–122, 128, 130, 131, 157, 167, 169
Mohammed, Farhi Saeed Bin, 118
Mohammed, Jamil Qasim Saeed, 92, 93
Mohammed, Khalid Sheikh, 45, 94, 96,
    100, 166, 171
*Mohamed v. Jeppesen Dataplan*, 97, 117–134
    *passim. See also* Jeppesen Dataplan. Inc.
Morocco, ix, 2, 8, 10, 14, 25, 45, 59, 65, 95,
    96, 101, 117, 118, 122, 170
Mossad (Israeli intelligence agency), 67
Moussaoui, Zacarias, 153
Mukasey, Michael, 38
Munich Olympics (1972), 69

Nasr, Osama Mustafa. *See* Omar, Abu
National Security Council, 27, 41–43, 135
National Directorate of Security (NDS)
    (Afghan intelligence service), 175–177
nation building, 152

NATO (North Atlantic Treaty
Organization), 143, 144, 172
Nazis, 10, 20, 32, 66, 86
Netherlands, 173, 175
New York, 44, 46, 89, 103, 104, 153
*New York Times*, 31, 114, 115, 127
Nicaragua, 140
Ninth Circuit Court of Appeals (U.S.), 97,
117, 123–126, 128, 129
nonderogable, 61, 62. *See also* derogation
nonrefoulment, 31, 33
Noriega, Gen. Manuel, 80, 81, 145
Northern Alliance (Afghanistan), 46, 47,
94
Nowak, Manfred, 39, 49
nuclear weapons, 12, 45, 125, 142. *See also*
weapons of mass destruction
Nureddin, Muayyed, 133
Nuremburg war crimes trials, 62, 67, 135

Obama, Barack, Obama administration,
43, 94, 99, 102, 116, 167, 178, 179
O'Connor, Dennis, 105, 109
O'Connor, Sandra, 47
OLC. *See* U.S. Department of Justice: Office
of Legal Counsel
Omar, Abu (Osama Mustafa Nasr), 10,
III–116, 121, 157, 159
OPEC, 69
Operation Enduring Freedom, 95
Osgoode Hall Law School, York University,
xi, 147
out-of-court settlements (U.K.), 167–169
outrages upon personal dignity, 62

Padilla, José, 12, 29, 44–48, 94, 96
Pakistan, 25, 45, 88, 92, 95, 96, 101, 116,
118, 119, 153
"Palestinian hanging," 39
Panama, 80, 145
Panama Canal, 80, 176, 177
Parliament (European), 159–162, 165
Parliament (Germany's Bundestag), III,
169
Parliament (U.K.), 129, 131
passive personal principle, 78
peaceful resolution, 145
penis (sliced with a scalpel), 25, 45, 95
Pentagon, 44, 60, 93
permanent resident, 102, 163
persona non grata, 113
Philbin, Patrick, 30
Philip II, king of Spain, 76, 81
Philippines, 22, 39
Phoenix Program, 42
Pinochet, Augusto Ugarte, 63, 80
pirates, 19, 20
plausible deniability, 8, 19, 42, 160
Poland, 10, 14, 162, 164–167, 170; Air
National Services Agency, 166
Pollari, Niccolô, 114
post-traumatic stress disorder, 5, 33, 40
Powell, Colin, 13, 41, 42, 154, 155

preemptive war, 136, 136, 137, 142, 150. *See*
*also* anticipatory war
Presidential Scholars, 60
pretext, 14, 123, 135, 136, 147
private bills, 124
proportionality (principle for conducting
a war lawfully), 81, 142, 144, 145
prorogation (of Parliament), 176
"pure heart, empty head test," 158

Qassim, Talaat Fouad, 92
"quaint" relicts of another age, 32, 173
Queen's Bench (U.K.), 101

*R (on the application of Mohamed) v.*
*Secretary of State for Foreign and*
*Commonwealth Affairs*, 98
Radsan, John, 64
*Rasul v. Rumsfeld*, 49, 50, 52, 54, 58
RCMP. *See* Royal Canadian Mounted Police
Reagan, Ronald, 60, 75, 78, 140
realpolitik, 148
Red Cross, 176
refoulement, 61–64, 173
refueling, 10, 14, 160, 162–164. *See also*
landing rights
Rehnquist, Justice William, 82
Reid, Richard, 153
Rejali, Darius, 11, 19, 21
rendition to justice, 10, 60, 66, 68–71,
73–78, 81–87, 91
Responsibility to Protect, 144
retroactive justification, 136, 151, 152
Rice, Condolezza, 41, 42, 70–72, 110, 160,
161
rogue state/regime, 13, 142
Romania, 10, 14, 162, 167, 170
Rome Statute, International Criminal
Court, 173
Royal Canadian Mounted Police (RCMP),
104, 105
Royal Jordanian airline hijacking, 78
Rumsfeld, Donald, 41, 44, 46, 49, 52, 54,
135
*Rumsfeld v. Padilla*, 44–46

"Salt Pit" prison (Afghanistan), IIO
Sartre, Jean-Paul, 18
Satterthwaite, Margaret, 87
Saudi Arabia, 46, 47
Savak (Iranian secret police), 24
Scheuer, Michael, 87, 88
Scotland, 10, 163, 164
Scott, Craig, xi, 9
secretary of defense (U.S.), 29, 41, 135, 151
secretary of state (U.S.), 13, 14, 41, 42, 70,
76, 98, 110, 154, 160
secret evidence, 29, 50, 53, 99–101, 104,
121, 125, 128–130
Security Council (UN), 13, 27, 43, 74, 135,
139–141, 143, 144, 146–150
self-defense, 135–137, 140–143, 146–148, 151,
152, 154

September 11, 2001, ix, 9, 25, 26, 28, 89,
91–93, 95, 135, 151, 162, 163. *See also* 9/11
SERE (survival, evasion, resistance, and
escape) training, 22, 23, 36
"sexed up," 151
shock the conscience, 36–38, 80
shoe bomber, 153
*Slate* magazine, 4
slavery, ix, 5, 31, 61–63, 75; slave traders,
ix, 19, 20, 62
sleep deprivation, 4, 21, 36, 42, 119, 177
Smith, Clive Stafford, 96, 97, 100
Sotomayor, Sonia, 103
South Carolina, 44, 46, 47
sovereignty, 49, 54, 66, 68, 72–76, 78, 84,
85, 112, 160, 161, 165
Spain, 10, 40, 76, 81, 170
Spataro, Armando, 115, 116
special rapporteur, 10, 39, 49, 161, 162
Specter, Sen. Arlen, 78
state secrets doctrine, 14, 97, 110, 111, 121, 126
station chief, CIA, 114, 164
Stockholm, Sweden, 163
Story, Dr. John, 76, 77
subcontracting interrogations, 174
Sudan, 69–71
suicide, 152–155, 157
Supreme Court (Canada), 133
Supreme Court (U.S.), 25, 29, 37, 38, 44,
49–59, 77, 82, 83, 85, 102, 103, 109, 110,
125, 126, 129, 130
survival, evasion, resistance, and escape
(SERE) training, 22, 23, 36
Suskind, Ron, 155
Sweden, 10, 14, 138, 162–164; Swedish
chancellor of justice, 163
Syria, ix, 2, 8–10, 14, 59, 64, 65, 88,
103–108, 133, 159, 161, 170, 174;
Palestine branch of the Syrian military
intelligence, 106

Taliban, x, 31, 47, 54, 95, 116, 147, 176
Tanzania, 94, 120
Temporary Committee on the Alleged Use
of European Countries by the CIA for
the Transport and Illegal Detention of
Prisoners, 162, 165
Tenet, George, 41, 86
terrorist training camp, 153, 154
Third Reich (Germany), 18, 68
Thomas, Justice Clarence, 38
ticking bomb, ix, 61
*Time* magazine, 41
torture lite, 1, 3–5, 16, 20, 21, 24, 26, 32,
38, 40, 46, 59, 107, 140, 154
torture memo, 32–37, 40, 42
*Torture Memos: Rationalizing the
Unthinkable, The* (Cole), 35
*Totten v. United States*, 125, 126
Tupamaro guerrillas, 23
Turkey, 161
twenty-first hijacker, 153

UCMJ. *See* Uniform Code of Military
Justice
Ulpian, 11
Uniform Code of Military Justice (UCMJ),
52, 58
United Kingdom (U.K.), ix, x, 7, 11, 14, 40,
62, 81, 85, 94, 95, 96–99, 101, 102, 117,
119, 128–132, 134, 139, 147, 149, 150, 161,
167–170, 171, 172, 173, 174; intelligence
service, 95, 97, 118, 128, 130, 131, 155
United Nations (UN), 13, 27, 39, 43, 49,
74, 135, 136, 138–141, 143–150, 154, 155,
166; inspections, 138, 145; Joint Study
on Secret Detention, 166; Security
Council, 13, 27, 43, 74, 135, 139–141, 143,
144, 146–150; Special Rapporteur on
Torture, 39, 49
United Nations Charter, 140; Article 2(4),
141; Article 51, 137, 141, 142; Chapter VII,
141
United Nations Human Rights
Committee, 61, 63, 64, 72, 163
United Nations Monitoring Verification
and Inspection Commission
(UNMOVIC), 138
United Nations Resolutions: Resolution
38, 74; Resolution 678, 148, 149;
Resolution 687, 148, 149; Resolution
715, 148; Resolution 1141, 149; Resolution
1154, 149; Resolution 1441, 139, 149, 150;
Resolution 1483, 136, 149; Resolution
1970, 144
*United States v. Alvarez-Machain*, 82–87
*United States v. Reynolds*, 125–127, 130
universal jurisdiction, 41, 43
UNMOVIC. *See* United Nations
Monitoring, Verification and
Inspection Commission
unlawful combatant. *See* enemy
combatant; illegal combatant
Uruguay, 23
U.S. Congress, 25, 34, 36, 44, 49, 50–54,
58, 78, 79, 124, 126, 154; Judiciary
Committee, 78
U.S. Department of Justice, 3, 26–28, 35,
43, 54, 73, 87; Office of Legal Counsel
(OLC), 3, 5, 6, 8, 17, 26–28, 30–32,
34–38, 57. *See also* attorney general
U.S. Department of Defense, 27, 46, 50.
*See also* secretary of defense
U.S. Department of State, 88, 105. *See also*
secretary of state
USS *Cole*, 92, 94

*Vanity Fair* magazine, 5
Vienna Convention on Treaties, 148
Viet Cong, 42, 48
Vietnam, 22, 48

wall slamming, 4, 37
War Crimes Act (U.S.), 30, 31, 42, 43, 54,
57, 67

war on terror, x, 2, 3, 8, 12, 17, 19, 20, 22, 25, 26, 29, 30, 38, 44, 48, 54, 57, 61, 62, 65, 91, 95, 103, 109, 113, 115, 122, 127, 130
war powers resolution, 25
Washington, D.C., 152, 168, 178
*Washington Post,* 93
waterboarding, 3–6, 12, 17, 27, 36, 39, 40, 42, 51, 112, 166
Watergate, 175
weapons of mass destruction (WMDs), 135–139, 142, 148, 150–152, 154–156, 158; chemical and biological, 135–139, 142, 148, 150–152, 154–156, 158
White House, 26, 31, 40–42
WMDs. *See* weapons of mass destruction

Wolfowitz, Paul, 151
World Court (International Court of Justice or ICJ), 72, 140
World Trade Center, 44, 60, 87, 88, 93, 94
World War II, 32, 39, 73, 77, 141, 143

Yemen, 92, 94
Yoo, John, 30
Yousef, Ramzi, 87, 88
Youssef, Mamoun, 155
Yugoslavia, 40, 62, 143, 146
Yunis, Fawaz, 78, 79, 81

Zimbardo, Phillip, 17, 18
Zubaydah, Abu, 12, 155, 166

# ABOUT THE AUTHOR

ALAN W. CLARKE is a professor of integrated studies at Utah Valley University. He has a Ph.D. from Osgoode Hall Law School, York University, an LL.M. from Queen's University, and a J.D. from the College of William & Mary. He has taught at Ferris State University and the University of Wisconsin, Parkside, was a visiting scholar at Michigan Technological University, a visiting research associate at the University of Manitoba Faculty of Law, and held a visiting endowed chair in Criminology and Criminal Justice at St. Thomas University.